WALTER BAGEHOT

WALTER BAGEHOT

BY

WILLIAM IRVINE

*Assistant Professor of English at
Stanford University, California*

LONGMANS, GREEN AND CO.
LONDON : NEW YORK : TORONTO

LONGMANS, GREEN AND CO. LTD.
39 PATERNOSTER ROW, LONDON, E.C.4
17 CHITTARANJAN AVENUE, CALCUTTA
NICOL ROAD, BOMBAY
36A MOUNT ROAD, MADRAS

LONGMANS, GREEN AND CO.
114 FIFTH AVENUE, NEW YORK
221 EAST 20TH STREET, CHICAGO
88 TREMONT STREET, BOSTON

LONGMANS, GREEN AND CO.
215 VICTORIA STREET, TORONTO

First Published 1939

Printed in Great Britain by the KEMP HALL PRESS LTD.
in the City of Oxford

TO

Ç. S. I.

PREFACE

To the late Mrs. Russell Barrington I wish to express gratitude for much kind and instructive conversation on Walter Bagehot and his friends, and for permission to see many of his unpublished letters. To the publishing house of Faber and Faber in London I owe the valuable gift of a copy of *The Love Letters of Walter Bagehot and Eliza Wilson* before they were published in 1933. To the late Professor Irving Babbitt of Harvard University I need hardly indicate my debt. It is evident on the pages of my book. To Professor Hyder E. Rollins I owe the good effects of much searching and painstaking criticism, as well as such habits of accuracy as I have acquired. To Professor Arthur G. Kennedy I am grateful for a host of particular suggestions, both stylistic and bibliographical, and to Professor Norman Foerster for several valuable general ones. I desire also to express thanks to Professors Hardin Craig, William D. Briggs, John W. Dodds, and Francis R. Johnson.

TABLE OF CONTENTS

Chapter I

YOUTH'S GREY HAIRS

WALTER BAGEHOT was not one of the great Victorian heroes. He neither founded an economic empire in Africa, nor agitated a great cause, nor received primroses from a queen. He was not, like Carlyle, as the voice of one bellowing in the wilderness, nor did he, like Arnold, go through the world proclaiming his own elegant aloofness and bidding the multitude aspire to become an Athenian aristocracy. He was the crusader against no abuse, the apostle of no reform, the prophet of no new religion. A quiet body of readers are aware that in his time Walter Bagehot decently occupied a prominent position in the financial world, that he made money unobtrusively, that he gravely edited a grave journal and wielded a powerful influence in the " City," that he published a few sedate tomes in later years and a few dashing essays in youth, and that in middle life he wrote dignified love letters to his future wife. What could relegate a man more rapidly to oblivion? Yet contemporaries who knew have declared that he was a fascinating man to meet of an evening. " Is it going too far," asks Lord Bryce, " to say that he was the most interesting man in London to talk to? "[1] His works reveal that he was also a brilliant man, and his life, less deeply buried than many in the decent obscurity of Victorian biography, that he was a wise one. Nor did prudence entirely exclude crisis and tragedy from his career. In the following sketch I shall attempt, as briefly and vividly as possible, to depict the drama of an active and thoughtful existence, to present a personality, to give to a body of prose the commentary and the illustration of biography, and above all to indicate a plan, for it is everywhere evident that Bagehot's life was in peculiar degree influenced by an idea —by Aristotle's idea of working towards happiness through the full and varied exertion of the whole intellectual and moral nature. His career, as well as his writings, was dominated by the concept of a life that should be practical without being worldly or sordid, religious without being narrow and visionary, and without being superficial— many-sided, rich, and human.

Walter Bagehot was born on February 3, 1826, at Langport, a quiet little town tucked away in the centre of Somersetshire. Its tranquil, circum- scribed past extends far back into the larger past of England itself, providing many a curious, out- of-the-way glimpse at great events. Situated on a hill, at the point where the River Parret ceases to be navigable, excelling alike in its facilities for defence and trade, it was a place of some importance even before the Roman occupation. It survived the coming both of the Romans and the Saxons, and was in Saxon times a royal borough, having in 1086 thirty-four resident burgesses.[2] In the early fourteenth century the town returned two members to parliament, until the burgesses, reckoning, as Bagehot himself delighted to explain, that money in their pockets was better than representation in London, petitioned Edward I to relieve them of the expense of paying their members.[3] But if the worthy burgesses refused to make history in London, they could not prevent its being made at their very door. The self-sufficient, prosaic little town is closely surrounded by some of the most romantic memories in English history and legend. At Athelney Alfred the Great is said to have burned the famous cakes that he was left to bake, and to Aller in his time of triumph he led Guthrun, the Danish king, to Christian baptism. At Sedgemoor the youthful Churchill defeated the Duke of Monmouth, and Lord Goring fled with his Royalist army across Kingsmoor after the Battle of Langport. At Burton Pynsent, Lord Chatham, upon whose son Bagehot wrote an essay, began the great mansion which he never finished and in which he lived out the tragic end of a brilliant career. All of these landmarks can be distinguished on a clear day from Bagehot's boyhood home, a large, comfortable house situated in the midst of a pleasant garden on the summit of Herd's Hill, just outside the town.

About the year 1772 Bagehot's great-uncle, Samuel Stuckey, founded in Langport the Somersetshire Bank, and the little town became the headquarters of a company which grew to be the largest private bank of issue in England. Of this establishment Bagehot's father was for thirty years managing director and vice-chairman, a position in which he was later succeeded by his son.[3] For one hundred and fifty years since the beginning of the eighteenth century, two families, the Stuckeys and the Bagehots, had dominated the affairs of Langport. Through their river and sea trade they had maintained and increased prosperity and population in a southern town at a time when prosperity

and population were rapidly moving northward.
Through the bank which the Stuckeys founded
they had made a small rural community into a
considerable financial centre. Long connected in
business, they were several times allied by marriage,
and Walter Bagehot was the only child of one of
these unions, his mother having been, before her
first marriage to Joseph Prior Estlin, a Miss Edith
Stuckey. One hundred and fifty years of success
in commerce and finance may be taken as an indication both of hereditary ability and energy, and of
sound traditions of rearing and training. Of the
two families, the Bagehots, though certainly no
more distinguished and capable in business, were
more devoted to artistic and intellectual pursuits.
" Their ancestors," says Mrs. Russell Barrington,
Bagehot's sister-in-law and biographer, " can be
traced back to the fifteenth century, when one
Richard Bagehot, *alias* Badger or Baghott, possessed
the family property at Prestbury, Gloucestershire—
a property held uninterruptedly by the Bagehots
till the last century. Several of the members of
the family were Knights, many were High Sheriffs,
some were soldiers, others ecclesiastics."[4] About
1747 Walter Bagehot's great-grandfather came to
Langport, and the family quickly became prominent
in the community. Whether they retained, together with the dignity and culture of gentility,
some of the cavalier spirit which belongs to that
condition, I have not the means of determining.
Certainly the cavalier spirit was very prominent
in their last and most famous representative.

Walter's father, Thomas Watson Bagehot, carried
conscientiousness to the singular extravagance of

being a wise and careful parent. Perhaps his greatest achievement was the rearing which he gave his son. Though much less the conscious Levite, he was after all a kind of gentler Dr. Arnold. He had the same strong, earnest, masculine intellect, which, naturally preoccupied with man and his more serious affairs, deals sensibly and vigorously with business, politics, religion, and the broader principles of human nature, particularly in their moral aspects. Perhaps no type of intelligence is better suited to the instruction of the young. There is nothing abstract or "profound" in such a mind to build a barrier around itself and alienate the child, nothing whimsical or unsteady to awaken his ridicule. Thomas Bagehot was tempted neither to wild theory nor to rash experiment, and his very limitations secured him against any attempt to maintain a permanent influence over so exceptional a pupil as Walter. He could mould and develop the boy; he could not hope to overshadow the man. Logical, concrete, and sound in an obvious and fundamental way, his intellect is the kind which a boy understands and appreciates, the kind which wins his confidence and admiration from the first. It has the clarity and simplicity of an elementary principle, and is an excellent introduction to thought.

Morally, Thomas Bagehot was an impressive man. Behind the stern Victorian, of rigid convention and pedantic punctuality, there was a truly large and ample nature, in which the stern necessity of conscience was tempered by " singularly deep and warm affections."[5] His powers of understanding, of tact and adjustment, especially when guided by love, are surprising, and no one can read of him

in Mrs. Barrington's book without seeing that he
was a man who could win a boy's confidence without losing his respect, who could descend to intimacy
without sacrificing authority.   Grimly conscientious,
he urged Walter on in a programme of study severe
even to the prejudice of his health.   Yet he never
permitted that study to seem barren and uninterest-
ing, nor his manner to be for long other than tender
and affectionate.   " I travelled on to Cheddar,"
he writes to his son after leaving the latter at Bristol
College, " with my thoughts wholly fixed on you
and with a parent's prayer for your happiness, and
I believe I have thought of little else since my
return; and both Mamma and I are longing to hear
from you."[6]   With rare tact he succeeded in assuming toward his son the role of an older and wiser
fellow student.   When they played at tops they
were boys; when they discussed politics they were
men.   As a parent he frequently delivered moral
advice, but never, one supposes, obtrusively.   He
thought modesty " a great charm in boys, and the
more so, the cleverer they are."[6]

He was a man nearly as much of liberal accomplishments as of business.   He had something to
teach.   Always a lover of beauty in nature, he was
a tolerable artist in water colours;   and upon his
own property, a very successful landscape gardener.
A wide and retentive reader, he excelled particularly in his knowledge of recent English history.
According to Hutton, Walter Bagehot often said
that " when he wanted any detail concerning the
English political history of the last half-century, he
had only to ask his father, to obtain it."[7]   Doubtless
Walter's early love of natural and poetic beauty,

his confident opinions on art and painting, and his precocious brilliance as a writer upon politics were in no small degree due to his father's efforts.

Of the fascinating but unfortunate Mrs. Edith Bagehot little need be said at the moment. If Walter resembled his father in those qualities which gave stability to his genius, in those which gave it brilliance he was like his mother. Both mother and son possessed the same buoyant, sensitive nature and quick, imaginative mind, the same humorous insight into character and manners, the same zest for all kinds of intellectual activity. Mrs. Bagehot was a loving and assiduous teacher to her son in his earlier years; in his later, a worthy and sympathetic confidante. Walter's peculiar idiom of wit and racy humour, no doubt somewhat mysterious to his father, was completely intelligible to her, being in large measure her own. She was a devout High Anglican, and Walter's youthful letters contain many dutiful echoes of her own pious reflections.

Especially in his earliest years, Walter could on occasion be a high-spirited, unregenerate little fellow, impatient of control, fond of danger, and devoted to play. G. H. Sawtell gives an interesting glimpse of him at a Sunday gathering in the garden of the Stuckey house, " swarming up a great tree," when his mother sought to exhibit him, " and there glaring down on the assembly from the topmost bough in a surprising manner and to the detriment of his Sunday raiment."[8] Mrs. Barrington relates that " he used to terrify his mother by climbing to the top of Burton Pynsent Monument and there running around the coping which was

unprotected by any rail or guard."[9]   He enjoyed
playing games with his father, and like many
clever boys who have few companions of their own
age, he lived much in his imagination, being a
great slayer of Saracens in Herd's Hill garden.
Many years later he wrote:

> But generally about this interior existence children
> are dumb.   You have warlike ideas, but you cannot
> say to a sinewy relative, " My dear aunt, I wonder
> when the big bush in the garden will begin to walk
> about; I'm sure it's a crusader, and I was cutting it
> all the day with my steel sword.   But what do you
> think, aunt, for I'm puzzled about its legs, because
> you see, aunt, it has only *one* stalk; and besides, aunt,
> the leaves."[10]

But in the main Walter's was a rather sombre
boyhood.   Tragedy loomed over it.   In Sawtell's
interesting account there is a pathetic little picture
of him, in the company of his imbecile half-brother,
Vincent Estlin, " ' doing sums ' with about twenty
clocks all ticking in unison and striking to the
minute around him (such being Vincent Estlin's
whim of the hour), while his mother read *Quentin
Durward* in as high a key and as rapidly as was
possible for the benefit of poor Vincent."[11]   Despite
some adventuresome tendencies, Walter was a studious, industrious, obedient boy, remaining up until
the time when he entered the university largely
under the influence of his parents. While he was still
quite young, his mother read him Scott and
Dickens, and instructed him in the Greek Testament, to which she added her own notes.   Through
many years, even after he had gone away to
school, his father assigned and corrected essays on
historical subjects, did mathematics with him, and

encouraged him in the extremely valuable habit of being *au courant* upon contemporary political questions.

Walter was a prodigy from the first, and associating constantly with earnest and sagacious adults, he of course became earnest and sagacious beyond all belief. In some respects he seems never to have been a boy, as in others he never ceased to be one. At the age of six, he writes his Aunt Reynolds, an ardent low churchwoman who was in the habit of distributing religious tracts among her relatives, please to send him " another Daily Food for Christians, because keeping this sometimes in my pocket and reading the text and poetry in it every morning, it is nearly worn out, and I am afraid I shall lose the leaves."[11]

At five Walter was placed in the charge of Miss Jones, a governess. At eight or nine, he became a day scholar under " the notable Mr. Quekett, for fifty-six years the able master of the anciently endowed Langport Grammar School."[12] At twelve, he was sent to Bristol College, a secondary school for boys at Bristol, where he remained for three years, from August 1839 to the summer holidays of 1842. Mrs. Barrington gives almost no information concerning this college, except that Walter's course of study for the first year consisted in four subjects: classics, mathematics, German, and Hebrew. Some further knowledge may be gleaned, however, from Chilcott's *Descriptive History of Bristol*, a contemporary publication:

> Bristol College is situated in Park Row, at the top of Lodge Street. The object of this Institution is to afford the inhabitants of Bristol and its vicinity, and

to those who come from a distance, the advantages of
a classical and scientific education of the highest kind,
and on the most moderate terms.   It is under the
superintendence of a *Vice-Principal*, and *Mathematical
Professor*.

The college course includes the classical education
afforded at the public schools of Winchester, Eton,
Westminster, and Harrow; with so much instruction
in mathematics and in ancient and modern literature,
as the time to be spent by each student at the college
will allow of his acquiring.

The age of admission is twelve to thirteen years;
when an acquaintance with the rudiments of the
Greek and Latin languages, and the elementary
branches of arithmetic, may in general be presumed.

Examinations are held publicly once in each year,
at which, medals, or other suitable prizes, are distri-
buted to those students who by their talents and
application distinguish themselves.[13]

Up until 1864 classics was the only subject taken
seriously in most secondary institutions and even
Rugby, the most progressive of the great public
schools, did not make French and mathematics
regular subjects until the headmastership of Thomas
Arnold (1837–42).   It is probable therefore that
Bristol College, offering these studies not later than
1838, was one of the newer liberal foundations of
which there were a number in England at that
time.   That it was efficient and well-managed is
very likely.   At least it grounded Walter Bagehot
in mathematics and classical grammar, subjects
in which no boy, however extraordinary, can easily
drill himself, with such thoroughness that he later
won the highest honours at London University.
And while it may not have escaped all the barbarism common to schools of the time, it was at

least sufficiently free from the more conspicuous
evils of drinking, gambling, fagging, and caning,
to win the approval of his father, who must not
only have been a shrewd observer, but had special
means of gaining information.[14] The city of Bristol
was at that time the residence of a circle of distinguished scientific men, including among others
the elder Addington Symonds and Dr. James
Cowles Prichard, the ethnologist, to whom Mrs.
Bagehot was related by her first marriage. Doubtless this connection not only afforded Mr. Bagehot
expert information on Bristol College, but largely
determined him to send his son there, for though
lodging with other students at a minister's house,
Walter spent most of his spare time with the family
of Dr. Prichard, from whose conversation his father
had counselled him to derive the greatest possible
benefit. Apparently he profited even beyond the
pious wish of his father, for on one occasion he
writes to Mrs. Bagehot perhaps with *naïveté*, and
perhaps with a touch of his later malice: " I dined
at the Prichards' on Thursday. Mrs. Prichard was
very much out of spirits, but the Doctor seemed not
so much so, and talked pretty much as usual about
Niebuhr and the origin of the Etruscans."[15]

His constant association with the Prichards, the
high expectations of his parents, his own inclinations—everything contributed to fasten him to his
books. He developed an enormous zeal to excel
in scholarship, and succeeded so well that he usually
came out first in all four of his chosen subjects.
His spare time was devoted to desultory reading,
which ranged all the way from *A History of Palestine*
lent him by Mary Prichard, to Byron, Moore, and

Johnson. His comments upon the latter are surprisingly precocious. He was " struck particularly "
with Dr. Johnson's " amazing " fear of death,
gravely commends him for " having been the very
first to consecrate poetry to the reprehension of
vice," but wonders at his " preferring Goldsmith's
history of Greece to any composition of Robertson
or Hume."[15] He distinguishes between the two
phases of Lord Byron's pessimism and opines that
the poet got rather more than he deserved when
" he was driven by the out-cries of the world from
his native land and the heath of fame on which he
had before lived was turned to wormwood." He
concludes: " Lady Byron was certainly a ' orrid un '
and that ' exactly '; but Moore was too much
Byron's friend not as far as ever was possible to
throw a veil over his errors."[15]

Needless to say, this monk-like devotion to study
and reading, however gratifying to his teachers,
scarcely won approval from the majority of his
schoolmates, especially when another player was
needed for a game of ball. There were incidents,
sometimes indignities. Walter's behaviour was
apparently very manly, his attitude not only surprisingly sensible, but most philosophically objective. He speaks of these encounters without the least
anger or resentment, merely regretting them as incon-
veniences which keep him from his studies. It is somewhat as though a grave and sensible old man, myster-
iously set down amid the conditions of schoolboy life,
were describing his experiences, quite unaware how
unusual they were. Walter writes to his mother:

I was carried out just now to play with some of the
other boys, I wanted to do my mathematics, and to

mug China; but they took me out, and because I
would not play when I got out there, tied me up to the
railings and corked me as hard as they could with a
ball which made me play whether or no. They very
often beg me to come out, when they have not enough
to make up their game; and it is hard to spoil their
game; and if I do; I get a kick every now and then;
and sometimes a blow for every time I open my
mouth. It is not at all a pleasant thing to be on bad
terms with any of one's schoolfellows much more with
all. This has prevented me from doing as much mathematics with Mr. Bromly lately as before.[16]

Yet boys could scarcely remain on ill terms for long
at a time with one who was so ready to see his own
folly: " I got into the water yesterday for the first
time, and like a goose as I was, I bundled in with
my flannel waistcoat on. For which I got soundly
laughed at as was of course to be expected."[16]
Walter had other recommendations. " The easter
cakes," he informs his mother, " went down amongst
the mob with great éclat, and were thought the best
cakes that were ever made."[16] Undoubtedly
Walter's position at the college, whatever it might
have been, was not that of a timid and shrinking
" grind." Perhaps as Mrs. Barrington says, " His
exceptional gifts, combined with natural modesty,
high spirits, and the curiously powerful influences
his individuality and original humour exercised,
gave him from early youth a very distinct position
of his own."[17]

Walter's reference to his fellow students as the
" mob " is significant. In his youth he was often
supercilious. This fault proceeded not from any
overvaluation of his own merits, for no one saw
them in a colder and clearer light than he, but from

a singular vigour and detachment of mind, from a curious inaccessibility to the play of casual feeling. He perceived that his schoolmates often behaved strikingly like a mob, that in comparison with himself and his select friends they were a mob, and therefore he did not scruple to make use of that vivid expression. Nor did he ever greatly trouble to conceal his observations from those upon whom they were made. The clear, vigorous action of his mind often jarred rather sharply against more placid understandings. G. H. Sawtell, who, if he was as easily submerged in argument as he sank under the intricacies of his own grammar, could not have been a very aggressive person, speaks of Bagehot's having, at fourteen, a " conversational freshness, chiefly, as far as I was concerned, interrogatively as to what I, three years older, learnt and saw and heard in the great city, always with the result of making me feel that I had got hold of the little end of the stick."[18]

Walter had only two close friends at Bristol—Sir Edward Fry and Killegrew Wait, who was in later life a Member of Parliament, and even these he mentions seldom in his letters. He enjoyed the company of his parents in the holidays. At school he had his studies and his books. His library grew, and sometimes scholarly extravagance wrestled with middle-class thrift. " Would you have any objection," he writes his father, " to my getting Donnejan's Greek Lexicon it is the best work on the subject I believe, and Mr. Booth strongly recommends it and indeed I feel very much the want of some book of the kind. The price is the only objection, as it is about 35 shillings; I am

afraid you will think this very expensive, especially
as I have lately bought a large Latin dictionary."[19]

He was so successful a student that during a part
of his last year he was placed in a class by himself.
Even earlier he had " found time out of school hours
to take private lessons with the Mathematical
Master of the college . . . and to attend lectures
given by the well-known Dr. Carpenter on Natural
Philosophy, Zoology, and Chemistry," sciences
little taught then even in the universities.[20] But
most of all he profited from his daily association
with Dr. Prichard, to whom we may trace, according to Hutton, " that interest in the speculative side
of ethnological research, the results of which are
best seen in Bagehot's book on *Physics and Politics*."[21] Indeed Bagehot was exposed to nothing
in vain.

Up until the time when he entered the university,
Walter was, as I have said, chiefly under the
influence of his parents. They guided and controlled him, and the education which he received
was virtually their work. Undoubtedly he derived
the very greatest advantages from this education.
It provided him at an early age with a large body
of knowledge, developed extraordinary powers of
industry and concentration, schooled him in self-
restraint, as well as in habits of orderly living and
thinking, and was probably a great force in keeping his life so singularly free from the error and
vacillation which turns to clay the feet of many a
literary idol. Yet Thomas Bagehot, with all his
admirable discretion and loving kindness, was
perhaps too severe. Like most Victorians he seems
to have felt that life is iniquitous save where it

exhibits much stress and strain. Walter was under a constant pressure, which in moments of exhaustion must have become intense. Frequently his whole attitude, like that of a fast runner in a long and difficult race, is strained and nervous, pathetically unlike the robust carelessness of the unprodded boy. It is a great tribute to the tact and perception of his parents that he never was led to rebel, that he always strove eagerly to satisfy their high expectations of him and the high standards which they set. Yet these same high standards and expectations hung on him at times with the intolerable weight of a second conscience. He writes to his mother at thirteen, while at school: " We had a holiday yesterday to enable us to go to church being Ash Wednesday. I think Papa will storm at our having so many holidays."[22] Again, in a letter to his father, having explained that he has more leisure time, because of the break-up of a class which he had attended, he says: " I am afraid you will think this too much holiday for me, and if so I will give it up and work on as usual."[22] His own conscience had grown to be almost as much a petty tyrant of the passing instants as his father's was. " My heart smites me to talk of sleeping," he confides to his mother, " since I fell asleep in the most curious way last night over my books, and slept ever so long."[23] He has taken his father's recommendation of modesty so much to heart that he shrinks from speaking of himself with approval and when he does so, brushes the subject aside with almost pathetic abruptness.[24] His whole attitude toward scholastic honours is strained and anxious.

I am ashamed of myself for not having sent this

letter before, but I think now it is as well to keep it till tomorrow when I shall know my marks and order. Grace is at present ten above, and I am thirty above Wait. If I could be top in classics, I should be at the head of the Junior Department in 3 things, viz. German, classics, and Theology, and second in Mathematics; but I am afraid I am building castles in the air: tomorrow will decide. I scold myself for being so anxious.[24]

Sometimes this tendency to worry manifests itself comically enough. Always the little mid-Victorian, he succeeds at times in being the little old man, and even the little old woman. At eleven he writes his father with charming earnestness: " I heard a few days ago of poor Uncle Watson's death, it will be a great trial to his daughters as well as to Aunty; as there will be a blank created in the object of their life which it will take some time to fill up. Have Mary and Sarah fixed any future plan of life, I cannot at all imagine them without Uncle, as all their existence seemed wound up in his." He concludes, in a paroxysm of care and anxiety: " I hope you will not go down to the counting house after dinner this winter."[24]

Yet one should not lightly criticize an education which brought forth such excellent results. It was not painless education, but neither was it profitless education. Walter's fretful turn of mind rapidly disappears in his maturer letters. What was induced by the pressure of a severely Victorian household evaporated when that pressure relaxed. G. H. Sawtell notices that between the ages of twelve and sixteen his outward manner underwent a decided change. By the time he went away to the university, the change was complete. The grave

c

and anxious boy had become, perhaps partly by
way of compensation, a rather jaunty young man.
When thirty-two he told his *fiancée*, " Though I
have a very anxious and distrustful judgment, I
never have suspicions beyond my judgment."[25]
Overcautious perhaps in making a decision, he
never fretted once it was made.

Chapter II

THE WILD OATS OF A VICTORIAN

BAGEHOT did not go to Oxford or Cambridge. His father objected to institutions that required religious tests. The only remaining choice was University College, London, which he entered in the beginning of October 1842. No place of learning could have been better suited to his peculiar needs. It offered him a broad and liberal curriculum, competent professors—above all, the immediate proximity of a great city.

Walter Bagehot was a man made to flourish in a great city. He was not one of those solitary, lyric, anti-social geniuses, who live entirely in the realization and expression of their own inward being, who must have a beautiful but vacant world —except perhaps for a few adoring women—into which to expand their æsthetic and insatiable egos, and who compensate us with wonderful descriptions of nature for the interest we take in their exaggerated sorrows. There was no heroic selfishness in Bagehot, and not much poetic imagination. Nor again, had he that bookish sort of mind which views mankind from across the abyss that separates the quiet study from the busy world. He was not like Guizot, who could walk down a street without ever knowing what he saw, and pass through a great experience without being affected by it; who was amazing not so much because he wrote brilliantly of politics without any practical

knowledge of them, but because he wrote of them no
more brilliantly after he had been for many years
the first minister of a citizen king, and had led a
great party.[1] A person of this type learns from
books with such a fatal facility that he hardly thinks
of looking at life. The mature man is the victim
of the clever schoolboy, whose mind crystallizes
early and sparkles ever after with the same precocious, immature brilliance. Bagehot was not such
a man. He had, as he says of Shakespeare, an
experiencing nature. His life was a continual
growth and expansion. He actually knew something of the great prosaic, urban world in which
he lived, for he used his eyes and his ears, and never
forgot that behind it all was that familiar mystery
—human nature. There were no artificial barriers
between him and his chosen study. He was gay,
witty, and amiable, one who enjoyed society and
whom society enjoyed. He loved the multiform
excitement of a great city, and he had the courage,
energy, and alertness to play an important and
active role in its noisy, perilous drama. At the
same time, he maintained within himself a small
region of quiet and detachment. All thinkers must
have a solitude, and Bagehot's was an interior one,
which apparently was disturbed neither by the
hurry and confusion of an active career nor by the
strongest personal emotion. His love letters to
Eliza Wilson are an extraordinary example of a
man's observing himself coolly while under the
greatest emotional stress.

At the beginning of his first term at University
College Bagehot met Richard Holt Hutton, later
to become a prominent editor and literary critic.

" I was struck," says Hutton, " by the questions put by a lad with large dark eyes and florid complexion to the late Professor De Morgan."[2] The two young students became fast friends and were soon launched on the exploration of London. They went to the Chartist and Anti-Corn Law meetings, delighting in the motley spectacle of humanity about them and thrilling at the stir of political excitement in the air. They heard Cobden, Bright, and O'Connell, and compared their oratory with that of Burke and Macaulay. They attended the House of Commons, and followed almost with the interest of fellow politicians the careers of Peel, Russell, Disraeli, and Gladstone. At the breakfasts of Henry Crabb Robinson they became acquainted with a distinguished literary circle, of which Arthur Hugh Clough, also Bagehot's close and lasting friend, was a member. They read the writings, and later made the acquaintance, of Dr. James Martineau, one of the most notable figures in contemporary religious controversy.

University College, London, was the result of a movement begun in 1825 by such groups as objected to the religious tests of Oxford and Cambridge, and to the narrowness of their curricula. The founders represent singularly diverse elements in the nation. There was Campbell, the poet and idealist; Lord Brougham, the great agitator; Isaac Lyon Goldsmid, a Jewish business man; the Duke of Norfolk, representing the Catholics; important Dissenters like John Wishaw; and finally the Utilitarians, among whom Bentham was prominent. According to Mr. H. Hale Belliot:

The strongest single influence on the new founda-

tion in London was that in Edinburgh. . . . The
extended range of the subjects of university study, the
lecture system, the non-residence of the students, their
admission to single courses, the absence of religious
tests, the dependence of the professors on fees and the
democratic character of the institution, were all
deliberate imitations of the Scottish practice.[3]

—and of German and American practice, it might
be added, for the University of London was also
modelled after those of Bonn and Virginia.
" The university was divided into a medical department and what was known as a general department, comprising arts, laws, and sciences. . . .
For the general department the Council drew up a
regular course of study, although it did not require
that all students should follow it."[3] This course,
which Bagehot seems to have followed, included
Latin, Greek, logic, the philosophy of the human
mind, chemistry, natural philosophy, moral and
political philosophy, and political economy. To
the common danger of so broad a curriculum, that
of merely acquiring a smattering of many subjects,
a person of such thorough preparation, such tireless energy, such powers of rapid acquisition as
Bagehot, is scarcely exposed. The extraordinary
soundness and many-sidedness of his education is
evident throughout his writings. Oxford might
have made him more of a stylist, more of a Newman-
ite and a conservative, but University College
confirmed him in what he was.

The professors under whom Bagehot studied
were Augustus De Morgan, of mathematics and
philosophy, Henry Malden and George Long, of
Greek, and T. Hewitt Key, of what we should call

classical philology. Bagehot's own account of
these men is undoubtedly the most enlightening:

> Professor De Morgan has *one* eye, and a large white
> face, rather like Mr. Paul in his manner. He lectures
> very well, and seems as interested in mathematics, as
> if he were lecturing on them for the first time, and had
> not been going continually over the same ground these
> ten years.
>
> Mr. Malden, they say, was a moderately pleasant
> looking man before he had the small pox, but certainly
> now he is, as pitiful a looking creature, as man ever
> saw. I like him, I think the best of all; he gives us
> an immense quantity of information on all manner
> of subjects; and seems quite delighted, if you go and
> ask him a question which I have done once or twice.
> He dresses in clothes which look as if moths had been
> long their familiar inhabitants. Professor Long I
> don't like so much, he is by no means *so* interesting,
> *and* is exceedingly minute, not to say almost tire-
> somely so, but he may improve as he gets more accus-
> tommed to the class, and we get more accustommed
> to him. [4]

At another time he writes more favourably of
Mr. Long, from whom his mother had received a
letter:

> He is as you say the very opposite of a learned
> booby. He is a dry, withered looking man, who seems
> to be ready to go through any amount of labour. He
> is very clearheaded, though with rather a narrow
> disciplinarian mind, and is very suspicious and rather
> sceptical. He has a dry humour which used to make
> me cry with laughing. [4]

Again Walter observes rather superciliously: " He
is always quoting Aristotle, whom he considers
as the greatest thinker who ever lived."[4] But
perhaps Mr. Long's enthusiasm was not altogether
lost upon his student, for no writer is more truly

Aristotelian. The most eminent of these professors
was undoubtedly Mr. De Morgan, who is remembered for his controversy on formal logic with
Sir William Hamilton. He is accredited with a
sense of humour and that same contempt for
careless and shallow thinking which appears so
strongly in Bagehot at this time.[5]

At University College, as at Bristol, Bagehot was
an extremely conscientious student, invariably
going into examinations with the gloomiest fore-
bodings and coming out with very high, if not the
highest, honours. He did not fret and worry so
much about his scholarship as before; but, for a
variety of motives, in which a sense of duty and
an eagerness in competition were prominent, he
was none the less bent upon succeeding. He
spared no effort, persevering at times even in the
face of an imminent danger. His health, always
delicate, and scarcely much benefited by a boyhood of hard study, gave cause, in the summer of
1843, for serious alarm. He developed a cough,
and was persuaded to remain away from the
university during the autumn term. Frequently,
throughout his college career, he pursued his
studies while in severe physical suffering:

> I have chosen not to go in for classical honours and
> this is the case. After writing that note to Papa on
> Saturday I determined on a last trial to see how I
> should get on. But after an hour's work I got
> thoroughly exhausted and went to sleep over my
> books, and when I awoke, really felt as though I had
> not two ideas—and this decided me. I had persevered
> all day against a pain in my shoulder, and a slight
> difficulty in breathing, which are by no means incen-
> tives to hard study.[6]

In this instance his health improved slightly on the next day and he continued with his preparation, eventually obtaining third highest honours. On another occasion he describes his efforts in an examination:

> I went but I am sorry to say did very badly. It was with a very painful effort that I collected my thoughts to *understand* the questions which I had been preparing for and some of which I had learnt up only a couple of days before. The effort of doing sums was still more painful as my head was terribly hot and aching and the whole room spinning round with me.[7]

In later years Bagehot learned to keep his efforts somewhat nearer the bounds of his physical endurance, yet quiescence was the last thing of which he was capable, and it was a favourite opinion of his that intense and absorbing activity was the best cure for a bad headache.

At this time Bagehot found himself in one of those ugly situations in which even the bravest and most forthright course seems a little ignominious. Shortly after taking up his abode with a Dr. Hoppus, who boarded and lodged students of the university, he became aware that two inmates of the house were carrying on certain immoral proceedings, the exact nature of which Mrs. Barrington does not disclose. Bagehot tried to disbelieve the fact as long as he could, and when that was not possible, " expressed his abhorrence " to the students, but in vain. At length, deciding after many sleepless nights that further silence was fair neither to the young men themselves nor to Dr. Hoppus, he conquered his repugnance of performing " the office of tale bearer," and revealed the whole affair.[8] Bagehot was only sixteen at the time.

Four years after his graduation from University College, Bagehot wrote that the more vital part of education consists

> not in tutors or lectures or in books " got up," but in Wordsworth and Shelley; in the books that all read because all like—in what all talk of because all are interested—in the argumentative walk or the disputatious lounge—in the impact of young thought upon young thought, of fresh thought on fresh thought— of hot thought on hot thought—in mirth and refutation —in ridicule and laughter—for these are the free play of the natural mind, and these cannot be got without a college. [9]

The rhetoric is Macaulay's, but the feeling, Bagehot's; nor is the sentiment ungraceful in one who had already received a solid grounding in the routine subjects. That period at which ideas are new and large and mysterious, at which the mind, first feeling its strength, looks out with a thrill of delight on the universe of thought, is one which he left with regret and always remembered with pleasure. His letters of this date are as full of poets and philosophers as another youth's might have been of horses and racing. Hutton recounts:

> Once, I remember, in the vehemence of our argument as to whether the so-called logical principle of identity (A is A) were entitled to rank as " a law of thought " or only as a postulate of language, Bagehot and I wandered up and down Regent Street for something like two hours in the vain attempt to find Oxford Street. [10]

Bagehot had passed most of his life in a sequestered country home. He had been carefully trained. He was full to bursting with the stores of many years of eager and lonely reading. Suddenly he

was emancipated from the dominion, however
welcome, of his parents and plunged at once into
the great real world of London life and the even
greater unreal world of intellectual discovery.
Together with comrades of his own age he found
himself embarked on a magnificent adventure. Is
it any wonder that he glorified this adventure, that
he regretted its passing, that he envied Pitt the
illustrious descent which permitted him, without
fear of the ridicule and laughter of the world, to
speak " in the grand style," and to retain through
his later years the same magic youthful confidence
in the greatness of his abilities and his future?
" We try to be sensible, and we end in being
ordinary; we fear to be eccentric, and we end in
being commonplace." Only a William Pitt the
Younger receives " from fortune the inestimable
permission *to be himself*."[11] And yet to Bagehot
also, though perhaps in lesser degree, fortune
granted that permission, as we shall see.

His vigour of mind and skill in argument quickly
made him a leader among his fellow students. In
debating, which was held in great esteem at
University College, he was an acknowledged master,
and together with Hutton and W. C. Roscoe
organized the New Debating Society.

Hutton observes of Bagehot as an undergraduate:

In those early days Bagehot's manner was often
supercilious. We used to attack him for his intellectual
arrogance . . . a quality which I believe was not
really in him, though he had then much of its external
appearance. Nevertheless his genuine contempt for
what was intellectually feeble was not accompanied
by an even adequate appreciation of his own powers.
At college, however, his satirical " Hear, hear," was

a formidable sound in the debating society, and one
which took the heart out of many a younger speaker;
and the ironical " How much? " with which in conversation he would meet an over-eloquent expression,
was always of a nature to reduce a man, as the mathematical phrase goes, to his " lowest terms."[12]

Hutton attributes his friend's behaviour partly to
high spirits, partly to

his remarkable " detachment " of mind—in other
words, his comparative inaccessibility to the contagion
of blind sympathy. . . . He certainly had not in any
high degree that sensitive instinct as to what others
would feel, which so often shapes even the thoughts
of men, and still oftener their speech, into mild and
complaisant, but into unmeaning and unfruitful,
forms.[12]

All this is very kindly and true so far as it goes,
but Mrs. Bagehot put the matter much more
plainly to the offender himself: " Mr. Reynolds
says your faults at present remind him of his at
your age, namely, that you are much fonder of
finding out and attacking all authorities where they
are wrong than you are of humbling yourself to
obedience and deference, and learning of them
where they are right."[13]   In all his writings Bagehot
is perhaps never so dashing and clever as in adverse
criticism.   Those who attack heroes are seldom
averse to annihilating dunces.   Between the quick
man and the slow man there is often, especially
in youth, a natural antipathy.   Citing the observation of Hazlitt that " Measure for Measure," more
than any other of Shakespeare's plays, seems to
have been written "con amore, and with a relish,"
Bagehot himself remarks:

Now the entire character of Angelo, which is the

expressive feature of the piece, is nothing but a successful embodiment of the pleasure, the malevolent
pleasure, which a warm-blooded and expansive man
takes in watching the rare, the dangerous and inanimate excesses of the constrained and cold-blooded.
One seems to see Shakespeare, with his bright eyes and
his large lips and buoyant face, watching with a
pleasant excitement the excesses of his thin-lipped and
calculating creation.[14]

One seems also to see the youthful Bagehot, " with
his bright eyes and his large lips," watching some
pretentious debater with an " excitement " equally
" pleasant." And indeed it is very dull to be
mere " social cement," to shape one's speech into
" mild and complaisant forms " and connive at
stupidity and folly. How infinitely more amusing
to bait and mystify, to shock and awaken, to dismay
and dumbfound! One has the power to shatter
pompous platitude and eloquent fallacy, and one
delights in exerting one's power. One has a knack
for pulverizing fools, and one would like to develop
that knack. One is eager in the pursuit of ideas,
and dullards are very much in the way.

Time taught Bagehot to conceal and moderate
his ὕβρις. He took to Socratic questioning and
learned how to slaughter a dunce almost without
visible bloodshed. Very early he developed a
technique of social experimentation, remaining all
his life an inveterate drawing-room naturalist.
The tedious, the hypocritical, and the pretentious
always received his particular attention; but even
his best friends sometimes became his guinea pigs,
though they seem never to have suffered any
painful vivisection:

" An aberrant form," I believe, the naturalists call

the seal and such things in natural history; odd shapes
that can only be explained by a long past, and which
swim with a certain incongruity in their present
milieu. Now "old Crabb" was (to me at least) just
like that. You watched with interest and pleasure his
singular gestures, and his odd way of saying things,
and muttered, as if to keep up the recollection, "And
this is the man who was the friend of Goethe, and is
the friend of Wordsworth!" There was a certain
animal oddity about "old Crabb," which made it a
kind of mental joke to couple him with such great
names, and yet he was to his heart's core thoroughly
coupled with them.[14]

Indeed not merely "old Crabb" Robinson, but
many others were often but strange animals in an
aquarium to Bagehot. Robinson's famous literary
breakfasts offered unusual opportunities for experiment. The friend of Goethe and Wordsworth was
not an entirely satisfactory host. He forgot to
make tea, he lost his keys, he delayed the preparation of the meal with an infinity of long stories,
and brought the hunger of his guests to the point
of extremest agony before serving them.

> The more astute of his guests [says Bagehot] used
> to breakfast before they came, and then there was
> much interest in seeing a steady literary man, who did
> not understand the region, in agonies at having to
> hear three stories before he got his tea, one again
> between his milk and his sugar, another between his
> butter and his toast, and additional zest in making a
> stealthy inquiry that was sure to intercept the coming
> delicacies by bringing on Schiller and Goethe.[14]

Hutton comments:

> The only "astute" person referred to was, I imagine,
> Bagehot himself, who confessed to me, much to my
> amusement, that this was always his own precaution
> before one of Crabb Robinson's breakfasts.... It

was very characteristic in him that he should not only have noticed—for that, of course, any one might do —this weak element in Crabb Robinson's breakfasts, but that he should have kept it so distinctly before his mind as to make it the centre, as it were, of a policy, and the opportunity of a mischievous stratagem to try the patience of others.[15]

Hutton does not mention that his own foibles were sometimes under the experimenter's eye. Though a very kindly and generous person, he was a little narrow in his views of morality and rather foolishly severe in his censure of others. Bagehot often jarred him to moral explosion by assuming " a cynically tolerant view towards most of the weaknesses of human nature."[16]

Bagehot was graduated from the University of London with the highest honours, taking the mathematical scholarship with his Bachelor's degree in 1846, and the gold medal in intellectual and moral philosophy with his Master's in 1848. Shortly after, though with some preliminary doubts as to the value and morality of the profession, he began to read law with Mr. Hall, and later with Mr. Quain, both prominent barristers of the time.

During this period he was troubled with melancholy. The causes are not far to seek, and one was very grave and real—the great tragedy which befell his mother, of whom it is now necessary to speak more fully. This pathetic and rather mysterious lady was certainly a person of extraordinary charm. Even the grave and serious Hutton, with whom she had never been friends, speaks of " a very pretty and lively woman, who had, by her previous marriage with a son of Dr. Estlin of Bristol, been brought at an early age into an intellectual atmosphere by which she had greatly profited."[17]   G. H. Sawtell describes her as being at thirty-eight, just before her marriage to Walter's father, a " very lively widow, brilliant and fascinating."[18]   Mrs. Barrington, who knew her when she was seventy-two, expatiates on her " lovely complexion and other traces of beauty," her voice " soft and persuasive " with " an emphatic ring which made people attend," her " intellectual vivacity," her " keen relish for intellectual pleasures," her " power of infusing life into the atmosphere about her," of stimulating it "with the invigorating tonic of humour."[19]   The testimony of Mrs. Bagehot's own letters is even more enlightening.   They reveal piety and humour, simplicity and cleverness, gentle perversity and high moral principle mingled in that curiously illogical manner which admits of but one explanation—that the ultimate logic was in feeling, and that the writer was very much of a woman. Doubtless it was not the least part of her charm that, behind her formidable cleverness and beauty, she remained a creature of the emotions and the affections, whose ruling principle was worship and love.   The person upon whom these treasures of devotion were bestowed was not so much her husband as her son Walter.   Natural affection, close similarity in character and temperament, mutual talent and charm—everything contributed to strengthen the bond between them.   But no amount of explanation can indicate so well as the following letter the extraordinary appeal of Mrs. Bagehot's personality and the effect which it must have produced upon her son:

11th June, 1845.
Day of St. Barnabus and my
beloved Stuckey's death.

My own Blessing,

A line I must dash off to thank you for yours. I was a *leetle* disappointed to hear that you thought we had better not have the pleasure of your company before next week, and, being thankful you feel well enough to stay, must not, I suppose, say a word against it upon my principle of "trimming the lamps" vigorously, and "watching in our various duties and callings with our various talents that we may return those 'who have the rule over us' and our Lord His own with usury"; but if Dr. Bright recommends a quicker transition to purer air, which he might, as there is now quite a change in the weather and you suffer from the heat so much, how fervently we shall delight to welcome you. I need not say I love and value you as much as I loved and valued Stuckey [a son by her first marriage, who died] at the same age, more I cannot; but I think my love for you has been happier, more roses and fewer thorns, because you have been since your birth so much more happily situated, and from the least boy ever joined with joy and pleasure in the same mental pursuits I have ever followed the most myself—not that I must ape the literature that you have (though I have always been fond of books, since, as a child, it was often a loud sentence of reproach to me—"Edith Stuckey, do not sit so lost over a book "), for when I was talking over your argument with William Wood, not only Papa had told me I was stupid, by giving me your explanation of the fact about Burke, but Aunt Reynolds gravely said, " now Edith, you are not to infer that Walter was wrong because you think him so, for you know you *are* ignorant," which I am quite ready to admit, only I thought to myself— I do like Walter to make that clear to others what is clear I dare say to his own research, so rapidly improving and telling; and when he does, I think I can *sense him*, though profundity in the subject may still

D

be wanting. . . . My elastic mind is daily recovering from the loss of my beloved brother. My mind, like his *must be cheerful*, from its vivid enjoyment of blessings left. . . . I think of my own brother constantly as if, in the transfer to a purer state, conversation and communion, that I thank God I sought on earth, are still carried on with him.[20]

The tragedy which darkened Mrs. Bagehot's life, as well indeed as her husband's and her son's, was that in her later years she was subject to frequent attacks of insanity, the result, partly at least, of a succession of heavy misfortunes. Her first husband died when she was still quite young. A few years later the eldest son of this marriage died of some illness, the second of the effects of a coach accident; the third was growing up an imbecile. These events unhinged her mind, and though she largely recovered, insanity returned upon her with approaching age. What this calamity must have meant to a man like Walter Bagehot need not be dwelt upon. One of the greatest joys of his life became at the same time his greatest sorrow, the more awful and terrible because the knowledge of it seems to have broken upon him gradually, and while he was still growing up. In his earlier letters there are pitiful passages in which he wonders at a strangeness in his mother that he cannot understand. At twelve he writes to her, apparently in answer to queries strangely insistent:

I know not why you should want me to answer to the question whether I wished to see you. I forbore answering it because I thought the thing spoke for itself. I do wish to see you or rather I long to see once more you and dearest, dearest Papa.[21]

This tragedy exerted a determining influence

upon his life and character. Undoubtedly it much increased his Englishman's sense of reserve. Few men so frank and talkative have revealed so little of their private and personal thoughts, and Disraeli in comparison is transparency waving the flag of secrecy. It deepened an experience otherwise peculiarly smooth and happy, and gave to a naturally cool, rational disposition a warmth and richness which it might not otherwise have possessed, and to which the essays on Hartley Coleridge and William Cowper, with their fine perception into delicate and sensitive character, bear eloquent witness. By inflicting upon him a constant nervous strain, by sapping his energies and destroying his peace of mind, it may conceivably, as Mrs. Barrington urges, have prevented him from attempting a more " creative " type of literature than the essay. Yet any such theory is extremely dubious. There is little evidence that he particularly aspired to loftier artistic fame, or that he had a genius suited to anything else than the admirable success which he achieved.

Bagehot met his misfortune characteristically. He never mentioned it, and seldom allowed his outward manner or way of life to be affected by it. Yet even more than his father, he fought the battle at his mother's side, patiently following her in the labyrinth of delusion, dispelling a strange notion now with tactful humour, now with cogent argument, comforting her when comfort seemed necessary, and when sternness, solemnly urging her to make, for her sake and her family's, a supreme effort to keep her mind in check. What this experience and these exertions must have cost a

sensitive man can only be imagined. All the
fascinations of a brilliant career, which might have
been his for the stretching forth of a hand, he
seems to have counted as little against the duty
toward his mother, and the desire to help her.
When in 1852 he was summoned to the bar, though
possessing all the talents which insure success in
the great professional world of London, he returned,
that he might be near his mother, to the paternal
counting house at Langport, and though ultimately
perhaps, his achievements would have been much
the same, whatever path he chose, his sacrifice was
not therefore the less noble. Up until the last seven
years of his life, he bore his burden of anxiety
without faltering, and when in 1870 his mother
died, he said, after the funeral, " The *worst* of it is,
that by many it was looked on as a relief."[22]

At no time, according to Mrs. Barrington, did
his mother's insanity prey upon him so painfully as
when he was studying law at London. In his essay
on " Hartley Coleridge," written about four years
later, he quotes from the preface to " Endymion ":
" The imagination of a boy is healthy, and the
mature imagination of a man is healthy, but there
is a space of life between, in which the soul is in a
ferment, the character undecided, the way of
life uncertain, the ambition thick-sighted."[23]
Bagehot went through such a period of ferment
at a peculiarly unfortunate time. His exertions
in obtaining the gold medal for the Master's degree
had left him once more in very poor health. His
most intimate friend, Hutton, had become a
student at Heidelberg. For the first time he was
living by himself in lodgings. In the loneliness of

a huge metropolis, remote alike from the wise counsel of his father and the charm of his mother's personality, he saw their tragedy in the darkest colours of reality and imagination. He was fully aware that in some respects he resembled his mother closely, and when, wrestling with his problem, he felt his nerves tighten and his thoughts grow wild and feverish, he must have believed that he tottered on the edge of an abyss. How serious the danger was, I have no certain means of determining. Such unpublished letters as I have seen yield no evidence on the point; yet the essay on " Hartley Coleridge " contains an ominous sentence: " Though it be false and mischievous to speak of hereditary vice, it is most true and wise to observe the mysterious fact of hereditary temptation."[23] If this observation refers to his own experience, it indicates not only the greatness of his peril, but the view which he ultimately took of it. It was not something fated and irresistible, but a " temptation," to be put down by the will, and put it down he did. It is both interesting and inspiring that a thinker whose most conspicuous quality is his steady and incorruptible sanity was once in some danger of going insane. Seldom has mind had so much power over mind.

But the fear of insanity, if he felt it, was not his only concern. The future looked very black. A legal career seemed for a number of reasons impossible. The only profession open to him appeared to be that of commerce, for which at the time he had no enthusiasm. The successes with which he met in writing, the publication in *The Prospective Review* of the paper on currency in 1847,

and that on John Stuart Mill, in 1848, did very little
to raise his spirits. Perhaps the sight of his own
thoughts, set down for the first time in the coldness
of black and white, was a little disappointing.

The tragedies of youth are seldom altogether
dignified. With deep and genuine suffering was
mixed not a little adolescent melancholy, of which
some playing with the ideas of Catholicism and
much dismal verse were the chief products. I
quote but one stanza of the verse:

> As an idiot mother prowling
>   For a lost and roaming brood;
> As a wild hyæna howling
>   For her foul and cankered food;
> So ravenous pain strays scowling
>   Round lean life's banquet crude.[24]

Many of his " poems " are obviously modelled
upon Newman's, and reveal the same romantic
playing of the imagination upon the colourful
antiquities of the Church. Both the character of
his early training and the natural inclinations of his
mind tended to give the melancholy into which
he had fallen a religious turn. The restrained
eloquence and the compelling logic of Newman had
made a profound impression upon him. According to Hutton, he was never really near conversion
to Catholicism. However he might indulge in
rhetoric upon occasion, he maintained at bottom
an extremely cautious and judicial attitude. He
feared the effects of authoritarianism upon the
conscience, and he " condemned and dreaded "
in the Church itself the " tendency to use her
power over the multitude for purposes of low
ambition."[25] Yet her grandeur and antiquity,

her system and order might have made a strong
appeal to a fatigued and feverish imagination. He
seems at this time to have had a sense of spiritual
isolation, of remoteness from religious truth. A
sentence from an essay of his, dating from this
period, runs as follows: " Gazing after the infinite
essence, we are like men watching through the
drifting clouds for a glimpse of the true heavens
on a drear November day; layer after layer passes
from our view, but still the same immovable grey
rack remains."[26] Weary and confused, oppressed
by loneliness, by the fading of earthly hopes and the
multiplication of religious doubts, Bagehot may have
looked toward the enduring, authoritarian security
of the Catholic Church with that same vague,
nostalgic longing, characteristic of so many readers
and followers of Newman. In " The Letters on
the French Coup D'État," written shortly after
this time, there is a passage which, though meant
mischievously to antagonize Unitarian readers,
may have some foundation in personal experience.
The Church is made to address such unbelievers
as himself:

> Shut yourselves up in a room—make your mind a
> blank—go down (as ye speak) into the " depths of your
> consciousness "—scrutinize the mental structure—in-
> quire for the elements of belief—spend years, your
> best years, in the occupation; and at length—when
> your eyes are dim, and your brain hot, and your hand
> unsteady—then reckon what you have gained: see if
> you cannot count on your fingers the certainties you
> have reached: reflect which of them you doubted
> yesterday, which you may disbelieve to-morrow.[27]

There is but one way out of the quandary: " No,
if you would reason—if you would teach—if you

would speculate, come to us. We have our *premises* ready; years upon years before you were born, intellects whom the best of you delight to magnify, toiled to systematize the creed of ages."[27]

It was at this time that Bagehot first knew Arthur Hugh Clough, who in November 1848 resigned his fellowship at Oriel College, Oxford, to become principal of University Hall, in London. Having subscribed for the erection of the Hall, Bagehot was now a member of its council, and in this capacity he saw much of the new principal. They became close friends and remained so until the poet's death. According to Hutton, Clough had " a greater intellectual fascination for Bagehot than any of his contemporaries."[28] This fascination did not depend so much on any fundamental likeness between the two men, though in animal vigour, natural reserve, hatred of hypocrisy, and in a mutual admiration for Wordsworth, they had much in common. Characteristically, Bagehot saw in his new friend not so much a congenial spirit as an interesting " specimen." He was the living illustration, both in his life and his poetry, of a fundamental truth which Bagehot had always felt very keenly, and never so keenly as at the time of which I write. As Hutton puts it:

> Clough's chief fascination for Bagehot, was, I think, that he had as a poet in some measure rediscovered, at all events realized, as few ever realized before, the enormous difficulty of finding truth—a difficulty which he somewhat paradoxically held to be enhanced rather than diminished by the intensity of the truest modern passion for it. The stronger the desire, he teaches, the greater is the danger of illegitimately satisfying that desire by persuading ourselves that what we *wish* to

believe, is true, and the greater the danger of ignoring the actual confusions of human things.[28]

And his life exemplified his doctrine, for he remained always in doubt. A letter to Hutton throws light, not only upon Clough, but upon Bagehot himself:

Clough you would like very much, I think. He is a man of strong, and clear though not very quick intellect: so that I feel like a gnat buzzing about him. He has a great deal of imagination, and has written a good deal of poetry; a proportion of which is good, though he unfortunately has been in the Highlands and talks of barmaids and potatoe-girls and other operative females there in a very humiliating manner as it seems to me though Roscoe defends it. You would, I think, agree with me in thinking that his mind was defective in moral feeling, and in the conception of law generally as applied to morals. But he is evidently a man of great honesty and moral courage with an immense deal of feeling. C. Prichard says his mind was injured he thinks by an overstrained ascetism when he first knew him at Oxford, and has never recovered from this evil. Roscoe and myself put him into the Principalship.[29]

Finding that his melancholy grew steadily deeper, Bagehot suddenly decided upon a change of air, and in the autumn of 1851 went off to Paris. The visit began as the modest and decorous fling of a serious youth about to assume the responsibilities of Victorian manhood. It ultimately resulted in one of the most curiously illuminating incidents in Bagehot's life, and perhaps the most brilliant single piece of writing which he produced. Shortly after his arrival Louis Napoleon's *coup d'état* occurred, and Bagehot was requested to write upon it by *The Enquirer*, the respectable and somewhat placidly idealistic organ of the Unitarians. *The Enquirer*

had itself recently been the object of a kind of
coup d'état, and the successful conspirators, Hutton
and a group of enterprising young intellectuals,
were in desperate search of lively material. Bagehot
gave them rather more than they bargained for.
The air of Paris was electric with revolution, with
the exciting dangers, the exhilarating fallacies, the
intoxicating drama of French revolution. A few
sniffs evaporated all melancholy; the residue was
an hilarious and theatrical cynicism. He spent his
days in assisting the republicans to erect barricades
in the streets, his evenings in preparing bomb-
shells for their sympathizers, the gentle readers of
The Enquirer. In so far as those readers had any
definite opinions upon the *coup d'état*, they doubtless felt that Louis Napoleon was a very immoral
man, that his destruction of the republican liberties
of France was a ruthless and wicked act, and that
if the truth were known, the Catholic Church
probably stood behind the whole affair. Bagehot
gave them a cool and cynical justification of
Louis, a brilliant defence of his suppression of
liberties, and tossed in an eloquent eulogy of the
Church, maliciously assuming the sympathy of his
readers at precisely those points where they were
likely to be most outraged. He argued that the
prince, who, he insisted, " was far better prepared
for the duties of a statesman by gambling on the
turf than he would have been by poring over the
historical and political dissertations of the good,"
had given the French that of which they had stood
most in need—a stable and arbitrary government.[30] For the French are far too clever a people
to rule themselves. They are too good at making

abstract, logical deductions. They prefer the vanity of thinking consistently to the hard work of thinking well—or the safety of not thinking at all. They are too keen at seeing the value of new systems and the pertinence of radical suggestions, ever to retain a republican consitution long enough to get used to it. They are too rational and adaptive ever to settle into republican habits. Only a great political people, like the English, has the sound stupidity for true self-government. Only the Englishman possesses that beneficent horror of ideas which restrains him "within his old pursuits, his well-known habits, his tried expedients, his verified conclusions, his traditional beliefs."[31] Such a man can be trusted to use his liberties in a thoroughly safe and unimaginative manner. But all men are not so fortunate, and the French, being cursed with intelligence, must congratulate themselves that they had a good tyrant to keep the peace.[31]

"The Letters on the Coup D'État" evidently stirred up considerable alarm, not merely among the readers of *The Enquirer*, but among its revolutionary management as well. Bagehot returned to London a cheerful man.

Chapter III

BUSINESS AND ROMANCE

HAVING been called to the Bar in 1852, Bagehot promptly gave up law as a profession, and settled at Herd's Hill to learn the banking business with his father. This decision was probably the result of several considerations. The study of law, somewhat too dry and abstract for a lively and vivid mind, had not been altogether congenial; his health was not of the best; his mother desired his presence at home. Finally, he decided that banking would afford him more leisure to pursue such cultural and scientific studies as he had already become interested in. Mrs. Barrington informs us:

> He had acquired a footing on the ladder of authorship with the articles on Currency and on John Stuart Mill, published in the *Prospective Review*; he had sprung boldly ahead in the letters on the *Coup D'État*, escaping once and for all from what was expected of him in Unitarian circles, and he was more than ever aware on returning to London from Paris, that the practice of law was incompatible with literature, though he never for a moment thought of making literature his avowed profession.[1]

Mrs. Barrington's last remark, that Bagehot never thought of making literature his profession, is significant. The peculiar circumstances of his life, his family tradition, the natural tendencies of his mind and temperament rendered the quiet existence of the professional writer unattractive

44

to him. He was a man who required the excitement of action, the sense of dealing with an immediately tangible reality. The son of a stoutly
commercial family, he felt, as he wrote his friend
Hutton, that " a fulcrum and a position in the world
. . . is quite necessary to comfort in England."[2]
Moreover, as Mrs. Barrington says, he probably
needed a narcotic for the trouble which was constantly preying upon his mind. A quiet and
leisurely life would have invited brooding, but the
absorbing routine of business afforded an escape.

But in my opinion there is an even deeper reason
and broader basis for his preference of a banker's
life to a lawyer's. As in the field of thought he
assumed upon all subjects almost instinctively a
humanistic attitude, so in life he naturally gravitated
to a profession which would not confine him to a
single activity, but would permit him to develop
that versatility and human breadth of experience
for which he is known. How conscious this motive
was, it is impossible to say, but it is significant that
in his later writings he often speaks of the banker's
life as being, for precisely the reason which I have
indicated, the happiest and richest possible in our
modern civilization.

The early years of his business career were both
full and exciting. His days were spent at the
counting house, his evenings in the study, and the
awful solemnities of book-keeping by double entry
were alternated with the pleasant follies of Shelley
and of Hartley Coleridge. In spite of much ill-
health and the frequent mental aberrations of his
mother, he went about both tasks with inexhaustible
high spirits, for he was one of those whose state of

mind is not dependent on their fortunes. He writes
to his friend Sir Edward Fry:

> I have in general pretty good health, though at the
> present time I am a good deal troubled by rather severe
> headaches. But I verily believe I am the happiest
> person living. I have such a flow of good spirits as
> no calamities I think could long interrupt, much less
> exhaust. As for melancholy without apparent cause
> natural to some minds, I do not know what it means.
> I am not over-sanguine as to the future in general, but
> I have a sort of reckless cheerfulness that gets on very
> well without the aid of hope.[2]

Bagehot's entry into the counting house threw
him once more into daily contact with his father,
and the association must have caused the kind old
gentleman nearly as much grief as happiness, for
Walter, though in essentials at once brilliant and
reliable, had no perception of the religious aspects
of banking. His father, though a simple and unpre-
tentious Unitarian in religious belief, invested
business with something of the elaborate sacerdota-
lism of a more formalistic creed. Business was his
golden calf—not that he expected any extraordinary
returns for his idolatry. An adequate maintenance
for his family was all that he ever desired. The
truth is, Thomas Bagehot was by nature a curious
mixture of the idolater and the eremite. The very
breath of idolatry is ceremony, and for ceremony he
seems to have had a modest and unobtrusive fondness. His son when still very small refers in a letter
rather elaborately to Sir Robert Peel as "the right
Hon. Baronet."[2] One suspects he was imitating a
habit of his father. But even more than he loved
ritual, the elder Bagehot longed for exercises of self-
denial and self-sacrifice, for mortifications of the

flesh and the spirit. His own religion denied him such extravagances. Flagellation was popish, and therefore abominable. What recourse had he but to business? To business he turned and quite unsuspectingly set it up on an altar. It became the source of solemn and exacting duties, the object of abstemious and ceremonial devotion. In the name of business he made his life into a ritual of ascetic punctuality and pious exactitude. He was infallibly regular in his times for coming to work. He was minutely accurate in keeping his accounts. He was scrupulously faithful to all the old complicated forms of making transactions, never taking the slightest short-cut, even when it seemed perfectly safe to do so. He was heroically relentless in his application to labour, and allowed himself so little leisure that he came thoroughly to enjoy an illness, for during convalescence, when the pain and the suffering were over, he might give himself up to the intellectual and literary pursuits which were his chief pleasure. Unfortunately, perhaps, his illnesses were few, and the years of pious routine many. How far he had carried his curious fanaticism, how greatly thereby he had restricted the scope of his mind became pathetically evident in a remark which he made almost at the end of his days, after the death of his son, " I should never have known how great a man Walter was, had I not survived him."[3]

Perhaps Walter himself, at twenty-seven, felt that he was not fully appreciated. At any rate his manner in the inner sanctuary was jaunty and careless. He failed to see the enormous spiritual importance of mastering unnecessary details. He transgressed against the sacred law of exactitude and cheerfully kept bad books.

> My dear Hutton,
>
> I have devoted my time for the last four months nearly exclusively to the art of book-keeping by double entry, the theory of which is agreeable and pretty but the practice perhaps as horrible as anything ever was. I maintain too in vain that sums are matters of opinion, but the people in command here do not comprehend the nature of contingent matter and try to prove that figures tend to one result more than another, which I find myself to be false as they always come different. But there is no influencing the instinctive dogmatism of the uneducated mind. In other respects I approve of mercantile life. There is some excitement in it, if this does not wear off; always a little to do and no wearing labour, which is something towards perfection.[4]

And again he complains to his friend Wait:

> Here am I in my father's counting-house trying (and failing) to do sums, and being rowed ninety-nine times a day for some horrid sin against the conventions of mercantile existence. My family perhaps you know are merchants, ship-owners, and bankers, etc. etc., here and elsewhere. Out of their multifarious occupations I hope to be able to find, though I cannot precisely say that I have yet found, some one to which I am not contemptibly unequal. As to your notion of doing anything *well*, it is so many years since I abandoned the idea, that I can't now quite enter into the feeling. My difficulty is in doing anything *at all*. The only thing I ever really knew was Special Pleading, and the moment I had learned that, the law reformers botched and abolished it. It was a very pretty art, and the only trade in which the logical faculties appear to be of any particular service, and was therefore the champagne of life, but this people which knoweth not the law, went and abolished it.[4]

Apparently Wait had written a letter of lofty aspiration, and the faint note of accusation in Bagehot's own rather ironical modesty is typical. It is interesting to observe how much pleasure he took in being an infidel to his father's creed. He seems to have been nearly as elaborate in his carelessness as his father was in exactitude. The sensibilities of a kindly old man were cheerfully—no doubt harmlessly—sacrificed, and a grave and sedate boyhood was revenged with a boyish and recalcitrant manhood.

Bagehot was never addicted to light amusements. The serious business of life was sufficiently diverting. Hunting alone he enjoyed, for the open air and the exercise:

> He was a dashing rider, and a fresh wind was felt blowing through his earlier literary efforts, as though he had been thinking in the saddle, an effect wanting in his later essays, where you see chiefly the calm analysis of a lucid observer. But most of the ordinary amusements of young people he detested. He used to say that he wished he could think balls *wicked*, being so stupid as they were, and all " the little blue and pink girls, so like each other,"—a sentiment partly due, perhaps, to his extreme shortness of sight.[5]

The great bulk of Bagehot's literary, biographical, and religious essays were written during the years between 1852 and 1858; that is, from the time he entered business up until that of his marriage. They were published in *The Prospective*, later *The National, Review*, with the management of which he was for several years closely connected. The success of the essays may be indicated from a newspaper cutting of 1858, which Mrs. Barrington quotes:

E

Several years ago, " Advanced Socinians," the Rev.
Messrs. Taylor and Martineau, founded the *Prospective
Review* with the conspicuous motto from St. Bernard,
Respice, Aspice, Prospice. From something narrow
and sectarian in its tone, the *Prospective* did not prosper,
and in the hope of a better future, its conductors
re-baptized it the *National Review.* During the last
twelve months, a series of papers, critical and characteristic, evidently from the same pen, have attracted
considerable interest to the quiet pages of the *National
Review.*[6]

" These papers," Mrs. Barrington adds, " were
by Bagehot."

In 1858 Bagehot gathered together " the most
striking " of his early essays, and published them
in a volume called *Estimates of some Englishmen and
Scotchmen.* As to its reception by the public,
Hutton writes: " I have never understood the
comparative failure of this volume of Bagehot's
early essays; and a comparative failure it was,
though I do not deny that, even at the time, it
attracted much attention among the most accomplished writers of the day."[7] But such notice was
what Bagehot prized. When the essays came out
he was too much in love to be concerned with the
trivial eventualities of literary fame; nevertheless,
he writes Eliza Wilson:

I am afraid I am callous, possibly proud, and do
not care for mere general reputation. Of course it
would be a pleasure if it should come, but it is a thing
which no sane man ought to make necessary to his
happiness, or think of it but as a temporary luxury,
even if it should come to him. First-rate fame, the
fame of great productive artists, is a matter of ultimate
certainty, but no other fame is. Posterity cannot take
up little people, there are so many of them. *Reputation*

must be acquired at the moment and the circumstances of the moment are matters of accident. In my case I have had a good deal of newspaper praise for these essays—at least some of them—when they first came out, and I must expect very little more. Besides I know they will be abused and by whom, and if one puts aside the unfavourable criticisms in newspapers carelessly, one has scarcely a right to set much store by the favourable ones. I do care however a good deal for some kinds of reputation. In proof of which I send you a letter we received in the course of the *National Review* operations from Mathew Arnold.[8]

The pertinent passage in Arnold's letter follows:

It was only a day or two ago that I read the article on Shelley in the last number; that article and one or two others (in which I imagine that I trace the same hand) seem to me to be of the very first quality, showing not talent only, but a concern for the *simple truth* which is rare in English literature.[9]

This is scarcely the place to discuss Bagehot's reputation as a writer, yet I cannot forbear to express my agreement with Hutton, that the literary and biographical essays have never received the notice which they deserve. When Bagehot died, newspapers all over the world had much to say of his economics and journalism, but scarcely anything of his literary criticism.[10] And though it may be granted that newspapers never evince great interest in letters, as late as 1915 so respectable a thinker as Mr. J. M. Keynes declared that Bagehot's literary studies were hardly " up to the level of his reputation," and provided " only a superficial interpretation of Shakespeare, Milton, and Gibbon."[11] On the other hand, he has had among later critics a few very genuine admirers, of whom Augustine Birrell and the late Irving Babbitt are

not the least. Though his name is little known to
general readers, it is seldom absent from the biblio-
graphies of discriminating writers upon nineteenth-
century literature and politics. He has been, in
both fields, something of a critic's critic, and if his
general fame is not great, we must remember that
specialists do not lightly forgive their colleagues for
competence in other fields.

Bagehot's activities in banking naturally gave a
spurt to his interest in contemporary economic
problems. In 1856 his friend Hutton became
editor of *The Economist*, a financial newspaper
owned by James Wilson, then Secretary of the
Treasury for the Liberal Government. Hutton's
connection with this journal suggested to Bagehot
the idea of writing for it. He communicated with
Mr. Wilson, who replied with an invitation to his
country house of Claverton. It was during this
visit that Bagehot met the statesman's daughter,
Miss Eliza Wilson, whom he later married. Their
love letters, recently published by Mrs. Barrington,
reveal Bagehot more intimately than any of his
other writings.

If strong men dare not read their youthful love
letters, and blush and sigh at the thought, what must
be the courage of the biographical student, who
reads not one, but many correspondences? Nor
is the mark of time upon such writings, the suggestion of faded ink and yellowed paper, their most
depressing feature. Rather it is their likeness to
each other, their uniformity. Everything is so
new and wonderful to the young people themselves.
They live on the crest of the exclamation point.
And yet the story of separated love is ever the same.

In every correspondence there is the same wonder at mutual love, the same ecstatic joy of possession, the same itch to provoke jealousy, the same delicious sense of unworthiness, the same bright dreams of the future, and where, as in most respectable affairs, marriage is the conclusion, the same invading note of the prosaic future—an increasing rattle of teaspoons and clatter of dishware. To read many such correspondences is to live in the monotony of perpetual spring, to behold Cupid peering out from a thousand disguises. Upon the present occasion he appears tied to the apron strings of propriety—and yet at times he tugs noticeably. Few romances have been at once so passionate and so pure. Few " virtuous romances " have been so interesting.

On the very evening of his arrival at Claverton, Bagehot had the mysterious good fortune to take Miss Wilson in to dinner.[12] Though a determined bachelor, and, because of his aversion to " little blue and pink girls," prejudiced against young women generally, he was at once much struck. She seemed so much a part of the distinguished and brilliant surroundings in which he found her. She had " a certain shy dignity which," as he later confided, " is inexpressibly attractive to me." When he offered his arm, she took it in a manner " which seemed to say, ' Well, I *must* touch it, but I won't touch it *much*.' " And when she talked to the Claverton physician, he observed on her face " a profoundly dignified expression," which quite implied, " *As* you exist, I *ought* to bear with you a *little* while." But she did not look at Bagehot in that way. Indeed, at two or three clever things he said to her sisters, she actually smiled. He spoke very little to her, " not knowing the *text*." So the first encounter passes not unfavourably, and thereafter his progress is rapid—according to Victorian notions of speed. Both in town and in the country he contrives to see much of Miss Wilson, but particularly during the autumn season at Claverton. Then the real love-making begins. There are " walks on the terrace by moonlight, readings *tête-à-tête* " of favourite poems, excursions in the downs, " games of battledore in the picture gallery, where Walter's characteristic eyeglass " floats in the air on its black string, as he runs here and there after the shuttlecock. There is a sombre meeting in the conservatory. Bagehot feels obliged to speak of his mother's insanity. Some time after, he asks Mr. Wilson's permission to propose, and having obtained it, encounters his fate in the library. But again there is the ominous suggestion of lurking tragedy. The knowledge of Mrs. Bagehot's condition has not changed Eliza's feeling, but has " complicated somewhat her vision of the future, and having no rash tendencies, she wavered as to taking a definite step then and there." A few days later, in London, she consents and Bagehot is off to tell Hutton.

His first love letter comes from the west. There is a financial panic, and he has gone to Somerset to watch over the interests of the bank. He is little concerned about the panic, but immensely concerned that he may not see her before she leaves for Edinburgh, where she is to be cured of her headaches by a famous Scotch physician. He must see her, talk with her more; he must have " detail."

Otherwise, her reality will vanish with her physical presence and his happiness appear an incredible dream. Nervously he attempts a little wit, then hastens to apologize. She must not think him irreverent: " Do not think I feel lightly because I write rubbish in jests. I wish you could read the bottom of my heart. If you were here I would try to whisper to you how *fearful* what I feel for you is, but I could not do it on paper, and it would be glaring." She replies that she does not mind his jesting. He must not fear to be himself. She is a little surprised at the vehemence of his feeling. For herself, she is quite cheerful, and has " not *moped* for five minutes." She will try to " soothe " him with her letters, for they have both agreed that " soothing " is to be her mission toward him. He protests she must not think, because he tells her of the " wild, burning pain " which he sometimes feels, that his love for her has been " mere suffering." " Even at the worst there was a wild, delirious excitement about it that I would not have lost for the world." But now his feelings are more endurable. At times he goes about murmuring to himself, " ' I have made that dignified girl *commit* herself, I have, I have,' and then I vault over the sofa with exultation. Those are the feelings of the person you have connected yourself with. *Please* don't be offended at my rubbish. Sauciness is my particular line. I am always rude to everybody I respect." She uses some of his favourite phrases, and becomes motherly, urging him to relieve the strain of financial worry with hunting, and advising him where he can borrow good horses near Bristol. She is amazed at the things which she is able to

say to him, though now and then, indeed, a shadow
of alarm crosses her mind.

Walter is horrified to learn of the dullness of her
life in Edinburgh. Nothing is worse than dullness.
" What is life relieved only by a piano? " People
have been complimenting him upon a recent
article in *The Economist*. He is pleased, but reputation is not his greatest temptation:

> The wish to be estimated at your value is nearly as
> important for good in a character as the wish to be
> estimated at *more* than your value is for evil, but I am
> not exceedingly prone to it myself. I am afraid I
> covet ' *power* ' influence over people's wills, faculties
> and conduct more in proportion than I can quite
> defend. I think this is a very good thing too in many
> ways, but I do not quite approve the intensity with
> which I feel it. Until I knew you it was certainly the
> strongest feeling I had ever known. Now it certainly
> is not, but it is stronger than is good for my happiness
> or my goodness.[13]

Such a revelation is rather startling, for the quality
is not one which readily appears in a man's literary
character, nor is it attributed to Bagehot by his
biographers. Yet, once confessed, it seems to
explain much. His choice of a best friend, the mild,
complaisant, and adulatory Hutton, his habit of
submitting his acquaintances to social experimentation, his preference of an active to a meditative life,
his repeated attempts to embark on a public career
—possibly even his enthusiastic defence of the
Emperor Louis Napoleon, and the strong element
of gusto in his most effective and trenchant writing
—all point to a steady and decent pleasure, sometimes to an exulting delight, in the exercise of
power.[14] This tendency appears no less in his

choice of a wife, for, as the love between the two
deepens and both grow more frank, Eliza confesses
what indeed is clearly revealed by all her letters:
" I believe my real nature is very womanly, I mean
that I love to lean on a stronger nature, though I
may appear to be somewhat independent on the
surface. I *can* stand alone if I must, but it makes
my heart heavy to have to do it." She is imposing
and dignified in manner, in nature soft and yield-
ing. Her mind is apparently quick and receptive,
without being deeply original. Could any woman
be better suited to a gallant, dominating gentleman? In his eyes she has at once the glamour of
beauty and that charm of inaccessibility which
goes with a stately dignity and a high social position. Moreover, her yoke is mild. She is a goddess
who returns worship with obedience. In her,
the lady may be adored and the woman
commanded.

Gradually Eliza awakens to the full significance
of her love. She had been in love once before—
youthfully, and not very deeply, and had " gathered
up her feelings and passed on." It was a humiliating
experience: " I began life with the wish and intention (there was the mistake and I had to learn my
weakness) to be so pure-minded, as never to like
anyone but the *one* I should marry, if I married, and
if not, *no one*." She had long been conscious, even
before meeting Walter, of depths in her heart that
had not been reached, " of a power of affection
which had as yet lain dormant, but I dared not
dwell upon it for fear it were fated I should not
meet the soul that could take possession of those
depths." Now she has met that soul and she is

deeply thankful. The experience is even greater than she had imagined:

Affection like ours *is* awful and gives such new significance to life—at least to me it does. It seems such a power in life, instead of the mere episode I fancied it to be. I cannot say that the feeling is different to what I imagined it, except in being infinitely more intense, but its effect upon life, even to its furthest horizon, seems *startlingly* strong. I feel our existence through time and even eternity bound together in a manner I could not have imagined. It is such a comfort to me to be able to write to you unreservedly, which I can *quite* do now, and I am getting on with your *name* as fast as you could wish. I find myself holding your letters fast and murmuring over them with the superlative adjective.[15]

Amazed and immensely grateful, Walter replies:

I too have long felt *my* soul bound to yours for *eternity*, but I should not have liked to say it to you lest it might frighten you, and you might think me exaggerated, or excited, but ever since for a moment you laid your head on my shoulder in the library at Claverton, I have found myself inexpressibly bound to you. It passed in my mind that I was yours for time and beyond time. Before that I felt wild, eager passion and in some sort deep affection, but there was nothing so consecrated, so soft and eternal as there is about my love for you now. Is there not a verse in the Bible, " My soul loves thee and what shall I say "? It is some odd end of a chapter somewhere, and it expresses what I mean and my difficulty too in saying it. I could not have dreamed that you could as yet feel for me anything at all like the same intense eternal bound that *I* feel myself. I had a nervous idea too that there was something about me too secular and jesting to admit of your feeling it, and it is *awful* happiness— almost too awful and chastening to *be* happiness—to hear that you *think* you feel it. I know your deep and constant nature and all that it implies. I hope you won't mind my writing to you in this way or let it *alarm* you. I do not mean anything you would dislike though the words may be in fault. I fear if I were to tell you how often I have had *tears* in my eyes over your last letter and how often I have kissed it (perhaps that is rude) you would think me the most *absurd* person, but if you knew how firm and stoical I am commonly thought, and how indifferent to everything at all like this, you would not quite adjure me.[15]

And oddly enough, she is not horrified. Her love has made her bold, and the awful monster of Victorian convention is slain, or at least severely wounded, by the gentle hand of a woman.

Do not be afraid to write what you like [she replies]. I can bear everything you have said as yet, for you are revolutionising my mind somehow, and the deeper what you say is, the more real my feelings about you seem. Why should it be *rude* to kiss my letters *now?* Would you like to hear that I have done the same? If so, I will own to it; if not, suppose I have retracted my words.[15]

In another letter Eliza writes, no doubt quite innocently, that Lady Kinnaird, a woman married for twenty years, whom the Scotch doctor has marvellously rejuvenated and cured of her headaches, is much prettier than herself. Walter is beside himself with indignation: " It is all nonsense about Lady K. or any woman who has been married twenty years being so pretty as you are, Dearest—utter rubbish—I have a very severe taste in beauty. They say at home I never allow any one to be pretty. You had better believe what I tell you and not set up foolish notions of your own." But she maintains her point, and when

Walter criticizes another lady in his trenchant manner, she replies:

> Are you not somewhat hyper-critical about women, dear? They must not be stupid; they must not talk and they must not be silent, and whatever else they are or are not, they *must* be pretty! I shall begin to fancy I must be a wonderful "*juste milieu*" in everything to be right in your eyes, and I shall be getting vain in spite of myself.[16]

Eliza expresses repeatedly the fear that she is not clever enough for him. He fears that he is much less clever than she thinks. She reads Hutton's estimate of his genius in *The National Review*, and is aghast. He is much amused, and hastens to assure her that she has both " more culture " and a " deeper nature " than he.

Even at this advanced stage of their correspondence Walter is racked and haunted by the fear of offending.

> I write to you without the slightest effort, but the moment the letter is gone I get anxious and fancy I have said something you might not quite like, and I am vexed at not being there when you read, to explain it and clear away the least shadow of annoyance from you.[16]

Gradually he becomes more assured, and finds at length that he can actually " chat " with her. He grows bold and " *whispers* " his ideas for the future. Desperately she attempts to be brave:

> I should very much prefer your *whispering* your ideas and wishes for the future to me, but if there is anything you would like me to know soon, I *will* brace my mind to think of it and even to write you what I think. I am very glad now that you told me what you wished about the spring, for though I do not see my way clear, it does not look so impossible as

I thought at first, and it has given a kind of definiteness to what before appeared nothing but vagueness. When Papa in urging me to take time to consider well what I was doing, said: " You will leave a very happy home," the idea appeared to me quite irrelevant to the subject, or so distant at least that if he had said: " You will have to leave home when you die," it could not have seemed more so.[16]

In some mysterious manner April 1, 1858, is set as the all-important day. Pressing his advantage, Walter presents another problem of fearful delicacy:

Really something must be done about a house. The practicality of my relatives is something *awful* to bear. Having never seen you, and having no other topic to let loose their minds upon, they have taken up this, and they make suggestions to me, and state difficulties. They evidently do not feel any confidence in the matter and until they can see a definite enclosure of wall they will never embody their ideas.[17]

Eliza confesses her family are equally practical. The search for a house has begun, and now the tension of reserve noticeably relaxes. Walter jokes sacrilegiously about the wedding; Eliza timidly follows suit. His letters bristle with domiciliary statistics, while she goes forth heroically to look at candlesticks and price salt cellars. There is a growing bustle of preparation and finally a quiet, witty letter from Walter to his mother. He and Eliza are on their honeymoon.

CHAPTER IV

ACHIEVEMENT AND DEATH

His marriage opened up to Bagehot the brilliant world of higher London society. It was through his connection with Mr. Wilson that he obtained that intimate knowledge of politicians and the workings of government which imparted freshness and vividness to *The English Constitution* and to *Physics and Politics,* and which formed the very substance of the long list of his biographical and historical studies. Mr. Augustine Birrell has attributed the peculiar virtues of his work to his experiencing nature.[1] They are also due to his great experience, which in the larger and more worldly sense, he began to acquire from this time forward. The guests at Mr. Wilson's house, Claverton Manor, included politicians, bankers, painters, musicians, authors—celebrities all the way from Matthew Arnold to the successor of Beau Nash at Bath. And in this brilliant society no one was better fitted to take a place than Bagehot. He had received a sound education in both the arts and the sciences. He had undergone the full course of legal study. He was already a considerable authority on government, literature, and political economy. He had acquired much practical experience as a banker. Above all, he was a keen and penetrating observer of human nature. Entering this larger society to which his marriage introduced him, Bagehot received, as he said of Pitt, " the inestimable permission to be himself."

Several years after his marriage Bagehot described his father-in-law in the language of the "City" as "a stern bullionist and an ardent Free-trader," a financial author of strong "business imagination" and valuable intelligibility.[2] Bagehot had a talent for explaining plain men subtly, but James Wilson can be explained very simply as a person of clear, logical mind, strong common sense, enormous energy, and warm affections. The son of a small Scottish woollen manufacturer, he rose after prodigious labours and heartrending vicissitudes to be an influential publicist and a minister of the government. It is wonderful that a man could work so hard and so fast as James Wilson did, but it is even more wonderful that in his intervals of leisure he could be an entertaining host and a loving father. Between this Victorian Hercules and his son-in-law an intimacy grew up such as seldom exists between men of ages and characters so different. Bagehot's "Memoir" of Wilson is critical, to be sure, and yet, despite its financial gravity and its Lombard Street jargon, one of the warmest and most sympathetic sketches he ever wrote.

He quickly became at home in the political world, and made close friends of many of his father-in-law's colleagues — particularly of Sir George Cornewall Lewis, once Chancellor of the Exchequer for the Liberals, whom of all the statesmen of the day Bagehot seems to have known best and admired most. Certainly no other public figure, except Wilson himself, has been praised so warmly by so cool a critic. The friendship was unique. It is scarcely too much to say that Bagehot found Lewis interesting because he was a dry and prosaic man. Sir Leslie Stephen observes: " He admired no one more than Sir George Cornewall Lewis, the very type of the thoroughly prosaic, solid, utilitarian mind; and not the less that he was himself imaginative, and, if not a poet, had very marked poetic sensibility."[3] Lewis, like Clough, belonged to the group of Bagehot's botanical friendships. Indeed these two must have constituted an extraordinary study of opposites. The latter exemplified the paralysis of a great mind; the former, the smooth efficiency of a limited one. Clough was bewildered by the complexity of truth and never came to an opinion. Lewis was " complication-proof," and moved through oceans of data to clear and simple opinions on nearly every subject. Sir George had a " born love of dry truth." " His mind was like a registering machine with a patent index."[4] He was always right and nearly always tiresome. In short, he was a brilliant example of Bagehot's favourite theory that truth is very dull and best discovered by very dull people. In justice to Bagehot, it should be said that he also esteemed Lewis for what he was—a worthy gentleman, a learned scholar, and a cautious statesman. What the friendship of such a man, and of public men in general, must have meant to the son-in-law of Mr. Wilson may be gathered from an entry, made shortly after his marriage, in one of his notebooks: " Living really in the political world is the greatest possible gain in a political country; knowing at first hand what others know at second hand only, the characters and the play of political life are not otherwise accessible."[5]

In 1860 Bagehot stood for Parliament and last

the London University seat to Sir John Romilly by four votes. The advice and assistance of his father-in-law, who was an extraordinarily successful canvasser, might well have turned the scales, but Wilson was not in England. In 1859 he had been offered the newly created post of Financial Member in the Council of India. The offer had been substantially an invitation to create in the eastern empire a whole new financial system, the old having fallen into irreparable chaos. Though reluctant to leave the political arena at a time when the highest offices in the realm were opening to him, Wilson had accepted. Of the tremendous difficulties which he encountered in India, of the impediments thrown in his way by jealous English officials and unscrupulous native merchants, of the enormity of the task itself, of the problems arising from the vastness, disorder, and strangeness of the country, as well as from the amazing complexity, diversity, and confusion of the old financial system I cannot properly speak here. It is sufficient to say that he performed a great labour with a great spirit. On July 4, 1860, he wrote with characteristic simplicity:

> You have no idea of the increased capacity of the mind for undertaking a special service of this kind when removed to a new scene of action, and when one throws off all the cares of engagements less or more trivial by which one is surrounded in ordinary life, and throws one's whole soul into such a special service, and particularly when one feels assured of having the power to carry it out, I cannot tell you with what ease one determines the largest and gravest question here compared with in England; and I am certain that the more one can exercise real power, there is by far

F

the greater tendency to moderation, care, and prudence.[6]

During the early months of his sojourn Wilson seemed hardly to feel the heavy burden of toil which he laid upon himself, but from the commencement of the rainy season at Calcutta, his health began to decline. He was warned to remove for a while to a better climate, but refused. His reforms were not yet satisfactorily set in motion. He sank rapidly and on July 11, 1861, he died, his mind busy to the very last with the great work to which he had sacrificed his life. The vacant seat in the Council of India was offered to Bagehot. Acceptance would have meant, with good health, almost certainly a brilliant political career, but it would have involved grave risk for a delicate man; it would have necessitated the giving up of an enviable position in London, and perhaps even more important in his eyes, a separation from his mother. Bagehot declined the offer without hesitation. This refusal, together with Wilson's death, marks a turning point in Bagehot's career. Had his father-in-law lived, Bagehot would certainly have been more of a politician and less of a writer than he was.

For some time editor in fact, Bagehot now became in title also director and editor of *The Economist*, and at the same time he was appointed supervisor of the London branch of Stuckey's bank. Thus he acquired the " established position " which he felt " necessary to comfort in England." For a while it seemed likely that the position might be augmented by honours even more considerable. Three times more he stood for a seat in parliament, at Manchester in 1865, at Bridgwater in 1866, and at the University of London in 1867. In no attempt did he succeed. His failure was ironical. Between him and a great public career there stood only what many a vociferous politician and dull country gentle-man had obtained with ease. Unknown to the voters, and apparently unable to make an impression upon them, he was nevertheless greatly respected and admired, and sought after in council, by the most celebrated statesmen of the day. Throughout the latter part of his life he acted as an " advisor behind the scenes of the Ministers and permanent heads of departments who consulted him " to such an extent that he has been called " a sort of supple-mentary Chancellor of the Exchequer."[7] When he travelled up to Manchester to stand for election, he carried with him a letter of recommendation from Gladstone, which declared:

> If thorough acquaintance with economic science, extensive and accurate knowledge, ready and practical habits of business and a conciliatory disposition, go to fit a man for the representation of these great national interests, it certainly appears to me that your fitness must stand without dispute in the first rank.[8]

And upon the occasion of Bagehot's death he wrote:

> During the time when I was Chancellor of the Ex-chequer I had the advantage of frequent and free communication with him on all matters of finance, and currency. Nor have I in all my experience known any one from whom in this important province more was to be desired, or who was more free and genial in the communication of his large knowledge and matured reflection.[8]

Bagehot's repeated failures to obtain a seat have

puzzled his friends greatly. His own explanation is that he was " between sizes in politics." And it is true that, though a liberal in name, he was at heart far from the vague, emotional optimism of Gladstone, choosing rather like Burke to be a conservative in principle and a liberal in application. Yet mediators have ever been dear to English voters, and to be nicely representative is scarcely necessary in a profession where equivocation has been so successful and defection so little punished. Perhaps, unwittingly Bagehot has pronounced judgment on himself. The greatest impediment to a political career, he has declared in many passages, is cleverness and originality, which never fail to awaken suspicion and distrust in the public mind. Without these qualities Disraeli and Lowe would have succeeded in half the time. In Bagehot the defect was at least equally grave, for not only was he full of ideas, but he presented even safe and simple ideas in startling and ironical forms. Never has so sound a writer indulged so much in paradox. Though in *The Economist* he cultivated a grave and dull style—and succeeded so well that his later works are not nearly so readable as his earlier—yet in the excitement of personal contact clever men have great difficulty in concealing their cleverness, even for their own best interests, and least of all can they forbear to puzzle and mystify stupidity.

Indeed, Bagehot was by temperament and conviction, as well as by endowment, an aristocrat. Mrs. Barrington informs us that the essay on Pitt contains much autobiography. And certainly in both men there was the same precocity and early

self-confidence, the same alertness and strong
common sense, the same retentive memory, the
same high notions of honour and sensitive purity
of mind. Perhaps in a more democratic age Pitt
himself could not have mustered enthusiasm for
cajoling and flattering ordinary people in the
street. Bagehot was also unfortunate enough to
possess something of the great Tory's austerity of
manner. That kind of social intercourse which
consists in uttering pleasant nonentities to innumerable strangers exhausted him completely.
He was no more capable of bribing with smiles
than with money. In certain moods he, too,
walked " without looking to the right or to the
left," and would rather have made a man a " privy
Councillor than have spoken to him."[9] Knowing
these things, one can understand why he found it
hard to throw himself into a campaign, and why
" there was a grain of cynicism in his attitude
towards the electors which doubtless crept out and
which tended to damp enthusiasm when it came
to a contest."[10]

Bagehot had not even the obvious advantage of
a good voice. His wife admits that he was no
orator, and Hutton observes, though with loyal
ambiguity, that " as a speaker he did not often
succeed. His voice had no great compass, and his
manner was somewhat odd to ordinary hearers."[11]
He had all the qualities which make a great statesman; he lacked only those which make the ordinary
politician. He had the knowledge, the insight, and
the genius, and lacked only the strength, the voice,
and the manner.[12]

After an illness in 1867, Bagehot deliberately

gave up all thought of entering parliament, maintaining, " I believe rightly," says Hutton, " that his political judgment was all the sounder, as well as his health the better, for a quieter life."[13] Mrs. Barrington declares that he never really desired to obtain a seat, but attempted to do so primarily to gratify his mother. Personally, I feel that so practical and sensible a man could hardly have been quite so dutiful a son. Bagehot himself has written on " The Advantages and Disadvantages of Becoming a Member of Parliament," in which he decides that the member gains position, a certain power, and the possibility of great inside knowledge of government—but at the sacrifice of undergoing great physical strain, of listening to very dull debates, and of cutting his ideas down to the dead commonplaces of the electoral mind.[14] Bagehot made three of his four attempts to get into the House at the time that he was beginning to write his longer works on politics and public affairs. It is possible that he desired a seat chiefly for the knowledge and experience it would bring, as he later renounced it for fear of the toll it would take upon his health.

In 1864 Bagehot became a member of the Political Economy Club, an organization which, according to its records, " was founded in London in the year 1821, chiefly by the exertions of the late Thomas Tooke, F.R.S., to support the principles of Free Trade set forth in the well-known London Merchant's Petition of 1820, originated and written by Mr. Tooke."[15] The records also state: " The Club has from the outset been composed mainly of men of business. Next in order come those engaged in politics, public officials, men of letters, lawyers, and professional economists." During the time Bagehot was in the club, the roll was limited to thirty-five names. Lord Courtney of Penwith, also a member, gives an interesting description of Bagehot as he appeared at these meetings:

> I revert to a stricter economist in naming Mr. Bagehot. We met on Friday evenings, not a convenient day for the Editor of the Economist, but he came as often as he could, and was always a welcome debater. If I venture to say that he was perhaps too frequently betrayed into the examination of differences and discriminations of the second order every reader of his writings can appreciate without accepting the criticism. His manner of speech was correspondingly finical and fastidious, but his intervention in discussion was always stimulating and acceptable.[15]

No criticism of Bagehot as an author could be more unmerited. Either Lord Courtney had read very few of his writings, or he had heard rather too many of his speeches. At any rate, Bagehot's character as a speaker requires no further comment.

Perhaps the most interesting group of which Bagehot became a member was the Metaphysical Society, which joined highly combustible materials for a benevolent purpose. Lord Tennyson, James Knowles, and David Pritchard, the founders, were, according to Hallam Tennyson, " grieved at the scorn that the theological and agnostic parties showed toward each other, and considered that meeting on a friendly footing would do much toward the ventilation of new doctrines, and the clearing up of misunderstandings, as well as toward the cultivation of charity in controversy, and mutual esteem."[16]   James Drummond's *Life and Letters of James Martineau* offers an interesting description of the meetings of the society:

> The meetings were first held in Willis Rooms, but later in the Grosvenor Hotel. After dining together the members sat round a table with a sheet of foolscap paper before each one, which was not often used for notes, but sometimes served for other purposes. . . . Not only were the debates of high interest, but the mere spectacle of several highly gifted thinkers, of very different types of faculty and genius, and with such a variety of facial expression, was itself a treat of no mean order. Towards the close of the evening the debate often passed into a conversation, and the genial affability with which the most eminent among them freely exchanged ideas with the humbler members suggested the fancy that we in modern times were enjoying a feast of reason in somewhat of the old Athenian style.[17]

On December 13, 1870, Bagehot read a paper " On the Emotion of Conviction," which is included in Mrs. Barrington's edition of his works. It is like him that in a club where men of diametrically opposite belief were brought together in combat, he should have chosen to speak on the psychology of believing. Hutton, describing another of these meetings, mentions that he humorously reproved Ruskin for assuming too much an attitude of child-like wonder toward external reality.

After his marriage Bagehot had little time for polite reading and polished writing. In the ensuing six years he wrote only five literary essays, and after that, none at all. Living in the world of business and politics, writing at least two articles each week for *The Economist*, he fell into a rapid, more or less journalistic style, which has left its mark even upon his longer works on political and economic science. The first of these was *The English Constitution*, which appeared serially in *The Fortnightly Review*, then edited by Mr. George Lewes, from May 15, 1865, to January 1, 1867. It achieved a quick success among statesmen and scholars. Mrs. Barrington quotes appreciations, written either at the time, or at Bagehot's death a few years later, from Lord Bryce, Lord Goschen, Sir Robert Morier, and others.[19] The book was quickly translated into German, French and Italian and, evidently as an ultimate reward of permanent literary merit, was made a text book at Oxford and in several North American universities. It has remained, despite significant constitutional changes, the best popular treatment of English government.

After finishing *The English Constitution* Bagehot set directly to work on *Physics and Politics*, the first chapter of which appeared in *The Fortnightly Review* on November 1, 1867. This work also was well received by contemporaries. " Thank you very sincerely for your book on *Physics and Politics*," wrote Sir Henry Maine. " It is practically an old friend. I do not know that I was ever more struck with anything than with the essays when they first appeared."[19] Many years later Hutton declared in the *Dictionary of National Biography*: " ' Physics and Politics ' . . . is one of the International Scientific Series, has gone through four editions, and has been translated into six or seven different languages." Harry E. Barnes, a modern sociologist, pronounces a recent opinion: " Bagehot's *Physics and Politics* remain as valuable as ever, for he dealt with those

fundamental psychological foundations of group
action which time is not likely to change in any
material manner."[20]

This was the most active and productive period
of his life. In addition to his editorial duties, and
the preparation of two articles a week for *The
Economist*, he wrote frequently for other journals,
shared in editing *The National Review*, and within
the space of three years completed two books, both
of which required large knowledge, careful thought,
and painstaking composition. He was managing
director and vice-chairman of the Stuckey bank,
supervisor of its London branch, and frequently
acted as financial advisor to the Government.
Visiting his parents fortnightly at Herd's Hill, he
maintained his interest in local affairs and was at
his death deputy recorder for the corporation.
Since 1861 he had been a Justice of the Peace for
the county of Somerset and attended Petty Sessions
regularly. Nor did these multifarious duties prevent
him from devoting considerable time to his family.
He rode with his sisters-in-law in the park, drove
nearly every day with his wife in their phaeton,
and took extensive vacations with her on the
Continent. Together with his mother-in-law and
her unmarried daughters he kept a large establishment in Belgrave Street, where parties and balls
were continually being given. In these he took
part, as well as in many other activities of the
most distinguished London society, from the political
breakfasts of Gladstone to the elaborate parties of
Lady Palmerston. Perhaps the ultimate concomi-
tant of a rapid, efficient, and versatile intelligence is
natural calm and repose of mind. At any rate, such

calm Bagehot apparently possessed. He never
seemed to mind being interrupted at work. Whenever any member of the family was faced with a
problem, her first thought was to seek out Walter
in his study, who always had plenty of time for
gentle and kindly consultation. He radiated order
and good sense, and though he showed, even in the
bosom of his family, an elaborate and gentlemanly
respect for the privacy and dignity of others, important business, domestic arrangements, and marriage settlements somehow fell of themselves into
his hands. A review of his activities reveals another
important trait. He was as tenacious of old
interests as he was receptive to new ones. A true
conservative of his own past, he loved old ideas,
old localities, old friends. His friendship with
Hutton was as enduring as his adherence to Aristotelian principles, his connection with Langport
in the midst of London life as certain as his enjoyment of literature in the midst of political and
economic study. But equally characteristic was
the fresh interest which, late in life, he evinced for
new studies, such as for geology and biological
science; and Mrs. Barrington informs us that
shortly before his death he began even to feel some
curiosity regarding music, which he had always
disliked. For such a man, to grow older is to
grow broader.

Bagehot did not long enjoy the fullness of his
powers. In 1867, at the age of forty-two, he
suffered a serious illness, a variety of " internal
inflammation," from the effects of which he never
entirely recovered.[21] Soon after, he was obliged
to find an assistant editor for *The Economist*, and

secured the services of Robert, later Sir Robert, Giffen. His next long work, *Lombard Street*, was also much more slowly written, having been begun fully three years before its publication in 1873. True, it was carefully revised, but careful and anxious revision is sometimes an indication of failing powers. In any event, the book received speedy recognition, especially among politicians and practical men of affairs. Congratulating the author, Gladstone knew not " whether most to admire its clearness or its force." W. S. Jevens, a contemporary economist, wrote to Bagehot: " So far as I am able to judge it is by far the best account which we have of the working of our banking system."[22] Johann Plenge declared in the introduction to a German translation: " Die 1873 erschienene *Lombarden Strasse* ist das klassische Buch über die Vorgänge und den Aufbau des Geldmarktes eines grossen Landes."[23]

Bagehot's last work, *Economic Studies*, was never completed. It was to have consisted of three volumes, the first and third on political economy itself, the second, on famous economists. Only two instalments of the first volume, printed in the January and February numbers of *The Fortnightly Review*, and a few of the biographical sketches, were written. Sir Robert Giffen accords the *Economic Studies* very high praise, referring to them as " with all their incompleteness, the most important work which Bagehot left."[24] Mrs. Barrington also quotes appreciations from Sir Francis Galton, the scientist, and Lord Granville, who was long Colonial Secretary for the Liberals.[25] But in general, the *Economic Studies*, being unfinished, seem never to have aroused so much attention as Bagehot's other long works.

On April 13, 1875, Bagehot officially became a celebrity, being elected to the Athenæum, which in those days was a kind of earthly Valhalla of those " known for their Scientific or Literary attainments, Artists of any eminence in the Fine Arts, and Noblemen and gentlemen distinguished as Liberal Patrons of Science, Literature, or the Arts."[26] Some interesting glimpses of him are to be found in writings of prominent contemporaries. In his *Recollections* Lord Morley reveals himself more clearly than Bagehot, of whom he says:

> In public things he did not really share the notions or aims of the younger men, but he took abundant interest in friends more ardent than himself. His good natured ironies put them on their mettle. . . . I often ventured to say to him, " You have only one defect; you do not feel the inherent power and glory of the principle of Liberty." This notwithstanding, we who dissented most from his maxims on current affairs were well aware how much better we were for his Socratic objections, and what real acquaintance with men and business, what serious judgment and interest, what honest sympathy and friendliness, all lay under his playful and racy humour.[27]

Lord Bryce is more eulogistic:

> He was, some of us used to think far back in the seventies, the most interesting man in London to meet, so bright and stimulating was his conversation. It was always conversation, never declamation or lecturing. He could listen as well as talk. He put himself on a level with his interlocutor, and however much you might feel his superiority, he always seemed to be receiving as well as giving, striking out thoughts from others as well as bringing them from his own store. . . .

But Bagehot was always cheerful, natural, spontaneous, unaffected. You felt he was hunting for truth, and you enjoyed the sense that he allowed you to be his companion in the chase.[28]

Monologue, agrees Mrs. Barrington, is the last thing of which Bagehot was capable. There is every evidence that she was right. Monologue, he seems to have felt, might be poured into the merciful silence of a book, but it should never be spoken, and scarcely listened to. Next to fraudulent politicians, Bagehot detested continuous speakers. If he wrote of Crabbe Robinson less kindly than old friendship would seem to require, the explanation is doubtless that the companion of Goethe and Wordsworth was pitilessly loquacious —a peculiarity of which Bagehot often took playful advantage, but from which he seems nevertheless to have suffered. In "Hartley Coleridge" he declares with commendable vigour:

> In fact, the habit of common and continuous speech is a symptom of mental deficiency. It proceeds from not knowing what is going on in other people's minds. S. T. Coleridge, it is well known, talked to everybody, and to everybody alike; like a Christian divine, he did not regard persons. "That is a fine opera, Mr. Coleridge," said a young lady, some fifty years back. "Yes, ma'am; and I remember Kant somewhere makes a similar remark, for, as *we* know, the idea of philosophical infinity. . . ."[29]

And Bagehot continues to castigate two generations of Coleridges through the greater part of another page.

There was about Bagehot nothing of the professional wit, of the man who goes about meditating epigram, like murder, in cold blood. He maintained that "humour gains much by constant suppression," and had a reserve which, like Pitt's, was probably the armour of a delicate constitution against the dull oppression of many casual contacts.[29] And indeed, though a humorist, he was never an enemy to good serious conversation. " As an instrument for arriving at truth," says T. Smith Osler, " I never knew anything like a talk with Bagehot."[30] He understood how to develop the suggestions of others, how to make the discussion move forward to a definite goal, and above all, how to keep up " animation without combat."[30] For open combat he had no particular liking. He preferred truth to war, and being, like Socrates, in part a humorist and a social experimentator, he often amused himself with searching for truth among the vessels of error. He loved to inflate others to folly with professions of his own ignorance, to shock, confuse, and guide them with ironical questions. " My mind is ' to let ' on that subject," he would begin with great innocence. " Pray tell me what to think."[30]

" Don't tell me," Pitt is reported to have said, " of a man's being able to talk sense; everyone can talk sense; can he talk nonsense? "[31] Before an appreciative audience Bagehot, like Pitt, could talk excellent nonsense, and like Pitt he saved his nonsense for his most intelligent friends. During the family breakfast, at which intimate friends were often present, he was accustomed to pace up and down the dining-room at Belgrave Street, giving utterance in his peculiar, boyish way to whatever ideas came into his head. Even the grave Gladstonian breakfasts did not entirely dampen this early morning inspiration.

I think the only time I met Mr. Bagehot to speak
to [writes Miss Helen Gladstone in 1905] was a very
long time ago when he came to one of my father's
Thursday breakfasts at 11 Carlton House Terrace. . . .
I only remember distinctly one thing that he told us;
that he knew what a nut felt like when it was going
to be cracked, as he once got his head caught between
a cart-shed and a lamp-post.[32]

One of his principal friends of this period was
Lord Carnarvon, the conscientious and much-
resigning member of several conservative cabinets
—a peer who presented that combination of the
serious statesman and the refined gentleman which
was so congenial to Bagehot.   At Highclere, the
earl's beautiful country house, he met with a larger
variety of people than in his own rather grave world.
After his first visit he writes in a letter:

I have been at Highclere, Lord Carnarvon's, who
is one of my sort, and has run to mind, and wanted
me to help to keep his house more decently reasonable
while the fast people were there.   We had Lord and
Lady Ashley, Lord Stanhope (Lady Carnarvon's
brother), Lady Dorothy Neville—a pretty woman with
an old husband, and several young men.   The women
wore wonderful dresses, and we played cards rather
high, always in the evenings and sometimes in the
morning—at least some people played in the morning.
—I kept my character for wisdom and did not.   Lord
Carnarvon will be Secretary of State for the Colonies
when the Tories come in.   Lady Carnarvon is very
clever and literary—at least with *snaps* of Literature.
They will be *people* for some years to come, for they
are both clever, very ambitious and have a beautiful
place near London to entertain in.[32]

On Sundays he often lunched with Lord and Lady
Carnarvon.   The manner in which he spent his

afternoons was characteristic. On alternate weeks he would visit his Uncle Reynolds, an exponent of the most respectable Evangelical thought, and George Eliot, an exponent of the most disreputable German philosophy, and a member of society regarding whose moral standing his uncle must have entertained the gravest misgivings. What is perhaps most characteristic is that it would be difficult to say which visits he enjoyed more. George Eliot he greatly admired, and thought her both very amiable and an interesting psychological study, but too big and weighty for the ordinary world, and, Mrs. Barrington adds, " somewhat strange in respect to its small amenities."[33]

In 1874, says Mrs. Barrington,

the Bagehots decided to buy a house in London, and settled on 8 Queen's Gate Place, which they gave into the hands of William Morris's firm to furnish and decorate, De Morgan tiles, of course, being a feature of the decoration.

Walter wrote to me that " Wardle is doing most of the house, but the great man himself, William Morris, is composing the drawing-room, as he would an ode." Walter would at times meet William Morris at the Bloomsbury depôt when choosing papers and tiles, and the two would talk poetry as well as furniture. Walter's fancy was tickled at the quaint combination, and at William Morris's autocratic attitude towards all questions of taste. However amusing the culture of æsthetics might be they could not wean Walter entirely. He had always had a great fondness for children. Amidst the choice designs of an inner hall, which the Morris firm had treated as a special feature in the new house, stood a fine large rocking horse, crude in colour and carving as such things are, my sister's gift to my boy. As we were passing it one day Walter spurted out suddenly, as he used to do when he

G

enunciated something that was *really* true, " *That's* the best thing in the house."[33]

Bagehot delighted in showing his friends through the house, explaining in great detail Morris's views " as to the morality or immorality of certain colours and designs. The poet was composing a specially beautiful blue damask silk for the curtains and furniture of the drawing-rooms."[33] Apparently the task was arduous, for Bagehot received sample threads every two or three months, but no curtains.

Indeed he was never to see those curtains. The attacks of bronchitis were becoming more severe, and were rendered doubly dangerous by a disease of the heart. In March of 1877, at the end of the first winter in the new house, he caught a heavy cold, against which, although it grew steadily worse, he took no precautions. One day he told a member of *The Economist* staff that he did not think he would recover. Shortly after, he left his bed one night and, going up to his study, made his will. On March 20, he departed with his wife for Herd's Hill—under the circumstances a very reckless journey. The doctor was sent for, and found the right lung congested. Bagehot grew daily worse, until the twenty-fourth, when he was supposed to be better. His wife lay at his side all morning,

> cutting open the leaves of a new copy of *Rob Roy*, which he read. He spoke often of feeling extreme weakness, increasing as the day advanced. In the afternoon he exerted himself, moving his pillows, and when my sister tried to help him, he said " Let me have my own fidgets," but called her to him, then fell asleep, breathing loud and hard. Gradually the sound quieted,

till, as the sun was setting, the end came peacefully—painlessly.[34]

A few years after his death Sir Robert Giffen wrote:

> Mentally Bagehot was at his best when he died, and he looked forward to many years of happy toil, both in finishing the *Economic Studies* and other work beyond. So far from becoming absorbed in economic science as he grew older, though his later writings happened to be almost all economic, Bagehot to the last gave me the impression of only passing through one mental stage, which being passed through he would again leave political economy behind.[35]

In his death certainly a keen mind and a rich experience were deprived of their maturest fruits, and a brilliant and noble career cut short in its most distinctive stage. Had he lived longer he would perhaps have afforded us an interesting spectacle of old age, in many ways the most revealing period of human life. And yet it is difficult to imagine Bagehot as a decrepit old man patiently decaying into extinction. Despite all his moderation and control there was in him a youthful daring, a love of vivid life, and hatred of weakness which seems to render a short career inevitable. He took grave risks in his last illness and, though not eagerly —like Shelley—extended his hand to death.

CHAPTER V

LITERARY DOCTRINE: FUNDAMENTALS, DISTINCTION BETWEEN CLASSIC AND ROMANTIC

BAGEHOT was a man of several professions and one avocation. That avocation was literary criticism. When the serious business of banking and editing was over, he retired to his study, read literature and wrote upon it. Writing was chiefly a means of relaxation, and his attitude was somewhat that of the " tired business man "—not that he thought of art merely as idle recreation or as an opportunity for " emotional release." His study jacket did not, with a characteristically twentieth-century magic, transform him from a captain of industry into a gushing æsthete. He brought to bear upon literature, as upon economics and political philosophy, the same keen, disciplined intellect, the same rich and many-sided experience. But his state of mind was that of a man who wished not merely to instruct his readers but to amuse himself, who wrote not anxiously and laboriously, but with exhilaration and easy abandon. The literary essays represent that part of his mind which found no adequate expression in a column of figures, the ephemeral pages of *The Economist*, or the grave and sedate tomes of *Lombard Street* and *The English Constitution*.

This point should not be pushed too far, nor the literary essays too sharply distinguished from the rest of Bagehot's writings. His view of all subjects was serious and responsible, as his manner of discussing them was often frivolous and audacious. A man so vitally concerned, in so many fields of inquiry, with the liberal and human aspects of truth would hardly treat with lightness the most liberal and human of all studies. Yet his literary work suggests unmistakably the attitude of mind in which it was written. Its virtues are those of fine conversation. The mood is easy and confident, the tone witty and vivacious, the thought free and lively. The author gives himself up to flights of eloquence and sallies of humour which, in a more guarded and anxious moment, he would scarcely have attempted. He allows his ideas to take their own direction, and turns literature into economics and history with a boldness which disgusts the studious critic and delights the ordinary reader. Unconsciously he is drawn to the thoughts closest to his heart and the things deepest in his experience. "William Cowper" bears the dark suggestion of his mother's insanity, "Hartley Coleridge" the trace of his own childhood. The literary essays have some of the excitement of confession and all the charm of intimacy. They are as the conversations of a great man recorded by himself.

But they have also the faults of good conversa-tion. The industry, the keen self-vigilance of the more deliberate author are lacking. Bagehot retreats from tedious labour. He scorns exhaustive preliminary research, and having worked out the interesting parts of an argument, fails to tie them together with hard, solid logic. He elaborates airy metaphysical distinctions as readily as one might discuss the weather. In the exhilaration of thought he sometimes swallows large potations of theory pure, without any adulteration of truth. He is too much at the mercy of his talents, and in " Hartley Coleridge," for example, esteems an author highly because he understands him vividly. His prejudices sit too complacently upon him. He is too patronizing toward French art and French genius.[1] He is too little on his guard, for one naturally so cautious and detached, against the Victorian within him. He makes too great a virtue of Dickens's purity, too black a crime of Thackeray's " suggestiveness."[1] He is a little too much struck with Browning's " nastiness."[1] The literary essays have in them more vital personality and more careless thought—one is almost inclined to say—more truth and more error than any of Bagehot's other writings.

Perhaps the least impressive part of Bagehot's criticism is his literary theory. It is a curious mixture of solid conservatism and brilliant guesswork, of safe intuition and dangerous speculation. Seeking instinctively principles which have stood the test of time, he bases himself firmly on Aristotle. Upon fundamentals he is naturally, instinctively sensible, as upon particular and subsidiary questions he is frequently both reliable and profound. Altogether he is the broadest and most liberal Aristotelian of his age. Yet nearly everything he says is tinctured with fallacy. There is a carelessness in logic and definition, an eagerness to ascend to a paradise of speculation upon the backs of dazzling first thoughts. Indeed, he is not quite deeply enough in earnest always to resist an exciting inspiration. Consequently the mask is off. The vilifier of intellect, the eulogist of stupidity frequently gives himself up to a strong natural inclination—to the intoxicating pursuit of intoxicating ideas.   In the literary essays Bagehot might be said to arrive at error by logic and at truth by instinct.

As an Aristotelian he was considerably influenced by some of the great modern exponents of classic tradition, notably by Coleridge and Matthew Arnold, and to a lesser extent by Goethe.   A steady contempt for French genius seems to have blinded him to the depth and penetration of French criticism.

As I have suggested earlier, Bagehot is not one of those who would hide literature in an ivory tower dedicated to the worship of beauty.   Literature is indissolubly connected with life.   Under favourable conditions it is a cultural and moral force of the first importance.   " We need," he declares, " an intellectual possession analogous to our own life; which reflects, embodies, improves it; on which we can repose; which will recur to us in the placid moments—which will be a latent principle even in the acute crises of life."[2]   Literature should not be deliberately didactic in a narrow and immediate sense, but inevitably didactic in a larger sense.   Poetry, at its best, " is a deep thing, a teaching thing, the most surely and wisely elevating of human things."[2]   Moreover, " though pleasure is not the end of poetry, pleasing is a condition of poetry."[2]   Bagehot does not of course maintain the theory of the sugar-coated pill.   His interpretation of the words " teach " and " please " is both liberal and profound.   Of Browning's " Caliban upon Setebos " he writes:

An exceptional monstrosity of horrid ugliness cannot be made pleasing, except it be made to suggest—
to recall—the perfection, the beauty, from which it
is a deviation.   Perhaps in extreme cases no art is
equal to this; but then such self-imposed problems
should not be worked by the artist; these out-of-the-
way and detestable subjects should be let alone by
him. [2]

But if ugliness is something which is out-of-the-way,
exceptional, and monstrous, beauty must be something which is central, typical, and human. Such
beauty is also truth. In its grace there is meaning,
as in its meaning grace. Literature impregnated
with such beauty instructs while it pleases and
pleases while it instructs. Matthew Arnold observes
in the same vein: " To the elementary part of our
nature, to our passions, that which is great and
passionate is always interesting "—and, he might
have added, instructive. [3]

Arnold has another saying which goes straight
to the heart of Bagehot's literary philosophy.
" What is really precious and inspiring," he asks,
" in all that we get from literature, except this
sense of an immediate contact with genius itself,
and the stimulus toward what is true and excellent
which we derive from it? " [3] In all save the deep
reverence implied, which for men, however great,
so detached a critic could not feel, this sentence
might have come from the pen of Bagehot. His
instinct for the practical, the human, led him
always to the author as the great reality behind
every book. Created personalities interested him
infinitely less. A natural aristocrat, he was naturally
drawn to the great aristocrats of the mind who find
in literature their fullest expression and develop-

ment, and as he has a conception of highest beauty, so he has a conception of highest genius. As he gives the highest place to an art which is deeply and broadly founded in life, yet restrained and noble, so he esteems most an author who carries with him the discipline of a high and moral culture through the stress and excitement and rich experience of a worldly career. Shakespeare, the supreme artist and successful business man, he honours above all authors, yet deplores the wildness of his genius, even while admiring its breadth and magnitude. He writes with respect and approval of the versatile mind of Scott, with critical wit of the narrow and studious mind of Gibbon. He exalts the " symmetrical genius " of Plato above the " irregular genius " of Dickens.[4] His preference is, as always, for the Greek virtues.

" Poetry," says Aristotle, " . . . is a more philosophical and a higher thing than history: for poetry tends to express the universal, history the particular. By the universal I mean how a person of a certain type will on occasion speak or act; according to the law of probability or necessity."[5] Behind these observations lies the idea that the infinite variety of human nature groups itself into certain types, and that these types are themselves but aspects of a universal human truth. The object of poetry—and here Aristotle has particularly in mind narrative and dramatic literature—is to express that truth. It does so by a process of selection, portraying indeed the physical surface of life, but not all the pointless trivialities, the meaningless events, the inexplicable accidents and contradictions which appear upon that surface,

and which are described in history. Rather poetry
depicts only those manifestations of life which
point toward its inner logic, toward the large and
permanent forces, which, ultimately, govern and
determine it.[6] In the passage just quoted Aristotle
characteristically regards the universal from the
point of view of human action. Bagehot approached
it from the point of view of subject-matter. He
emphasized not so much that the universal is
probable, as that it is selective.

We have the word " picturesque," he says, to
describe such a scene in nature as includes all the
typical features of a landscape and is therefore a
fit subject for painting. Why not have a word
" literesque "?

> The word " *literesque* " would mean, if we possessed
> it, that perfect combination in *subject matter* of litera-
> ture, which suits the *art* of literature. We often meet
> people, and say of them, sometimes meaning well and
> sometimes ill: " How well so-and-so would do in a
> book! " Such people are by no means the best people;
> but they are the most effective people—the most re-
> memberable people.

Such people are typical:

> When we see the *type* of the genus, at once we seem
> to comprehend its character; the inferior specimens are
> explained by the perfect embodiment; the approxima-
> tions are definable when we know the ideal to which
> they draw near. There are an infinite number of
> classes of human beings, but in each of these classes
> there is a distinctive type which, if we could expand
> it in words, would define the class.

Such a type would form part of a purified reality,
a reality freed from the accidental and extraneous,

and " the poet must find in that reality, the *literesque* man, the *literesque* scene, which Nature intends for him, and which will live in his page."

But there are authors who do not see, or but imperfectly see, this typical reality. Some are too much fascinated by particular theories or systems of thought, and to these writers Bagehot would assign a lesser rank:

> A Schiller, a Euripides, a Ben Jonson, cares for *ideas*—for the parings of the intellect, and the distillation of the mind; a Shakespeare, a Homer, a Goethe, finds his mental occupation, the true home of his natural thoughts, in the real world.[7]

Some authors again seek strange and exciting subjects. They depict not the typical, but the exceptional, the peculiar, the marvellous. To these also Bagehot assigns a lesser place, because he feels they treat subject-matter of lesser importance.

Again, the typical is much affected by the circumstances in which it is delineated. Characters may be represented as talented or untalented, as of high or low rank, and all are not equally suitable for the best art. Men of exalted station who are involved in great crises and who decide the affairs of nations are more striking to the imagination than other men, and if they are also men of great and varied abilities, including within themselves a large portion of human nature, they seem, when represented in a work of art, to stand as gigantic symbols for all humanity. Their thoughts and actions have about them the majesty of abstract truth, and even their crimes have an awfulness which prevents us from turning away in disgust. In short, the noblest art depicts the universal in circumstances of solemnity and grandeur. Such art is to be found in the second book of *Paradise Lost*:

> The debate in Pandæmonium is a debate among these typical characters at the greatest conceivable crisis, and with adjuncts of solemnity which no other situation could rival. It is the greatest classical triumph, the highest achievement of the pure style in English literature; it is the greatest description of the highest and most typical characters with the most choice circumstances and in the fewest words.[7]

Yet Bagehot realized perfectly well that human nature is weak and high classic art neglected: " But little deep poetry is very popular, and *no* severe art."[7] The ordinary reader much prefers familiar prose to high poetry, and the serial novel to the Homeric epic. Bagehot's attitude is characteristically moderative. He judged all art critically, and that which pretended to be great, by the highest and most rigid standards, yet he excluded nothing that deserved the name, however trivial, from consideration. He was quick to point out the deficiencies of popular taste, but no less quick to reprehend the narrowness of an author who forgot that he wrote for human beings.

Arnold's exclusiveness aroused in him an almost Philistine resentment: " But I own I think a man ought to be able to be a ' Philistine ' if he chooses; there is a sickly incompleteness about people too fine for the world."[8] And about art too fine for the world, perhaps! At any rate, in a letter to Hutton, written during the period of his greatest interest in literature, he says of Arnold:

> I am glad you like Matthew Arnold's letter. I am reading his new tragedy which is clever, but too much

" high art " and not addressed enough to the common feelings and minds of ordinary people. I used to tell Clough he believed legibility to be a defect, and I am sure the high art criticism and practice tend steadily in that direction. [9]

Again he dwells at length on the absurdity of Arnold's idea that poetry should portray only great actions:

> Mr. Arnold, some years since, put forth a theory that the art of poetry could only delineate *great actions.* . . . Nobody in their senses would describe Gray's " Elegy " as the delineation of a " great action "; some kinds of mental contemplation may be energetic enough to deserve this name, but Gray would have been frightened at the very word. [10]

On the other hand he fully recognized the defects of contemporary taste and contemporary literature. " In truth," he says, " review writing but exemplifies the casual character of modern literature. Everything about it is temporary and fragmentary. . . . People take their literature in morsels, as they take sandwiches on a journey." And who was the reader of this literature but " the merchant in the railway with a head full of sums, an idea that tallow is ' up,' a conviction that teas are 'lively,' and a mind reverting perpetually from the little volume which he reads to these mundane topics, to the railway, to the shares, to the buying and bargaining universe? "[10]   Readers were many, ignorant, and unguided:

> We live in the realm of the *half* educated. The number of readers grows daily, but the quality of readers does not improve rapidly. . . . Without guidance young men, and tired men, are thrown amongst a

mass of books; they have to choose which they like; many of them would much like to improve their culture, to chasten their taste, if they knew how.[10]

But they did not know how, and therefore they preferred a strange and wonderful, a " glaring " art, to a sober and probable one. The supreme examples of contemporary art, Bagehot readily admitted, were very great. According to the late Mr. George Saintsbury, he was one of the first to point out the merits of Tennyson and Browning, yet he also recognized their defects, and though granting them a high place, he emphatically denied them the highest.[11]

Though maintaining that the best literature " is a deep thing, a teaching thing," Bagehot was far from excluding frivolous and superficial productions from the pale. Such books as the *Mémoires de Grammont*, though immoral, have their place. They are an offence against morality but not against taste: " Morals and policy must decide how far such delineations are permissible or expedient; but the art of beauty—art-criticism—has no objection to them. They are pretty paintings of pretty objects, and that is all it has to say."[12] On another occasion he might have had more to say. And indeed, though readily admitting the *Mémoires de Grammont* to be literature, he does not say they are great literature. He specifically calls them " pretty paintings of pretty objects." The phrase is in itself a judgment. A world which is distinguished from the animal kingdom chiefly by good taste necessarily appears somewhat trivial, and the book which reflects such a world must be trivial also. It might be thought pretty, but never beautiful, for beauty

in art, as Bagehot conceives it, is fundamentally
human or moral.

His dictum that " pleasing is the condition of
art " leads him to reprehend not only the monstrosi-
ties of Browning, but the paupers and beggars of
Dickens. As he ridicules a delineation of poverty
which is idyllic and unreal, so he condemns one
which is morbid and prolonged. The poor should
be depicted with caution. They present " an
unusual difficulty to artistic delineation ":

> A good deal of the character of the poor is an unfit
> topic for continuous art, and yet we wish to have in
> our books a life-like exhibition of the whole of that
> character. Mean manners and mean vices are unfit
> for prolonged delineation; the everyday pressure of
> narrow necessities is too petty a pain and too anxious
> a reality to be dwelt upon.[12]

Farther along he applies this objection specifically
to the poor of Dickens: " His poor people have
taken to their poverty very thoroughly; they are
poor talkers and poor livers, and in all ways poor
people to read about." As subjects for artistic
delineation, the poor are under two great disadvantages. First, their sufferings and misfortunes
have no grandeur or awfulness about them. They
do not " take " the imagination, but worry and
oppress the reader with the thought of a mean and
sordid reality. Second, they do not permit of profound and significant treatment.[12] Very much of
humanity but very little of human nature, in
Bagehot's opinion, can be crowded into stupidity
and ignorance. Now these are certainly strong
reasons against poverty, yet hardly strong enough
to exclude it from literary treatment. *Oliver Twist,*

however much it " dates," is after all still read by
the few that read the literature of the past. Moreover, it teaches a valuable lesson of sympathy,
though that teaching needs now to be corrected
by a little regard to common sense and justice.
Finally, any rigid exclusion of subject-matter in
literature is always dangerous. To say that certain
lives should not have been treated in art is somewhat like saying they should not have been lived.

In the essay on Shelley, Bagehot draws a distinction between classic and romantic by differentiating,
after the manner of Coleridge, between the imagination and the fancy.[13] Imagination is defined
as the faculty which produces large, bold, basic
ideas or images, fancy as the faculty which produces
" delicate " and subsidiary ones, or basic ideas
and images of weaker and fainter kind. He
continues:

> When we speak of this distinction, we seem almost
> to be speaking of the distinction between ancient and
> modern literature. The characteristic of the classical
> literature is the simplicity with which the imagination
> appears in it; that of modern literature is the profusion
> with which the most various adornments of the acces-
> sory fancy are thrown and lavished upon it.[14]

Bagehot's illustration—his contrast, for instance,
between the severe beauty of Sophocles and the
baroque beauty of Shakespeare—implies a principle
much broader than that which he has stated. In
suggesting that romantic literature is superior in
vividness, spontaneity, and sensuous appeal, classical literature in unity, idea, and restraint, he has
in my opinion shown some real perception of
the difference between the two. Indeed his

illustrations are what eventually reveal the narrowness of his formula. In neglecting the unreal, idyllic
quality of imagination so prominent in historical
romanticism, he has gone notably astray. One is
a little surprised, for example, to hear that the
imagination of Shelley is " classical," and the
account of it given is not reassuring: " Its sphere
is in what the Germans call the unconditioned—
in the unknown, immeasurable, untrodden. . . .
We cannot know detail in tracts we have never
visited; the infinite has no form; the immeasurable
no outline."[14] But Homer's imagination is generally
thought classical, and certainly its sphere is not in
" the unconditioned." His imagination does not
lack " form " and " outline." Rather I should
say that proportionateness is one of its most prominent characteristics, and a subordination to condition—in other words to principle or law—its most
prominent. Engaged in poetic composition, it
subordinates itself to the law of unity and restraint
in the use of artistic technique, to the law of fidelity
in nature description, to the law of probability
in character portrayal. Romantic imagination,
on the other hand, tends to be lawless, as Bagehot
himself, in a criticism of Disraeli, clearly implies.

Another and much more elaborate attempt to
distinguish between classic and romantic fails
through that want of rigid and systematizing logic
which I have already pointed out in Bagehot.
Both Arnold and Hazlitt may have furnished him
with a number of valuable hints for this distinction,
but essentially it is his own.[15] He founds his theory
upon Aristotle's doctrine of the universal, as interpreted in " Wordsworth, Tennyson, and Browning."

H

Having occasion to attack his arguments, I must, at the risk of tiring the reader, return to an earlier discussion. Bagehot begins by saying that we need a word *literesque* to denote " that perfect combination in *subject matter* of literature, which suits the *art* of literature." As he uses this new term, it seems to signify the typical, the generic, or the universal. A literesque character is one who possesses qualities typical of a large class of ordinary characters; a literesque sentiment is one which, under given circumstances, would probably be felt by a large number of people; a literesque action, one which a large number of people, under given circumstances, would probably take. He proceeds:

> The great divisions of poetry, and of all other literary art, arise from the different modes in which these *types* —these characteristic men, these characteristic feelings —may be variously described. There are three principal modes which we shall attempt to describe— the *pure*, which is sometimes, but not very wisely, called the classical; the *ornate*, which is also unwisely called romantic, and the *grotesque*, which might be called the medieval.

> . . . . . .

> The definition of *pure* literature is, that it describes the type in its simplicity—we mean, with the exact amount of accessory circumstance which is necessary to bring it before the mind in finished perfection, and no more than that amount. . . . There is a setting of surroundings . . . without which the reality is not itself. By a traditional mode of speech, as soon as we see a picture in which a complete effect is produced by detail so rare and so harmonized as to escape us, we say, How " classical "! The whole which is to be seen appears at once and through the detail, but the detail itself is not seen: we do not think of that which gives us the idea; we are absorbed in the idea

itself. Just so in literature, the pure art is that which
works with the fewest strokes.[16]

Pure art can treat " only the best subjects," " the
most literesque characters in the most literesque
situations." An art in which idea is everything
must contain a good idea. Pure art must adhere
closely to the universal, for through its transparent
surface all that is inconsistent, improbable, and
extraneous becomes glaringly evident. It is an
art which emphasizes the whole and not the part,
which reveals form and proportion. In short, it
is an art which defines, and which calms by definition. " That which is chaste chastens; there is a
poised energy—a state of half thrill, half tranquillity
—which pure art gives, which no other can give;
. . . an enobled satisfaction at what ought to satisfy
us, and must enoble us." As different manifestations of such art Bagehot cites three poets: Wordsworth as expressing " typical *sentiment*," Shelley as
maintaining perfect spontaneity, Milton as deline-
ating classic characters and action on a large scale.

But all art cannot treat the best subjects in the
best way. " Human nature could not endure such
a critical commandment as that." There must be
subjects which are less literesque, types which are
less perfect, and these are best represented by
ornate art. The ornate artist introduces into his
subject-matter an exciting and mysterious confusion, " a rich medley which does not exist in the
actual world." His method is exactly opposite to
that of the pure artist. He " wishes to surround
the type with the greatest number of circumstances
which it will bear." He "works not by choice and
selection, but by accumulation and aggregation."

Bagehot selects Tennyson's " Enoch Arden " as an example of the ornate style. The story itself is extremely simple: " A sailor who sells fish, breaks his leg, gets dismal, gives up selling fish, goes to sea, is wrecked on a desert island, stays there some years, on his return finds his wife married to a miller, speaks to a landlady on the subject, and dies." Told in the pure style, this tale would not fill three pages, but Tennyson extends it almost to a volume. He elaborates upon every scene, incident, and personage. By a complicated brilliance of language, by elaborate poetical descriptions, and by every other means of artificial enhancement, he casts a " mist of beauty " over what might have been a very dingy narrative. " Nothing is described as it is; everything has about it the atmosphere of something else." One feels a want, a " want of ' definition.' " All is surrounded with a blinding glitter and brilliance, producing upon the mind " an excess of fascination, a complication of charm."

The third kind of art, the grotesque, deals with the type " *in difficulties* ": " It gives a representation of it in its minimum development, amid the circumstances least favourable to it, just while it is struggling with obstacles, just where it is encumbered with incongruities. It deals, to use the language of science, not with normal types but with abnormal specimens." Grotesque art " works by contrast. It enables you to see, it makes you see, the perfect type by painting the opposite deviation." As an example Bagehot cites Browning's " Caliban upon Setebos," the hero of which he describes as typifying great mind placed in circumstances peculiarly unfavourable to mind.

Divorced from its formula, and regarded merely as a series of observations on classicism and romanticism, this discussion is invaluable. As sound and coherent theory it is open to serious objection. Certainly its results do not recommend it. Wordsworth and Shelley, for example, are referred to as pure, or classic, poets, yet they produce upon the mind—and here I should cite particularly Shelley—the effects which Bagehot assigns to romanticism. " To a Skylark," or even " The Isle," which Bagehot quotes as an example of pure art, does certainly exert " an excess of fascination, a complication of charm." Its " conciseness " does not " calm." Here, then, is an obvious inconsistency.

A much more fundamental one appears in the structure of the theory itself. Bagehot declares at the outset that " the business of the poet, of the artist, is with *types*; and those types are mirrored in reality." Toward the middle of the essay he describes Enoch Arden as an *unreal* type, such a character as a " casual traveller by the sea-shore, with a sensitive mood and a romantic imagination " might fancy a sailor to be. But, obviously, if the word *type* always signifies something real, it cannot apply to Enoch Arden, who is admittedly unreal, and the mere day-dream of a man. Bagehot declares that ornate art should deal with types which are " less literesque," " less perfect." Enoch is less literesque and less perfect only in the sense that he is no type at all. Between him and the Satan of *Paradise Lost* there is simply and plainly the difference between the fanciful and the typical, the unreal and the real, the improbable and the probable. Is such the distinction that Bagehot would draw between romantic and classic? If so, why has he not indicated his meaning in so many words? The truth is, no doubt, that he did not know what he meant. By faulty definition and by a careless use of terms, he has built up around his ideas just such a verbal screen as he once complained of in other writers. The basic fallacy of his theory lies of course in his use of the word *type*, the inconsistency of which he veils from himself by introducing the corresponding and broader term *literesque*. Literesque, closely identified with the typical, is defined as " fit to be put into a book." But what is fit to be put into a book may or may not be typical. It was therefore possible to use *literesque* correctly throughout the discussion and at the same time shift the meaning of *type* at convenience. Bagehot's strict employment of the one term probably blinded him to the loose employment of the other.

If for the sake of argument it is admitted that types may be real and unreal, the difference between pure and ornate amounts to the difference between realistic and unrealistic. And certainly, in their deeper understanding of man's moral nature, in their juster emphasis upon his peculiarly human qualities, the great works of antiquity— after all the best and truest examples of classical literature—are more profoundly realistic than the great works of modern romanticism. Yet they are not more realistic than Shakespeare, whom Bagehot properly describes as a predominantly ornate artist. In short, much that is real in Shakespeare cannot be reduced to classicism, just as much that is romantic in Tennyson cannot be reduced to unreality. Again, if Bagehot's theory is described purely in terms of the literesque, it amounts to the following statement: Pure art is produced when any subject " fit to be put in a book " is treated with simplicity and with a minimum of detail; ornate art, when such a subject is treated in complexity, or with a maximum of detail. Such a rule might serve rather awkwardly to explain certain variations between classic and romantic technique, but for any practical purpose it is hopelessly inadequate. Indeed, one cannot arrive at a satisfactory distinction in this matter by employing the methods of the schoolmen. A more thoroughly inductive definition, a more elaborate analysis of classicism and romanticism as historical movements are necessary. Bagehot's most serious limitation as a literary critic, and one very common in his time, was a want of scientific scholarship.

His account of " grotesque art " describes excellently, I think, the practice of a few poets in a few poems. Browning's " Caliban upon Setebos " does certainly present " mind in unusual circumstances," or " under difficulties." His " Pied Piper of Hamelin " presents the bourgeois nature " in the utmost difficulty, in contact with magic and the supernatural." And the *Fables* of La Fontaine, it might be added, represent human nature under difficulties, in strange and peculiar conjunction with animal nature, and with the animal world. Yet the examples of such art are few, and by no means sufficiently important to require a separate category, equal in status to the classic or romantic.

Chapter VI

LITERARY DOCTRINE: THE *GENRES* AND ELEMENTS OF ARTISTIC WRITING

THE distinction made by Bagehot between prose and poetry is essentially that made by Coleridge, who points out that it is not metre which makes poetry but what metre implies: " If metre be super-added, all other parts must be made consonant with it. They must be such, as to justify the perpetual and distinct attention to each part, which an exact correspondent recurrence of accent and sound are calculated to excite."[1] Bagehot elaborates:

> We need only say here that poetry, because it has a more marked rhythm than prose, must be more intense in meaning and more concise in style than prose. People expect a " marked rhythm " to imply something worth marking; if it fails to do so they are disappointed. They are displeased at the visible waste of a powerful instrument; they call it " doggerel," and rightly call it, for the metrical expression of full thought and eager feeling—the burst of metre—incident to high imagination, should not be wasted on petty matters which prose does as well. Verse, too, should be more concise, for long-continued rhythm tends to jade the mind, just as brief rhythm tends to attract the attention. Poetry should be memorable and emphatic, intense, and *soon over*.[2]

Bagehot perceived, much more clearly than Coleridge, that metrical language must be exalted and poetic because it is rhythmical, and rhythm has a strange, primitive power to excite passion.

In preferring poetry to be " soon over," does Bagehot mean to imply that the lyric is more truly poetical than the epic? Perhaps he felt, as I do, that lyrics are more human. Men can write great epics, but they can scarcely read them—at least not for long at a time. They are for angels to enjoy. Who dares cast a stone at Dr. Johnson?

It is natural that Bagehot, delighting in the clarity and definiteness of classification, has much to say of the *genres*. And he not only does full justice to those commonly recognized, but creates a good many new ones, some of which, it must be confessed, are not very significant. Though not arranging them into a definite hierarchy, he evidently does not consider them all of equal rank. In spite of Aristotle, epic is quite definitely placed above tragedy, and the poetry of meditation preferred to that of society. The *genre* is not merely an instrument of order. It is also a natural growth, having the cause of its rise and decline in the changes of civilization and human experience. It is to be studied, apparently, in terms rather of contemporary social conditions than of the evolutions of *genres*. Bagehot reveals here as elsewhere his indifference to the details of literary history. In order effectively to be what it is, a *genre* develops certain laws and restrictions. The writer breaks these, and mixes the *genres*, at his own peril. Elizabethan drama, with the exception of Shakespeare, would have been much greater, had it not attempted to include within itself the merits of prose fiction.

Bagehot's principal description of the various *genres* of poetry occurs during the unfolding of a theory that " poetry begins in Impersonality " :

Homer is a voice . . . and this is all we know. The
natural subjects of the first art are the scenes and
events in which the first men naturally take an interest. They don't care . . . for a kind old man; but
they want to hear of the exploits of their ancestors—
. . . of the founders of their own land—of wars, and
rumours of wars—of great victories boldly won—of
heavy defeats firmly borne. . . . So in all countries
—Siegfried, or Charlemagne, or Arthur—they are but
attempts at an Achilles: the subject is the same—the
κλέα ἀνδρῶν and the death that comes to all.

The epic, then, is heroic, martial, and impersonal.
It is superior to drama because it deals not only
with character " in motion," like the drama, but
with character " *in mass* ":

If a thoughtful person will compare the character
of Achilles, as we find it in Homer, with the more sur-
passing creations of dramatic invention, say with Lear
or Othello, he will perhaps feel that character in
repose, character on the lonely beach, character in
marble, character in itself, is more clearly and perfectly seen in the epic narrative, than in the conversational drama.

In this respect, the epic resembles that type of
lyric poetry in which the poet delineates his own
character " in repose," or in isolation. And so
Milton, a great master of both kinds, " did not
hesitate to turn aside from his ' high argument ' "
and speak of his own thoughts and sentiments.
Unlike Aristotle, Bagehot stresses the non-dramatic
element in the epic.[2]

But in the course of time the old heroic age,
with its incessant warfare, passes away. Life
becomes less turbulent, and men grow in refinement and civilization. Yet they still remember the
old world; they still worship the old heroes, and are

ready to receive from the poet " a new telling of
the old tale—a new idealization of the legendary
tradition. This is the age of dramatic art, when
men wonder at the big characters of old, as school-
boys at the words of Aeschelus, and try to find in
their own breasts the roots of those monstrous, but
artistically developed impersonations."[2] The
drama is a more limited, more difficult *genre* than
the epic. It is restricted by its brevity, by the
limitations of stage production, and most of all
by the inadequate expressiveness of dialogue, for
enormous skill is necessary to exhibit character by
" mere talk." The Elizabethan dramatists ven-
tured to go beyond these restrictions, but of them
all Shakespeare alone succeeded. He alone could
delineate in a play " a whole list of *dramatis personæ*,
a set of characters enough for a modern novel, and
with the distinctness of a modern novel." A
lesser dramatist should be more than content if,
like the ancients, he " can give two or three great
characters in solitude and in dignity," or " catch a
monarch in a tragic posture."[2]

Bagehot has made a few other observations on
tragedy. One, on the nature of tragic effect, is
very general: " The pleasure of high tragedy is also
painful: the whole soul is stretched; the spirit
pants; the passions scarcely breathe: it is a rapt
and eager moment, too intense for continuance—
so overpowering, that we scarcely know whether
it be joy or pain."[3] In a more lengthy and interesting passage on the " Samson Agonistes " of
Milton, he declares

that catastrophes require a comic element. We appear
to feel the same principle in life. We may read solemn

descriptions of great events in history,—say of Lord
Strafford's trial, and of his marvellous speech, and
his appeal to his " saint in heaven "; but we compre-
hend the whole transaction much better when we learn
from Mr. Baillie, the eye-witness, that people ate nuts
and apples, and talked, and laughed and betted on
the great question of acquittal and condemnation.

The reason for this peculiar phenomenon in the
psychology of belief, says Bagehot, is that the
imagination is " a glancing faculty. It goes and
comes, and comes and goes, and we hardly know
whence or why." We cannot concentrate it.
Therefore, in depicting a catastrophe, the poet
should contrive by " artistic contrasts," and " skil-
fully disposed opposites " to let the imagination go
" in such a manner as to ensure its coming back
again." The spectator realizes more perfectly a
great tragic idea when he sees the effect it has on
petty minds.[3] The explanation is metaphysical,
but the line of thought pretty clear. Bagehot is
deeply convinced that human life is for the most
part petty and prosaic. The author who excludes
these elements from his scene is bound to repel the
discriminating reader. A great tragic catastrophe,
the most inhumanly heroic of all the spectacles of
art, should be ingeniously framed in the humdrum.
The spectator must feel his feet firmly on the ground
before he permits his mind to soar into the clouds.
This theory is in part at least but another example
of Bagehot's limited appetite for the heroic.

Lyric poetry appears, says Bagehot, with the
coming of civilization: " Men wish not only to tell
what they have seen, but also to express what they
are conscious of. . . . As time runs on, arise gentler

emotions and finer moods and more delicate
desires which need expression, and require from
the artist's fancy the lightest touches and the most
soothing and insinuating words." Lyric poetry "is
designed to express, and when successful does
express, some single sentiment, some isolated longing in human nature."[4] These passages appear in
the essay on " Hartley Coleridge " written in 1852.
In 1853 and 1854 Arnold brought out the first
and second editions of his poems, containing the
famous prefaces, which Bagehot shows many evidences of having read with particular attention.[5]
In the preface to the first edition Arnold declares
that the excellence of a poem greatly depends on
the choice of subject-matter. A great poem should
deal with a great action—such an action as by its
passion and significance must permanently interest
mankind. In short, a great poem must imitate
the universal. In the preface to the second edition
he briefly remarks that the earlier preface " leaves
. . . untouched the question; how far and in what
manner the opinions there expressed respecting
the choice of subjects apply to lyric poetry."[6] The
inference is obviously that lyric poetry should also
treat the universal. Bagehot seems to have caught
at this suggestion in " Wordsworth, Tennyson, and
Browning," for in describing lyric poetry, he applies
to it, as Arnold had applied to narrative poetry,
the doctrine of the universal. The peculiarity of
lyric poetry is

> that the poet does not describe himself *as* himself:
> autobiography is not his object; he takes himself as a
> specimen of human nature . . . he takes such of his
> moods as are most characteristic, as most typify

certain moods of certain men, or certain moods of
all men. . . . The essence is that such self-describing
poets describe what is *in* them, but not *peculiar* to them,
what is generic, not what is special and individual.[7]

Bagehot may seem to contradict this view in erect-
ing another *genre*, that of " self-delineative " poetry,
which in the course of time arises out of the lyrical.
Here the author is concerned

> with his mind viewed as a whole, with the entire
> essence of his own character. The first requisite of
> this poetry is truth. It is, in Plato's phrase, the soul
> " itself by itself " aspiring to view and take account
> of the particular notes and marks that distinguish it
> from all other souls. The sense of reality is necessary
> to excellence; the poet being himself, speaks like one
> who has authority; he knows and must not deceive.[7]

Would Bagehot have accounted for self-delineative
poetry by the doctrine of the universal? The
passage quoted above, with its romantic insistence
upon the holiness of individuality, would not lead
one to think so. Yet questioned, he would probably
have given somewhat the same explanation that
he gave for the success of eccentric characters in
Sterne. The self-delineative poet must show his
" relation to our common human nature; . . . how
we were related to it, how in some sort and in some
circumstances we might ourselves become it."
He must reduce his abnormal formation to the
normal rules.[7]

In an attempt to get at the original ballads of
which the epic is composed, a famous German
scholar once butchered and expurgated the *Niebe-
lungenlied* into something very much his own. His
reputation was so impressive, his results so " scienti-
fically " exact, his argument so free from reason

and so confidently dogmatic that the learned world half inclined to accept the amazing new " songs " —until it was discovered that their erudite creator was a septomaniac. Every element in his results had some clearly demonstrable relation to the number seven. Bagehot himself probably had just a touch of duomania. He found a strange fascination in making dichotomies. Of these the ones relating to human psychology—such as the distinctions between seer and groper, the symmetrical and irregular genius, the experiencing and inexperiencing nature—are real and perspicacious; but those relating to literary theory have so little basis in reality that I am persuaded their chief value is rhetorical. They serve to mark off sharply the matter to be discussed, to establish a contrast between the subject in hand and the rest of the universe—though usually at considerable damage to the truth, for, despite many brilliant individual remarks in the elaboration, they constitute perhaps the weakest chapter in his thought. Lacking the same full knowledge, he does not possess the same sure tact in the field of literary history as in that of human psychology. Feeling less responsibility than in discussing politics or economics, which perhaps he considered weightier and closer to his reputation, he seems more recklessly to indulge his native love for theories and ideas. His virtue of sharp analysis and striking statement often falls into the excess of over-simplification, and as passion frequently speaks in the severest logic, so here bias and prejudice take the imposing language of Socratic dichotomy.

In his essay on Shelley, Bagehot divides the lyric

into the human and the abstract. The human deals
" of course with the actual life, passions, and actions
of real men," the abstract lyric, coming later in
time, with the " large number of half-personified
abstractions," which " from the deposit of the
débris of a hundred philosophies " have become
" part of the familiar thoughts and language of all
mankind." In most minds these abstractions,
" remote altogether from the eyes and senses of
men," arouse no great emotion, but " in some
peculiar minds " they call forth " an almost dizzy
intensity of excitement."[8]   Such a peculiar mind
was Shelley's, and its characteristic product is such
an abstract lyric as the " Epipsychidion." This
dichotomy, if indeed legitimate, is certainly not
very new. The abstract or philosophical lyric is
no discovery of Bagehot's. And what precisely
does he mean by " abstract "?   Apparently he
refers to certain unreal concepts produced by the
romantic imagination, like the perfect equality
which Rousseau describes in the *Discours sur
L'Inégalité* and the ideal woman which Shelley sees
in the Emilia Viviani of " Epipsychidion." But
these idyllic abstractions, which, as Bagehot observes, are usually accompanied by the most intense
emotion, represent a comparatively narrow phenomenon in great literature, and should be defined
with a little more attention to their real essence
and their historical origins, before logical distinctions are erected upon them. Moreover, such
abstractions arouse excitement not merely in the
few, but in the many. The French Revolution has
taught us that almost nothing has more power
over a dull mind than a clear idea. The dichotomy

has but one tangible value. It throws upon a few poems of Shelley, which are the subject of discussion, the spotlight of antithesis.

Another dichotomy distinguishes between " poems of this world and poems not of this world." The first variety, which might also be called *vers de société*, is concerned with the social sentiments; with the thoughts and feelings clustering upon the surface of life, about the *salon*, the theatre and the café; " which are half superficial and do not touch the inmost soul, but which nevertheless are unspeakably important in the actual constitution of human nature." But down below this level, within each man, " we fancy . . . a primitive immovable essence, which is modified into all the ever-changing phenomena we see, which is the grey granite whereon they lie."[8] From these experiences are made the poems not of this world. Horace and Béranger are poets of the first school, and as a poet of the second, Wordsworth would doubtless have been named, for from Bagehot's phraseology, and particularly from the frequent use of the word " primitive," one suspects that he was influenced by the opposition Rousseau had set up between society and the individual, between the superficial inhabitant of the drawing-room and the lonely, deep-souled man of nature. He had on another occasion drawn just such a contrast between Jeffrey and Wordsworth in " The First Edinburgh Reviewers."[8] If indeed he founded his dichotomy upon this romantic opposition, he has asserted in effect that lyric poetry is divided into social verse and the nature poetry of Wordsworth—scarcely an exhaustive division. But if the division is to be more broadly interpreted, as separating all poetry of the inner life from all poetry dealing with the outward world, it is certainly admissible—though not striking nor indicative of the very hazy border-line between the two *genres* defined. Milton's sonnet "On His Being Arrived at the Age of Twenty-three," while mainly concerned with the individual alone, has, like all true ethical poetry, the closest relation to outward life.

Society affords subject-matter for many kinds of poetry, two of which Bagehot describes at length. These are concerned with "the expression of the feelings which are called out by the accidents of society; next, the harmonized expression of that philosophy of indifference with which the world regards the fortunes of individuals and its own." The first kind of poetry, typified by the songs of Béranger, deals with the more trivial aspects of love, with "society's light expression of its light emotions." The second, typified by the odes of Horace, celebrates that worldly creed which regards "with easy equanimity . . . the fugitiveness of life, the necessity of death," which conceives "of goodness as a mean and of sin as an extreme." Here Bagehot has marked out *genres* distinctly worth defining and made many excellent individual remarks:

> The world, such as it is, has made up its mind what it is. Childishly deceivable by charlatans on every other subject,—imposed on by pedantry, by new and unfounded science, by ancient and unfounded reputation, a prey to pomposity, over-run with recondite fools, ignorant of all else,—society knows itself. [9]

Yet the discussion is marred by what seems to me

a very definite tendency to regard the *vers de société* of Béranger as a symbol for the whole of French genius and of French literature. Bagehot saw one aspect of French character too clearly and could see no other. The spirit of his argument is tainted with the complacency of insular prejudice.

About the *genres* of prose he has very little to say. In " The Waverley Novels " he works out a dichotomy which at once indicts the present and prescribes the future novel. Fiction is " sentimental " and " ubiquitous." The sentimental is that variety, immensely the more popular—as Bagehot felt—in which all else is subordinated to a more or less shallow love interest. The ubiquitous aims at describing the whole of human life "in all its spheres, in all its aspects." " It searches through the whole life of man; his practical pursuits, his speculative attempts, his romantic youth, and his domestic age. . . . If there be any lineaments which it forbears to depict, they are only such as the inevitable repression of a regulated society excludes from the admitted province of literary art."[9] The ubiquitous novel is plainly something of an ideal. It is to be a *Wilhelm Meister* without the placidity and the coldness, and not so much like " a menagerie of tame animals." It is a *genre* which, upon the plane of fiction, is to include everything in human life except indecency. Unfortunately, the modern novel contains almost nothing else. In *The Forsythe Saga* and other more recent works, however, there is an approach to Bagehot's idea.

There are two dichotomies, neither very original, perhaps, referring to history and biography. History may be " universal " or " particular."

Universal history deals with the story of the human race, or with the story of a civilization, covering at the same time events in many nations. Such history, exemplified in the works of Gibbon, has sweep and grandeur, but, being wide in scope, must treat its materials in a rather dry and superficial manner. Particular history is concerned only with a single nation or a few nations. Here detail is possible, and the elements of drama and character may be brought out. The chief master in this class is Macaulay.[9] Again, biography may be " exhaustive " or " selective." It may contain all the known material on its subject, or it may contain what is vivid and important. The world is too small, says Bagehot, for many such works as Masson's *Life of Milton*.[10] And indeed I fear there is among certain scholars nowadays a tendency to rate biographical excellence according to the number of pages and the quantity of facts. An extended biography, well loaded with fact, is an invaluable book of reference, but it is seldom a great work of art. Life is a platitudinizer; it deals very much in the things of every day. Much that happens to very unusual characters is very usual, very tedious, very insignificant and unmeaning. Irreverent people meet great men and wonder why they are great. Probably Disraeli said many a dull thing to county delegations, and to many of his contemporaries Lincoln seemed just another American politician. In the same way biography, as it becomes more factual, approaches more closely the moment-to-moment commonplace of life, without acquiring life's vividness and immediacy. Interesting ideas, salient qualities of character, which the artist should select out and illustrate, are smothered and buried in the unceasing snowstorm of fact. At its best, exhaustive biography seldom presents a living picture. Even Lockhart's *Life of Scott* has scarcely survived the industry of its author, and Boswell himself is now commonly read in abridgements. At its worst, the lengthy biography is in no sense the imitation of a human existence; it is a tomb, a mausoleum, in which the corpse of the great man is laid out in state, among all his documents and affidavits, to rest upon a library shelf in the dusty immortality of four or five ponderous volumes. Exhaustive biographies of high literary merit do certainly exist, but they are fewer than some critics would have us believe. Too often the word *great* has been applied to mere collections of material carefully gathered and sensibly arranged.

Cautious and conservative in his formulation of principles, yet broad and liberal in their application, Bagehot is, in his conception of character portrayal, a true Aristotelian. His underlying belief seems to be that great literature delineates man in terms of the permanent and significant elements in his nature—primarily, therefore, in terms of that fundamental dualism, that struggle between his moral and carnal selves, which the most famous authorities have held to be the central fact in human experience. Character portrayal which disregards moral responsibility is but caricature. Mr. Pickwick, because he is not " a moral agent," is pronounced a " vivified accident." Falstaff, because no one dreams of holding him down to " the ten commandments and the statute-law," is declared not a man, but " a sort of sack-holding paunch." In general: " It is amusing to read of beings *out* of the laws of morality, but it is more profoundly interesting, as well as more in-structive, to read of those whose life in its moral conditions resembles our own." For this reason, the " grotesque exaggerations " of Dickens can never be compared with " the great works of the real painters of essential human nature."[10]

Yet important as it is, morality does not engross the whole of our being:

> The soul of man, and, as we necessarily believe, of beings greater than man, has many parts besides its moral part. It has an intellectual part, an artistic part, even a religious part, in which mere morals have no share. In Shakespeare or Goethe, even in Newton or Archimedes, there is much which will not be cut down to the shape of the commandments.

Unfortunately, Bagehot is disposed to go much farther. Continuing the discussion in the same essay, " Wordsworth, Tennyson, and Browning," he seems to deny the fundamental principle upon which most of his criticism rests, that character should be presented in terms of a moral dualism. " The internal metaphysics of a divided nature," he declares, " are but an inferior subject for art." But the contradiction is much less significant than it appears, for the whole treatment of character in " Wordsworth, Tennyson, and Browning " is vitiated by errors which I have already partially indicated. " Enoch Arden," says Bagehot,

> represents a bit of human nature—a good bit, of course —but a bit only—in disproportionate, unnatural, and revolting prominence; and therefore, unless an artist

use delicate care, we are offended. The dismal act of a squalid man needed many condiments to make it pleasant, and therefore Mr. Tennyson was right to mix them subtly and to use them freely.

A mere act of self-denial can indeed scarcely be pleasant upon paper. A heroic struggle with an external adversary, even though it end in a defeat, may easily be made attractive. Human nature likes to see itself look grand, and it looks grand when it is making a brave struggle with foreign foes. But it does not look grand when it is divided against itself. An excellent person striving with temptation is a very admirable being in reality, but he is not a pleasant being in description. We hope he will win and overcome his temptation; but we feel that he would be a more interesting being, a higher being, if he had not felt that temptation so much. The poet must make the struggle great in order to make the self-denial virtuous, and if the struggle be too great, we are apt to feel some mixture of contempt. The internal metaphysics of a divided nature are but an inferior subject for art, and if they are to be made attractive, much else must be combined with them. If the excellence of " Hamlet " had depended on the ethical qualities of Hamlet, it would not have been the masterpiece of our literature. He acts virtuously of course, and kills the people he ought to kill, but Shakespeare knew that such goodness would not much interest the pit. He made him a handsome prince and a puzzling meditative character; these secular qualities relieve his moral excellence, and so he becomes " nice."[10]

This discussion contains much that is sound and sensible, much that is interesting and revealing. The cynical treatment of hero worship is characteristic, and the animosity against priggishness does credit to the moralist. Yet there is throughout a large factor of error. Bagehot's argument is that " a mere act of self-denial can scarcely be pleasant upon paper," first, because human nature is revolted at the spectacle of virtue unrelieved, and secondly, because it likes to see itself " look grand." But an act of self-denial has frequently been made pleasant upon paper. Maggie Tulliver, in *The Mill on the Floss*, feels temptation, and feels it sorely, nor is her struggle elevated by circumstances of grandeur, yet she is far from being " an unpleasant person in description." Moreover, human nature does not always like to see itself look grand. Often it likes to see itself ridiculous. We love not only to feel our nobility in admiring the greatness of heroes, but to feel our superiority in laughing at the folly of fools. Indeed, so far from wishing to behold man dignified and elevated, we seem nowadays more often to prefer him degraded, debased, and reduced to the level of animalism. Throughout his argument Bagehot places far too much emphasis on " significance." Enoch Arden is objectionable not because he is " squalid " and " mean," nor because he represents virtue in " unnatural and revolting prominence." His primary defects are: first, simply that he is unreal; secondly, that he is a sentimental and immoral creation. His dismal and fantastic story is the excuse for an infringement of the marriage code. Tennyson sanctifies the breaking of a moral law in the name, not of a higher moral law, but of a pretty and sentimental emotionalism. He appeals to the heart by insulting the reason and the conscience. Neither Bagehot's argument nor his illustration is good, but his fundamental position, that literature is concerned not merely with morality, but with man's whole spirit, is both liberal and just.

Bagehot diverges from Aristotle in maintaining, together with most modern critics, that character in a work of art is larger and more important than plot, having not only an active element, which is expressed by plot, but a solitary or meditative element which cannot be so expressed. Epic is inferior to drama because it presents character not " in motion," but " in mass," that is, in both its active and inactive phases. Yet in one instance at least, Bagehot approaches very close to Aristotle's point of view, emphasizing aspects of the problem little appreciated in his day. In " Charles Dickens " he writes:

> Caricatures are necessarily isolated; they are produced by the exaggeration of certain conspicuous traits and features; each being is enlarged on its greatest side; and we laugh at the grotesque grouping and the startling contrast. But that connection between human beings on which a plot depends is rather severed than elucidated by the enhancement of their diversities. Interesting stories are founded on the intimate relations of men and women. These intimate relations are based not on their superficial traits, or common occupations, or most visible externalities, but on the inner life of heart and feeling.[11]

In other words, the most interesting elements in character are those which give rise to interesting and significant action, to action expressive of the " inner life of heart and feeling." Such action, Bagehot everywhere implies, is moral, and springs from the fundamental dualism of our nature. Latent in his remarks on Dickens is the Aristotelian concept that plot includes the most important qualities in character. " Plot in the drama, in its fullest sense," says Butcher, interpreting Aristotle,

" is the artistic equivalent of ' action ' in real life. . . . ' Action ' ($\pi\rho\hat{a}\xi\iota s$) in Aristotle is not a purely external act, but an inward process which works outward, the expression of a man's rational personality." Action is a form of " moral energy or activity."[12]

Bagehot demands persistently that plot, in the narrower sense, be orderly and coherent. In this respect he found little to delight him in the masters of English fiction. Sterne " never begins at the beginning and goes straight through to the end."[13] Thackeray's plots are insignificant.[13] Dickens's concept of character is not only unsuitable to a significant action, but his mind is incapable of putting together an orderly sequence of events.[13] George Eliot alone receives unstinted praise. Her novels are models of close and careful workmanship, of plan carefully conceived and admirably carried out.[13]

Bagehot's distinction between wit and humour, though revealing a characteristic Victorian preference for the latter, is in the main that which we now accept. G. K. Chesterton points out in the *Encyclopædia Britannica* that the word *humour*, derived from the Latin word meaning " moisture," was applied in medieval and Renaissance psychology to a ruling passion or dominating eccentricity. The humorist, or the man dominated by such a passion or eccentricity, was at first rather the unconscious than the conscious provoker of mirth:

> The blend, and the beginnings of the modern meaning, may perhaps be dated at about the time of the Waverley Novels, when Guy Mannering complains of Councillor Pleydell as a " crack-brained humorist."

For Pleydell is indeed laughed at for his little vanities or whims; but he himself joins in the laugh and sees the humour of his humour. Since then the word has come to be used more and more exclusively of conscious humour; and generally of a rather deep and rather delicate appreciation of the absurdities of others.

Distinguishing humour from wit, Chesterton says that humour

> involves some confession of human weakness; whereas wit is rather the human intellect exerting its full strength, though perhaps upon a small point. Wit is reason on its judgment seat; and though the offenders may be touched lightly, the point is that the judge is not touched at all.

Bagehot's distinction, though more loosely drawn, and lacking the completeness of an historical background, is essentially the same as Chesterton's. He also insists upon the close connection between wit and intellect and between humour and character, upon the detective sharpness of mind which underlies wit, and the large spirit of enjoyment, of generous participation in life, which lies behind humour. There is between wit and humour

> the distinction of dry sticks and green sticks; there is in humour a living energy, a diffused potency, a noble sap; it grows upon the character of the humorist. Wit is part of the machinery of the intellect. . . . Sidney Smith's mirth was essentially humorous; it clings to the character of the man; as with the sayings of Dr. Johnson, there is a species of personality attaching to it.

Swift is Bagehot's example of a wit: " Swift was a detective in a dean's wig; he watched the mob; his whole wit is a kind of dexterous indication of popular frailties."[14]

Preoccupied in his writings chiefly with the mind and character of the author, and with the larger aspects of literary doctrine, Bagehot has on the whole little to say of technique and form in the narrow sense. What he does says is, if not original, at least clear and sensible enough—with the single exception of his remarks on the sonnet, which are but another indication that rhetoric flourishes most luxuriantly in the absence of thought. Discussing " self-delineative poetry " in " Hartley Coleridge " he writes:

> Indeed, the whole series of sonnets with which the earliest and best work of Hartley began is . . . mainly and essentially a series on himself. Perhaps there is something in the structure of the sonnet rather adapted to this species of composition. It is too short for narrative, too artificial for the intense passions, too complex for the simple, too elaborate for the domestic; but in an impatient world where there is not a premium on self-describing, who so would speak of himself must be wise and brief, artful and composed—and in these respects he will be aided by the concise dignity of the tranquil sonnet.[14]

It is perhaps true that the sonnet is particularly adapted to self-delineation, but self-delineation is not always " tranquil." Certainly Mrs. Browning and Edna St. Vincent Millay have proved that the sonnet is not " too artificial for the intense passions." And what are the simple passions if they are not also intense? What precisely are the domestic? Rebuttal is unnecessary where definition is so vague.

The essay on " Mr. Clough's Poems " contains some sensible observations on metre:

> It is quite true that the metre of intellectual poetry

should not be so pretty as that of songs, or so plain and impressive as that of vigorous passion. The rhythm should pervade it and animate it, but should not protrude itself upon the surface, or intrude itself upon the attention. It should be a latent charm, though a real one. Yet, though this doctrine is true, it is nevertheless a dangerous doctrine. Most writers need the strict fetters of familiar metre; as soon as they are emancipated from this, they fancy that *any* words of theirs are metrical. If a man will read any expressive and favourite words of his own often enough, he will come to believe that they are rhythmical; probably they have a rhythm as he reads them; but no notation of pauses and accents could tell the reader how to read them in that manner; and when read in any other mode they may be prose itself.[15]

The warning is particularly apropos nowadays, and not merely for intellectual poetry. Many a modern poem sounds musical only from the lips of its author.

More solemn nonsense is written about style than about almost anything else. The reason is that it has been degraded into a light and frivolous subject, and men are never so heavy and ponderous as in discussing light and frivolous subjects. They are often gay about religion, clear about science, intelligible about metaphysics, but about teas, wines, and tobaccos, about the superfluities of the menu and the appendages to leisure, they propound theories that for pedantry might disgust a German professor and for subtlety stagger a medieval schoolman. Style also has become one of these profundities of individual whim and taste, and those authorities who do not generalize their personal eccentricities into universal laws come to rest on the mystic and imposing intuitionalism of the palate.

Style, says Bagehot, is a "*je ne sais quoi,*" but Buffon knew better and had the courage to utter a platitude: " Le style n'est que l'ordre et le mouvement qu'on met dans ses pensées."[16] The data of stylistic criticism indicate that he was right. Whatever Bagehot may declare in a flight of eloquence, practically he observes that the great merit of Gibbon's style is its continual forward movement and the great defect of Sterne's its distracting want of coherence.[17] Aided by Buffon, he might have gone further with Sterne, for certainly his style is the disorder and retrogression which he introduced into his thoughts. But at any rate it is clear that Bagehot searches for order and movement, and doubtless in their widest meaning these two qualities are the basis of all artistic technique. Bagehot writes:

> The art of narration is the art of writing in hooks-and-eyes. The principle consists in making the appropriate thought follow the appropriate thought, the proper fact the proper fact; in first preparing the mind for what is to come, and then letting it come. This can only be achieved by keeping continually and insensibly before the mind of the reader some one object, character, or image, whose variations are the events of the story, whose unity is the unity of it.

He then goes on to explain that Scott achieves this unity in the midst of change by keeping before the reader " the mind of some one person," Hume, by holding up a point of view or general idea, Macaulay, by presenting a picture which is continually fading into another picture.[17] Evidently, this theory, analysed to the bottom, maintains that the chief elements in narration are unity and progression, which are nothing else than order and movement. W. C. Brownell points out that there is in style, as indeed we might suspect nowadays, a subjective as well as objective element. The former is the element of personality: " How the artist subjectively handles—or neglects—the objective element of style is *his* style." Personality in style is the particular order and movement which a particular author gives to his thoughts. Emphasized too greatly, personality tends toward mannerism and affectation. It cannot be emphasized too little. In the deeper sense, perhaps, personality in style is, as Brownell remarks, not what you put in, but what you cannot leave out.[18] In spite of his definition, the whole tendency of Bagehot's criticism is to reduce the personal element to a minimum. A writer should begin not with rhetoric, but with truth. Style should never be an impediment to veracity. Gibbon was limited by illusions of grandeur. He could speak of very grand things and of things less grand, but like the French translator of " Othello," he could never have mentioned a handkerchief:

> Truth is of various kinds—grave, solemn, dignified, petty, low, ordinary; and an historian who has to tell the truth must be able to tell what is vulgar as well as what is great, what is little as well as what is amazing. Gibbon is at fault here. He *cannot* mention Asia *Minor*. The petty order of sublunary matters; the common gross existence of ordinary people; the necessary littlenesses of necessary life, are little suited to his sublime narrative.[18]

In another passage Bagehot is even more hostile to personal mannerism:

> We believe that the knack in style is to write like a human being. Some think they must be wise, some

elaborate, some concise; Tacitus wrote like a pair of stays; some startle as Thomas Carlyle, or a comet, inscribing with his tail. But legibility is given to those who neglect these notions, and are willing to be themselves, to write their own thoughts in their own words, in the simplest words, in the words wherein they were thought.[19]

Bagehot may seem here to prohibit not only mannerism, but art, from language. Such, however, was probably not his meaning and certainly not his ordinary view. To the artistry of Gibbon, Béranger, and Milton he does full justice. What he objects to in Macaulay's style is not its brilliance, its vividness, its variety—not its art, nor again any mannerism in it, but a deficiency in that deeper personal element which cannot be left out. Macaulay's style has a singular fault: " It is too omniscient. Everything is too plain. All is clear; nothing is doubtful. . . . This defect in style is, indeed, indicative of a defect in understanding. Macaulay's mind is eminently gifted, but there is a want of graduation in it."[19] In short, Macaulay's style over-simplifies the truth, because his mind over-simplifies it. His deficiency lies in the particular mind which gives a particular order and movement to its thoughts.

Bagehot, like Brownell, sees in style another and distinctive personal element, that of the soul, the spirit of aspiration and self-improvement which is present in a man's language as in his actions.

The words of some authors are said to have " hands and feet "; they seem, that is, to have a vigour and animation which only belong to things which live and move. Milton's words have not this animal life. There is no rude energy about them. But, on the other hand, they have, or seem to have, a soul, a spirit which other words have not. He was early aware that what he wrote, " by certain vital signs it had," was such as the world would not " willingly let die." After two centuries we feel the same. There is a solemn and firm music in the lines; a brooding sublimity haunts them; the spirit of the great writer moves over the face of the page.[20]

Good style is due partly to native aptitude, partly to care and effort. It is perhaps natural that a man of precocious childhood should stress the first element. Of *The Wealth of Nations* Bagehot writes:

> But the style has no intrinsic happiness; no one would read it for its own sake; the words do not cleave to the meaning, so that you cannot think of them without it, or of it without them. This is only given ... to the very few of those—the five or six in every generation—who have from nature the best grace, who think by inborn feeling in words at once charming and accurate.[21]

Yet those who have a native gift can improve their style by care. Béranger

> tells us that all his songs are the production of a painful effort. If so, the reader should be most grateful; *he* suffers no pain. The delicate elaboration of the writer has given a singular currency to the words. Difficult writing is rarely easy reading. It can never be so when the labour is spent in piecing together elements not joined by an insensible touch of imagination. The highest praise is due to a writer whose ideas are more delicately connected by unconscious genius than other men's are, and yet who spends labour and toil in giving the production a yet cunninger finish, a still smoother connection.[21]

Bagehot has a theory, suggested by Darwin's concept of natural selection, on how the characteristic style of a particular age originates:

K

The true explanation is, I think, something like this. One considerable writer gets a sort of start because what he writes is somewhat more—only a little more very often, as I believe—congenial to the minds around him than any other sort. This writer is very often not the one whom posterity remembers—not the one who carries the style of the age farthest towards its ideal type, and gives it its charm and its perfection. It was not Addison who began the essay-writing of Queen Anne's time, but Steele; it was the vigorous forward man who struck out the rough notion, though it was the wise and meditative man who improved upon it and elaborated it, and whom posterity reads. Some strong writer, or group of writers, thus seize on the public mind, and a curious process soon assimilates other writers in appearance to them.[21]

The " curious process " is imitation. The " strong writer, or group of writers," becomes the fashion, and is imitated, consciously and unconsciously, by the other writers of the time.

Bagehot has very decided views on the art of translation. In a criticism of Cowper's translation of Homer he writes that if the object of translation " is to convey an idea of the general tone, scope, and artistic effect of the original, the mechanical copying of the details is as likely to end in a good result as a careful cast from a dead man's features to produce a living and speaking being."[22]

Chapter VII

CRITICAL DOCTRINE

In Bagehot's occasional references to criticism there is a note of deprecation not altogether to be explained as the modesty of a practitioner. He seems to have had some grave misgivings both as to the value of the art and as to the amount of interest which it aroused. Of reviewing, which he himself practised, he observes—one feels with some wonder: " Many able men really give themselves up to it."[1] He refers to criticism as tedious, and declares that it " must be brief . . . because its interest is too weak to be prolonged." His most extravagant contention is that, " if an evil," it is " a necessary evil."[1] Here plainly, is no longing to convert the Philistine masses of England into a universal Athenian aristocracy of the intellect. Plainly the spectacle of millions of ignorant people reading millions of bad books did not infuse Bagehot with zeal to be a St. Paul of culture or a Jeremiah of literature. For if there was in Arnold a suppressed and inverted, in Bagehot there was a vein of open and healthy, Philistinism. He was after all a man of action and of affairs, who dealt all day long with solid, palpable realities. What, compared to business and budgets, are books, authors, and critics? What is an author but a man who sits in a quiet room sedulously building up an elaborate shadow of the noisy, exciting world outside? What is a critic but a commentator upon such shadows, a writer upon writers? Literature, however great its excellencies, is after all but an imitation; criticism but the reflection of an imitation, a thing twice removed from reality. These are reflections natural to the man of action, and though they seem extraordinary for Bagehot, there are indications that he may occasionally have entertained them. His explanation of the purpose of history as something upon which the idle, capable man might exert his ingenuity may not be altogether humorous.[2] Bagehot was always a little apprehensive of books, and he looked down upon the man who knew nothing else. Above all, he was profoundly suspicious of the purely literary career.[2]

But these prejudices did not, I think, run very deep. Certainly Bagehot could not have shown so much interest in books and authors, and expended so much energy in writing, had he not at heart been firmly convinced, despite temporary misgivings, of the great and constant value of literature. Probably he despaired less of criticism itself than of the form which it took in contemporary journals, and of the people who read them. He felt, far more than the secluded critic could feel, the pressure of the vast, unthinking Philistine world which read books. He realized that most readers were uncultivated, unintelligent. He knew that they took up their reading when they were tired and unwilling to exert themselves, that they expected to be told what they wanted to hear, and that journalistic critics obliged them. It is not extraordinary that, knowing he addressed himself to such readers, and contended against such critics, Bagehot was apologetic at times for what difficult matter he introduced

into his essays. Yet these apologies should not be
taken to indicate his real attitude toward criticism
of permanent merit. He observes of Jeffrey's
reviews: " You must not criticize papers like these,
rapidly written in the hurry of life, as you would
the painful words of an elaborate sage, slowly and
with anxious awfulness instructing mankind. Some
things, a few things, are for eternity; some, and a
good many, are for time."² The " elaborate sage "
whom Bagehot had in mind must almost certainly
have been Aristotle. And if he is described with
some malice, at least he is admitted to have instructed mankind, and " for eternity." Indeed
when Bagehot turned to Aristotle for the basic
principles with which, in his essay on " Wordsworth,
Tennyson, and Browning," he sought at least somewhat to clarify the artistic confusion of his age, he
must have felt that the immortality of the ancient
critic, even though a little dry and musty, was not
inglorious.

Bagehot's practice recommends criticism much
more than does his theory. His own essays are
certainly no mere accumulation of writing upon
writing, of papers upon papers. Rather he tears
away the multitudinous pages of a formidable
volume and shows you the living author behind it.
Such an essay as that on Gibbon is neither too
dull to be entertaining nor too narrow and specialized to have an independent interest. The fresh
breeze of a broad and worldly wisdom blows
through it. It is the brilliant, witty after-dinner
talk of a thinking and acting man, not the less
worthy of a hearing because it is informally spoken,
nor the less keen and profound because it is the

product not of a deliberate mind sharpened by anxious attention, but of a quick mind enlivened with enjoyment.

Bagehot remarks that " the critical faculty is as special and as peculiar almost as the poetical," but he does not explain his remark.[3] Whether he had any ideas beyond the usual platitudes, it is impossible to say. Upon the ultimate end of criticism he is explicit enough: " If in the following pages we seem to cavil and find fault, let it be remembered, that the business of a critic is criticism; that it is *not* his business to be thankful; that he must attempt an estimate rather than a eulogy."[3] The end of criticism, then, is *not* appreciation, but judgment.

What does judgment in criticism imply? A criticism which lays emphasis upon the judgment of books must obviously search out those elements which books have in common and by which they may be compared. As it aspires to judge consistently and reliably, it must develop principles and standards. As it would judge humanly and sympathetically, it must defer to the general taste. As it would have its judgments recognized by intelligent men, it must, in its whole theory and practice, appeal to those qualities which are general among intelligent men. In brief, judicial criticism tends to emphasize that which is common and permanent in human experience, as impressionistic criticism tends to emphasize that which is particular and evanescent. Bagehot himself exhibits, of course, the tendency of the judicial critic. He judges according to a taste which he believes fairly uniform in the great number of cultivated men, and according to standards implied in a theory of life and

literature which has been widely held through
many ages.

Yet he also shows a commendable interest, rare
among critics of his class, in the problems of understanding, as well as of appraising a work of art.
His ideas upon this subject, however, do less credit
to the keenness of his thought than to the breadth
of his view. In one instance he writes:

> In metaphysics, probably both taste and judgment
> involve what is termed " poise of mind," that is the
> power of true passiveness—the faculty of " waiting "
> till the stream of impressions, whether those of life or
> those of art have done all that they have to do, and
> cut their full type plainly upon the mind. The ill-
> judging and the untasteful are both over-eager; both
> move too quick and blur the image.[3]

Such a theory would serve as an excellent caution
to the critic of narrow principles, like Jeffrey, or of
violent prejudice, like Johnson, but it can scarcely
be considered an accurate description of the critical
process. The judicial mind tends to withhold
judgment only upon phenomena which it cannot
readily subject to a general principle. The familiar
type of book, the familiar type of man it judges
as it studies, though it may delay final sentence
until occasion requires.

In another place he writes:

> The only way to criticize a work of the imagination,
> is to describe its effect upon the mind of the reader—
> at any rate, of the critic; and this can only be adequately
> delineated by strong illustrations, apt similes, and
> perhaps a little exaggeration. The task is in its very
> nature not an easy one; the poet paints a picture on
> the fancy of the critic, and the critic has in some sort

to copy it on the paper. He must say what it is before
he can make remarks upon it.[4]

This passage has undeniably an impressionistic
sound. The critic is to remain passive while the
poet " paints a picture " upon his fancy, and then
he is to describe that picture " by strong illustrations, apt similes, and perhaps a little exaggeration." Parallels may be found almost at random
in the writings of Walter Pater and of Oscar
Wilde. A modern impressionist, Mr. J. E. Spingarn,
writes: " To have sensations in the presence of a
work of art and to express them, that is the function
of Criticism for the impressionistic critic."[5]   But
Spingarn and Bagehot would disagree fundamentally, I think, as to the nature of the sensations
in question. Spingarn is embarked upon an endless search for novelty and strangeness. Bagehot is
interested in discovering the basic principles of
art and the constant qualities in human nature.
Spingarn emphasizes the element of the many in
man's psychology. Bagehot attempts a just mediation between the many and the one. Spingarn
would say that the same book excites entirely
different sensations in each man; Bagehot, that, by
and large, it tends to excite the same sensations.
According to Bagehot the reader or critic must not
merely " emote " in the presence of a work of art.
He must also " say what the poem is," what in
general it means for all who read it with thought
and care. Finally, he must make remarks upon it
—in other words, pronounce a judgment. But if
Bagehot escapes the charge of impressionism, he is
still open to that of inaccurate observation, of
seeing an artificial separation between apprecia-

tion and judgment—nor is his theory borne out by his practice, if the criticism of *Paradise Lost*, to which the quotation of the preceding page serves as preface, may be considered an example. He does not progress beyond the twelfth line of his criticism without implying a major judgment; he does not progress beyond the second paragraph without making one. When a critic is ready to paint a picture on the fancy of the reader, he has already formed his judgment—if he has any to form—nor will he be able to keep it long from what he writes.

Bagehot's scattered remarks on the important subject of taste further reveal the ultimate principles, more implied than expressed, upon which his criticism rests. His conception of taste, though nowhere fully stated, appears to be essentially that expressed by Coleridge in the *Biographia Literaria*. The latter asks rhetorically how an author may regulate his style, and replies:

> by such knowledge of the facts, material and spiritual, that most appertain to his art, as, if it have been governed and applied by *good sense* and rendered instinctive by habit, becomes the representative and reward of our past conscious reasonings, insights, and conclusions, and acquires the name of TASTE.[6]

Preoccupied with the defects of modern romantic literature, Bagehot emphasizes that bad as well as good taste is the result of previous effort and training. " The will," he says, " has great though indirect power over the taste." If he desires it sufficiently, a man may acquire a liking for the strange and grotesque, as the hardened soldier acquires a thirst for blood. Thus people are led to consider even the poetry of Browning beautiful.

Contemporary English readers can purge themselves of such barbarism only by mastering sound principles of art and applying them in the study and enjoyment of good literature.[7]

Bagehot's principles and standards I have already discussed—in so far as they relate to books. But a great book is also the index, the record, at once intimate and puzzling, of a great mind. In its noblest phase criticism is the study of genius. Writing on " Shakespeare—The Man " Bagehot observes:

> Some extreme sceptics, we know, doubt whether it is possible to deduce anything as to an author's character from his works. Yet surely people do not keep a tame steam-engine to write their books; and if those books were really written by a man, he must have been a man who could write them; he must have had the thoughts which they express, have acquired the knowledge they contain, have possessed the style in which we read them. The difficulty is a defect of the critics. A person who knows nothing of an author he has read, will not know much of an author whom he has seen.[7]

A critic who has principles for the judgment of books will presumably have standards for the appraisal of writers. These standards Bagehot nowhere defines, yet everywhere implies. When he says that Clough makes the truth too complicated and uncertain, and that Macaulay makes it too simple and easy; when he observes that Shelley's imagination is too lawless and fantastic, Thackeray's too much bound down to the immediate, common-place world; when he ironically implies that Gibbon is too complacent, and declares that Burke is too passionate; evidently he had before his mind the

image of that broad, many-sided, moderate man of
the world whom I have already had occasion to
describe.[8] His standard of a man is the " symmetrical genius," the writer who possesses " animated moderation," who deserves most of posterity
by thinking of it least, and who attains the highest
literary power by a wise distrust of the book and
the pen.[9]

Such a man may serve not only as a standard
for the judgment of authors, but as a model for
the imitation of critics. Probably Bagehot never
asked himself with Longinus: " How would Homer,
had he been there, or how would Demosthenes,
have listened to what I have written, or how would
they have been affected by it? "[10] To such lengths
of hero-worship Bagehot could scarcely have gone.
And yet in one vigorous defence of classical and
humanistic principles he was moved to remark that
romantic art is like a " painted statue." It has " a
want of that inseparable chasteness which clings to
simple sculpture, an impairing predominance of
alluring details which impairs our satisfaction with
our own satisfaction; which makes us doubt whether
a higher being than ourselves will be satisfied even
though we are."[11] If Homer and Aristotle are not
his gods, at least they are acknowledged to be on
the side of the angels.

The ultimate test of literature is of course that
of time, and the ultimate judge, posterity. " A
stray schoolboy may still be detected," says Bagehot,
" in a wild admiration for the ' Giaour ' or the
' Corsair ' . . . , but the *real* posterity—the quiet
students of a past literature—never read or think
of them."[11] Perhaps quiet students are indeed the

real posterity—certainly for literature of secondary merit. Indeed these tireless annotators show a disquieting tendency nowadays to bury great authors alive and to disinter corpses, but in all ages they seem naturally to feel a sympathetic and often a discriminating interest in lesser authors long dead. Such authors probably find their due place and a respectable immortality in the accumulation of studious praise and castigation. And doubtless all literature receives judgment in the same manner. But in the larger sense the real posterity includes the stray schoolboy as well as the quiet student. Great literature becomes a tradition. It is not what the schoolboy likes to read—if indeed nowadays he likes to read anything—but what he is compelled to read, what the pupil skims and the master annotates, what the busy world forgets and the quiet world remembers. Great literature finds its surest perpetuation in the tranquil classroom.

In surveying as a whole Bagehot's theoretical ideas on literature and criticism, one is struck with their coherence. One is surprised that what are for the most part disjointed and occasional remarks, dropped in the course of a criticism, should, at least in broad outline, hang so well together. The basis of this consistency, as of all other consistency in Bagehot, lies ultimately in the concept of the moderate and many-sided man. To this personage I must return again and again because he lies at the very centre of Bagehot's thought, as the standard of all that is excellent and desirable. The best literature should be broad in its contact with life, moral and serious in its thought and tone, noble and restrained in its style, because the moderate and many-sided man, as a reader and critic, prefers such literature, and because, as an author, he produces it. This is the ultimate logic and meaning of Bagehot's literary theory.

Chapter VIII

THE INFLUENCE OF HAZLITT

IT is significant that although he had adopted the theory of the classicists, Bagehot admired the practice of a great romantic. Much that he aspired to be, both as critic and writer, he seems to have found in the essays of William Hazlitt.

Both Augustine Birrell and Professor Zeitlin have pointed out this debt, and in his " Henry Crabb Robinson " Bagehot himself records his conviction " that Hazlitt was a much greater writer than Charles Lamb—a harmless opinion which I still hold."[1] An essay on Hazlitt, reported to have been begun in 1867, has unfortunately not been preserved.[2] But the fact of this influence scarcely needs to be supported by external evidence. The elder writer's criticisms and ideas, quoted, paraphrased, and adapted—with and without acknowledgment—can be found from one end of Bagehot's essays to the other.

No doubt Hazlitt's great merit, in the eyes of his admirer, was that he was thoroughly alive. He was an ideal to set up against literary dullness and insipidity, the model of a critic with an experiencing nature. He was no mere bookworm, no pale spinner-out of idle words, who " is acquainted with the style and sentiments of the best authors," but " is out of the way of employing his own eyes and ears."[3] He was rather pre-eminently the example of a man who derived from books, as from life, not arid pedantry, but knowledge and power. It is true his life was not eventful, that he had never occupied " an established position," that he was a dreamer, a lover of solitude, a lonely, morose fellow, dull and phlegmatic at the thought of other people's brilliance—too shy, sensitive, and awkward to play a part in the world, even had he so desired. Yet the nature of his life and manners is no index to the energy of his mind and the quality of his writings. He describes a prize-fight as fiercely as another man might knock out an opponent. His comments on contemporary politics suggest at times the memoirs of a great statesman, and again the literary remains of a revolutionary martyr. Indeed, one is tempted to say that if he preferred his books to an active life in the world, it was not because he loved the world less, but because he loved books more, for few authors have written of life either in poetry or in prose, with so much passion and eloquence, so much subtlety and penetration, as he has expended on the analysis and criticism of other men's opinions and writings.

In another respect Hazlitt was just the kind of idol one would expect Bagehot to choose—an idol with feet of clay. He had the recommendation of possessing grave faults. There was no principle of restraint in his intelligence. He saw truth swiftly and passionately, but when passion proved a false guide and he saw wrongly, there was no pulling up for a sober second sight, no corrective in judgment. Indeed, thought was inseparable from feeling. He seemed to observe everything, as Bagehot himself remarks, " from a certain soreness of mind," and when the world grated on him too sharply, he burst into fits of irrational fury, or sullenly retreated into a wonderland of the imagination. In short, he was an ideal writer to borrow from—hasty and fertile, full of clever suggestions that needed thinking out and of brilliant theories that needed modification. He was moreover exactly the kind of writer for a cool critic to admire —complex and fallacious, full of subtle faults to diagnoze and of strange crochets to explain, which —to Bagehot—were the more fascinating because they were extremely English. For in spite of all his French revolutionary ideas, Hazlitt was after all a capital example of the English Tory. He maintained radical principles, but as a country squire might defend Cavalier prejudices—gallantly, fiercely, irrationally. He was so much a conservative at heart that the scandalously modern opinions which he advances appear ancient and respectable in his pages. As a literary critic he loved sound old books that had stood the test of time, and was ever recurring to them with the same keen, daily enjoyment with which the typical Tory, according to Bagehot's sympathetic description, celebrates old customs and old feasts.[4] Altogether, he was a man to talk about, to write about, to borrow from, to admire—a man suitable for everything but hero-worship, a man after Bagehot's own heart.

Most prominent in some of his very first publications, the influence of Hazlitt is conspicuous in practically all the literary and biographical essays of Bagehot's early and middle period, and is represented by a notable instance of borrowing even in such a work as *The English Constitution*, which not only was written late, but on a subject considerably removed from literature proper. An influence so strong at the formative period, so extended and persistent, must obviously go deep, and indeed it consists in much more than the mere taking over of specific ideas or than even an imitation of style and manner. The marked resemblance between the two writers in what are perhaps their most distinctive literary characteristics, their gusto and their emphasis on psychological interpretation, suggests an influence which cannot easily be measured.

I need scarcely say that, although Bagehot has borrowed, he has not copied. Even his closest imitation of Hazlitt, the description of Southey's personal habits, to which Birrell has called attention, bears a definite mark of individuality.[5] And in most instances Bagehot has not so much borrowed as corrected and adapted, expanded and developed. What Hazlitt exaggerated and confused in a fit of anger Bagehot has moderated and systematized with reflection and humour. What Hazlitt, the more compressed and poetic writer, hinted in an epigram, implied in a paragraph, or scattered through an outburst of lyric eloquence, Bagehot has carefully gathered up, elaborated, and explained to its ultimate possibilities in half a dozen pages. What Hazlitt has observed of an individual Bagehot has generalized into a type or a psychological law. Hazlitt hotly maintains that Sir Walter Scott lacks soul. Bagehot transforms the suggestion into an orderly criticism.[6] Hazlitt eloquently declares that the mind of Shakespeare " contained a universe of thought and feeling within itself. . . . He was just like any other man, but that he was like all

L

other men." Bagehot gives this idea a more specific application, and shows with somewhat prosaic minuteness that the mind of Shakespeare contained the minds of Goethe, Keats, and Scott.[7] Hazlitt writes a brief character sketch of Lord Brougham, emphasizing his extraordinary energy, his capacity for indignation, and his many-sidedness. Bagehot singles out the same qualities, adds certain others, and describes the typical agitator, naming Lord Brougham as the outstanding example.[8] Hazlitt panegyrizes the cool common sense and gentle optimism of Lord Jeffrey. Bagehot finds very similar traits at the basis of Whig character.[9] Such evidence as this suggests how much Hazlitt must have contributed not only to the development of some of Bagehot's most important doctrines, the very instruments of his thought, but also to the growth in him of psychological insight and of a psychological approach to all intellectual problems.

The subject of gusto, one of the most attractive features of Bagehot's style, has long suffered for the want of a proper man to deal with it. It does not require an intelligent man—several such have already treated it—but a courageous man, one who has the courage to utter the necessary platitudes. I presume to take upon myself the task. Etymologically, *gusto* is of course simply the Spanish and Italian word for "taste," going back, like the French *goût*, to the Latin *gustus*, which signifies "taste," "relish." And if one may judge from the definitions and illustrations listed in the *New English Dictionary*, the term must at one time have had a meaning very similar to that now given to taste. Both words must have signified, among other things:

first, a particular preference or liking for some object
in nature or art; and second, the faculty of the mind
which develops these preferences—a faculty which
perceives, discriminates, and enjoys. One could
have a taste for fine furniture, and one could have
a gusto for it. Fine furniture could suit one's taste
and it could suit one's gusto. But whereas taste
retains these uses and meanings, gusto has apparently tended, especially from the beginning of
the nineteenth century, to lose in the one use of
the original word the meaning of preference, and
in the other the meanings of perception and
discrimination; so that in its broadest sense and
according to the most brief dictionary definitions,
it appears to connote little more than enjoyment,
or the capacity for enjoyment—as the *New English
Dictionary* expresses it, " keen relish or enjoyment
displayed in thought or action; zest." The problem
of defining gusto in literature, then, is the problem
of analysing the causes and evidences of enjoyment
in writing.

Most writers refer to gusto parenthetically, as
though it were a very simple thing. Doubtless
they have stared into the awful maze of platitude
and drawn back. Deep within the tangled under-
brush of his style, Saintsbury ventures to speak of
gusto as " that amorous quest of literary beauty
and rapturous enjoyment of it," and Mr. P. E.
More hurriedly defines the term as a " power of
intense enjoyment based on understanding."[10]
But can the gusto of Hazlitt's " Letter to Mr.
William Gifford, Esq." be explained as an amorous
quest of literary beauty, or even a " power of
intense enjoyment based on understanding "?

Hazlitt himself has in his own definition considered almost exclusively what might be termed the active phase of gusto. " Gusto in art," he says, " is power or passion defining any object." His illustrations reveal how much better he understood the phenomenon than he defined it:

> The infinite quantity of dramatic invention in Shakespeare takes from his gusto. The power he delights to show is not intense, but discursive. He never insists on anything as much as he might. Milton has great gusto. He repeats his blows twice; grapples with and exhausts his subject. His imagination has a double relish of its objects, an inveterate attachment to the things he describes, and to the words describing them.[11]

In speaking of the power which Shakespeare " delights to show " and the " double relish " that Milton's imagination has for its objects, Hazlitt clearly implies that the ultimate basis of gusto is enjoyment—that essentially gusto is not power and passion, but an intense delight in the exercise of power and passion in writing—a delight which causes the author to insist upon his point again and again, to exhaust his subject, to linger upon his ideas and the words expressing them with a peculiar pleasure. Again, though in his statement Hazlitt asserts that gusto defines, he clearly implies in his illustration that it insists. And such is plainly the fact. Within a brief passage, Milton likens Satan to a tower, to the sun when dimmed by mists and when darkened by eclipse; he insistently suggests, but he does not define, Satan's fallen grandeur.

In one sense every good author writes with gusto, because every man feels some pleasure in

doing what he does well. Even Flaubert, faced
with the awful possibility of a repetitive *de* con-
struction, must have felt a thrill of tired relief in
escaping the catastrophe. But here we are speaking of authors peculiarly capable of enjoyment.
We are concerned with enjoyment which is not
anxious and fleeting, but intense and continuous.
What, then, are the causes and the manifestations
of such enjoyment? If accidental factors are left
out of consideration, the causes are two: an author
may enjoy his subject, whether it is a book to critize
or a theme to develop, and he may enjoy the act
itself of thinking and writing. Usually if he enjoys
the one he will enjoy the other, and in considerable
degree *because* he enjoys the other. An author
relishes his subject because it is great and uni-
versally interesting, because it is peculiarly adapted
to his talents, because it is associated in his mind
with pleasant recollections, because of a combination of these and a good many other more extraneous
reasons which might be assigned. Similarly, an
author delights in the act of composition, partly
because his subject has a particular merit in his
eyes, but much more, perhaps, because his writing
itself has some real or fancied quality, either of
excellence, power, or individuality, which gives
him extreme pleasure. Hazlitt enjoyed writing
" with power and passion"; Lamb enjoyed writing
quaintly; and the late Mr. Saintsbury, I think,
enjoyed writing strangely.

The signs and manifestations of gusto are such
as reflect the motives. Animation, excellence,
brilliance, and singularity are all indications, but
the peculiar mark of gusto is copiousness beyond

the requirements of the subject. The writer dwells upon his point with a lingering relish. He is reluctant to leave it until he has expressed it in every possible way, and rung every change upon it. He is perpetually recurring with unflagging pleasure to favourite topics, favourite ideas, favourite jokes, favourite words and phrases, finding in them always, or nearly always, added potentialities of meaning or application. But he is not always happy in his repetitions, nor always wise in his enthusiasms. Gusto exposes a writer to his talents, and thus great eloquence has sometimes tempted authors to write when they had nothing to say, and to convince themselves—as well as others—of much that they should never have believed.

But perhaps no writer exhibits more clearly than Hazlitt the vices, as well as the virtues, of a vehemently enjoying habit of mind. He could write about books and men in a way that makes one's mouth water, and indeed I think no one endowed with any love of good writing has assisted at the slaughter of Mr. Gifford without sensing the pleasurable odour of blood in his nostrils. But Hazlitt could slaughter a shadow with nearly as much ferocity. Perhaps the last infirmity of a passionate mind is to enjoy passion, and this infirmity he shared with the melodramatic washer-woman. Judgment had no place and truth no sanctity where passion was at such a premium. Wordsworth and Coleridge can be found both black and white in Hazlitt's essays, according as his mood at the time was suited to passionate praise or passionate abuse. And unfortunately his ravings are not merely malignant or boastful, but sometimes

simply inane, continuing long after he has nothing
more to say, as in *The Spirit of the Age*, where,
having uttered many telling things about Scott,
he concludes with several pages of mere roaring
against Toryism.[12] Perhaps the most amusing
example of the extravagance to which his gusto led
him is the passage in which he draws a contrast
between " King Lear " and any possible product of
Sir Walter Scott:

> I should like to see Sir Walter giving us a tragedy
> of this kind, a huge " globose " of sorrow, swinging
> round in mid-air, independent of time, place, and
> circumstance, sustained by its own weight and motion,
> and not propped up by the levers of custom, or patched
> up with quaint, old-fashioned dresses, or set off by
> grotesque backgrounds or rusty armour, but in which
> the mere paraphernalia and accessories were left out
> of the question, and nothing but the soul of passion
> and the pith of imagination was to be found.[12]

One is reminded at once of Hector shouting a
battle challenge and of a small boy boasting of his
big brother.

Between the gusto of Hazlitt and the gusto of
Bagehot there is a difference both of quantity and
quality. There is in both writers the same enthusiasm for literary beauty, the same thrilling joy
of discovery in psychological insight, the same
exultation in penetrating thought and powerful
writing. But whereas the gusto of one is like the
forest fire, a law unto itself, that of the other is a
definitely post-Promethean blaze, subject to a
rational use of the match box and the extinguisher.
Hazlitt's gusto is wild, violent, all-consuming;
Bagehot's is moderate, subtle, adaptive, showing
forth vigorously in the literary essays, and growing

pale and decorous in the dignified pages of the economic and political works. Tempted by lesser talents and an imagination less vividly poetic than Hazlitt's, Bagehot was at the same time more conscientious and controlled. The spirit of enjoyment led him occasionally into carelessness or complacency, but seldom into exaggeration. He considered the gift of eloquence a heavy responsibility, and mere rant, for its own sake, filled him with horror. He knew when he wrote well, and he evinces a discriminating enjoyment. His gusto is one more of thought that of feeling, and accompanies passages of intellectual brilliance rather than of poetic exaltation. The lyrical vein he seldom attempts, and of course with lesser success, and therefore with lesser enjoyment, than Hazlitt. Sometimes, moreover, his gusto exceeds what the excellence of his " poetry " would seem to warrant. Attempting to explain the psychology behind Wordsworth's nature worship by means of a " mystical sense," he writes:

> As we gaze on the faces of those whom we love; as we watch the light of life in the dawning of their eyes, and the play of their features, and the wildness of their animation; as we trace in changing lineaments a varying sign; as a charm and a thrill seem to run along the tone of a voice, to haunt the mind with a mere word; as a tone seems to roam in the ear; as a trembling fancy hears words that are unspoken; so in Nature the mystical sense finds a motion in the mountain, and a power in the waves, and a meaning in the long white line of the shore, and a thought in the blue of heaven, and a gushing soul in the buoyant light, an unbounded being in the vast void of air.[13]

The passage borders dangerously on the sentimental, and indeed, as I have said, Bagehot's is essentially an intellectual "prose" gusto. It appears to best advantage in passages of psychological analysis, of paradox and epigram, of humour and anecdote. Having outlined Wordsworth's nature religion, he describes Lord Jeffrey's reactions to it:

> But be this as it may, it is certain that Mr. Wordsworth preached this kind of religion, and that Lord Jeffrey did not believe a word of it. His cool, sharp, collected mind revolted from its mysticism; his detective intelligence was absorbed in its apparent fallaciousness; his light humour made sport with the sublimities of the preacher. His love of perspicuity was vexed by its indefiniteness; the precise philosopher was amazed at its mystic unintelligibility. Finding a little fault was doubtless not unpleasant to him. The reviewer's pen—φόνος ἡρώεσσιν—has seldom been more poignantly wielded.[13]

Of Hartley Coleridge he writes:

> When he was about five years old, he was asked, doubtless by the paternal metaphysician, some question as to why he was called Hartley. " Which Hartley? " replied the boy. " Why, is there more than one Hartley? " " Yes, there is a deal of Hartleys; there is Picture Hartley (Hazlitt had painted a picture of him), and Shadow Hartley, and there's Echo Hartley, and there's Catchmefast Hartley," seizing his own arm very eagerly, and as if reflecting on the " summject and ommject," which is to say, being in hopeless confusion. We do not hear whether he was puzzled and perplexed by such difficulties in later life; and the essays which we are reviewing, though they contain much keen remark on the detail of human character, are destitute of the Germanic profundities; they do not discuss how existence is possible, nor enumerate the pure particulars of the soul itself. But considering the

idle dreaminess of his youth and manhood, we doubt
if Hartley ever got over his preliminary doubts—ever
properly grasped the idea of fact and reality. This is
not nonsense. If you attend acutely, you may observe
that in few things do people differ more than in their
perfect and imperfect realization of this earth.   To
the Duke of Wellington a coat was a coat; " there
was no mistake "; no reason to disbelieve it; and he
carried to his grave a perfect and indubitable persuasion
that he really did (what was his best exploit), without
fluctuation, *shave* on the morning of the battle of
Waterloo.[13]

The gusto of paradox appears most strongly in
" The Letters on the Coup D'État," the first of
Bagehot's published writings, and those which
reveal, in thought, temper, and style, the closest
relationship to Hazlitt. Their argument, as I have
already said, depends upon the twin propositions
that clever people are peculiarly incapable, stupid
people peculiarly capable, of self-government. Upon
these he insists with infinite relish, never adverting
to them without the most fondly careful preparation, never leaving them without a luxuriant display
of his most telling phrases, his aptest illustrations,
and his most brilliant wit. Against intelligence as
a political vice he inveighs with great moral indignation, and praises stupidity with bland and
patronizing unction. And what is very remarkable, the result is not, I think, a sacrifice of sound
opinion to mere paradox. Bagehot's doctrine,
beneath its rather jaunty dress, is the most solid
and conservative Burke, his view of the French
situation, when the exaggerations of humour are
deducted, essentially the view of wiser and more
experienced statesmen at the time.[14] " The Letters

on the Coup D'État " are very much what the late Mr. Chesterton, with less soundness, equal gusto, greater brilliance, and more imposing unintelligibility, has done in our own day.

CHAPTER IX

THE PLEASANT AVOCATION OF CRITICISM

BAGEHOT's interest in books, like Hazlitt's, was immediate and direct. He was concerned with the human nature in them. A great book was for him primarily the vivid and beautiful record of a great mind. It was also history, but only in a limited sense. Its precise geneology, the multitude of earlier books and earlier ideas, subtly and deviously connected, which were its ancestors, did not arouse his curiosity nor strike his imagination. He wrote before the historical method was fully developed, and indeed he was much less interested in intellectual history than several of his contemporaries. In the literary essays he seems to have imagined the past, not, like Coleridge, as a vast network of ideas gradually expressing themselves in action, but as a series of societies, gradually —by a continuity of manners rather than of thought —merging into one another. No doubt this indifference to the history of ideas is only natural, for it was one of Bagehot's favourite theories, as I have already indicated, that a man is governed, not by reason and logic, but by habit, routine, prejudice, and tradition. Ideas may act as a spark to an occasional revolution, but humdrum soon obliterates the effects and reasserts its original tyranny. That many a dull prejudice was once a daring idea he does not seem sufficiently to consider. Moreover, his learning, such as it was, accumulated around economics and political philosophy rather than around literature. In the strict sense he was not so much deeply learned, as broadly read. He loathed a dull book and never fully appreciated that sometimes a great many foolish men must be read in order to understand a few wise ones. " After the long biography of Moore," he sighs in the essay on Shelley, " it is half a comfort to think of a poet as to whom our information is but scanty."[1]

Bagehot's ignorance of the platitudes of literary opinion has laid him open to the charge of repeating them tiresomely. Sir Montstuart Grant Duff complains of the elaborateness with which, in " Lady Mary Wortley Montagu," he observes that letter-writing has decayed, and Sir Leslie Stephen declares:

> He is sometimes commonplace because he tells us how things strike him, and not the less that they have struck every other competent writer in much the same way; he writes of Shakespeare and Milton as if he had discovered them for the first time; he can at times utter a crude judgment because he is too indifferent—if that is possible—to orthodox literary authority.[2]

There is some justice in these remarks. Undoubtedly Bagehot has made crude judgments, as in condemning Byron to " lasting oblivion " and in brushing aside French tragedy as mere " prosing rhetoric " and " attenuated oratory."[3] Perhaps also his essay on Shakespeare contains a little too much mere common sense; still, we should be grateful for a phrase like " experiencing nature," and for the illuminating explanation which accompanies it. The "John Milton" is likewise marred by commonplaces on style and technique, yet Bagehot seems aware of his weakness in dealing with these subjects and invariably slights them. Much the greater part of the essay on Milton is devoted to an analysis of character, nor will one easily find another forty pages containing so many essential and penetrating observations on the mind and personality of the great poet.

What Bagehot says, and what he does not say, of the romantic movement is a revealing test of his quality as a critic, and an interesting illustration of his attitude toward intellectual history. Of so important a phenomenon he manages to say surprisingly little, and indeed he seems to regard the word itself with considerable suspicion. In writing at length of ten romantic authors he scarcely uses it; and when compelled to do so, deliberately substitutes the expression "ornate," which he declares to be "unwisely called romantic."[3] The few passages in which he has dared to employ the term, however, indicate an extraordinary grasp of its essential meaning and content. Scott's imagination, he explains, has a "romantic tinge." It pictures the Middle Ages "as we should have wished them to have been," as the "'fighting time'" which is the ideal of boyish fancy. It conceives Mary Stuart as the beautiful martyred queen rather than as the decidedly human and rather foolish woman which in his more critical moments Scott recognized her to be.[4] In other words, romantic imagination deals with the fanciful, the idyllic. It sees things otherwise than they are, and escapes from reality into a dream. Even more

penetrating in its insight into romantic imagination is the following passage on Disraeli:

> No politician has ever shown, in the bad sense of
> the word, so *romantic* a political imagination,—in other
> words, a fancy so little imbued with the laws of real
> life, so ready to revolt against those laws, and put up
> feeble idealities in their place. His ideal measures,
> like his ideal heroes, have always seemed the inven-
> tions of a mind on the rack to produce something grand
> or startling instead of something true and life-like.[4]

" Wordsworth, Tennyson, and Browning " is
the only one of Bagehot's essays that deals with
romanticism as such. It reveals that he had a
keen understanding of the nature, and a considerable appreciation of the importance, of that
movement as a phenomenon of contemporary
literature. His explanation of the pecular appeal
of romantic poetry, his elucidation of its incidental
accompaniments, his analysis of the idyllic quality
in Tennyson and the eccentric quality in Browning,
are masterly. Nevertheless, he is somewhat confused on fundamentals. He fails to see that between
his classic poets, Wordsworth and Shelley, and his
romantic, Tennyson and Browning, there is in
basic mode of thought and feeling a striking
similarity. His error arises, not merely from
mistakes in formal logic, but from a tendency to
ignore his surest beacon in this maze—the history
of the movement itself. And this omission is the
more conspicuous in that Bagehot, though lacking as yet the modern scholarly treatments on the
subject, was a considerable student of such authors
as Burke, Goethe, Hazlitt, and Carlyle, who are
full of valuable hints and illuminating suggestions.

But it is only natural, as I have pointed out, that a thinker so suspicious of thought should be indifferent to the history of thought, and that a man of broad, practical experience should explain contemporary art in terms of contemporary social conditions, that he should trace the flashy, sentimental, fragmentary nature of modern literature—in part very rightly—to the exhausting tempo of modern business and industrial life, the want of sufficient leisure, the increasing number of ignorant readers, the lack of cultural background in the middle classes, the growing influence of women, and the absence of any authoritative group to impose an austerer taste.

Bagehot's analysis of individual romantics is more brilliant and reliable than his treatment of the movement as a whole. On Wordsworth alone has he erred and indeed he was scarcely the man to be critical of Wordsworth, for, having been young when the poet stood at the very zenith of his fame, Bagehot was exposed to the full force of a contagion from which, cool-headed as he was, he never entirely recovered. Nor is Wordsworth, as everyone knows, an author whom it is easy to docket and label. Some have considered him a great religious teacher, others the formidable disseminator of a pernicious doctrine. He has been called a profound philosopher and an idle dreamer, a great rationalist and a great obscurantist, a follower of Hartley and a follower of Rousseau. And of course everyone is partly right. The truth is a matter of emphasis. Yet few I think will now deny that whatever he was at the time of his death, and whatever else he may have seemed earlier, as a

poet he was predominantly romantic, that he
exhibits the characteristic sensitiveness, uncon-
trolled feeling, absorbed self-admiration, and
Arcadian imagination of the romantic, that his
attitude is not genuinely religious, but idyllic, that
instead of facing life and its problems he retreats
from them, seeking in lonely and musing communion with nature a spiritual peace and happiness
which he never really found there. For his worship
of the rocks and hills never taught him to be
humble and generous toward Coleridge after their
break-up, nor to bear with Christian patience the
death of his daughter Dora. Indeed, his Christian
patience was sometimes more than his fellow men
could endure, and he could turn the other cheek
in a very brutal manner. The Rousseauistic doctrine which in his influential years he preached so
beautifully, with its insistence on the innate goodness of man and its glorification of nature, can be
recommended by its effects neither upon his own
life nor upon life in general. Whatever it has
done, it has scarcely conferred the benefits of
genuine religion.

Into the treacherous sea of Wordsworthian
criticism Bagehot is a timid diver. There is a depth
of profundity—within easy distance of the bottom
or truth of the matter—below which he never
descends. Having reached that point, he rises
rapidly to the surface once more. Sensible observation gives way to rather vague and generalized
expressions of approval. Having observed that
Cowper uses nature merely as a background, he
continues, " To Wordsworth . . . Nature is a
religion. So far from being unwilling to treat her

M

as a special object of study, he hardly thought any other equal or comparable. He was so far from holding the doctrine that the earth was made for men to live in, that it would rather seem as if he thought men were created to see the earth." Here he seems on the verge of saying something very much to the purpose, but he continues, " The whole aspect of Nature was to him a special revelation of an immanent and abiding power—a breath of the pervading art—a smile of the Eternal Mind —according to the lines which everyone knows."[4] And Bagehot quotes the lines which everyone knows. Again, speaking of Wordsworth in " Hartley Coleridge," he begins very hopefully:

> It has been attempted in recent years to establish that the object of his life was to teach Anglicanism. A whole life of him has been written by an official gentleman, with the apparent view of establishing that the great poet was a believer in rood-lofts, an idolater of piscinæ. But this is not capable of rational demonstration. Wordsworth, like Coleridge, began life as a heretic, and as the shrewd Pope unfallaciously said, " once a heretic, always a heretic." Sound men are sound from the first; safe men are safe from the beginning, and Wordsworth began wrong.[5]

But the discussion ends on the same note of vague admiration. Wordsworth's religion is accepted at its face value. Indeed his poetry is raised up to the level of the Bible, as having upon the few the same moral influence which that book has upon the many:

> In truth, his works are the Scriptures of the intellectual life; for that same searching, and finding, and penetrating power which the real Scripture exercises

on those engaged, as are the mass of men, in practical
occupations and domestic ties, do his works exercise
on the meditative, the solitary, and the young. [5]

Evidently, then, fine feeling, æsthetic musing,
dreamy sentimentality, and religious meditation
are all much the same thing, equally productive of
the good life and of an exalted inward calm.
Other passages on Wordsworth, equally uncritical,
might be quoted—one in particular, which urges
to the poet's advantage the Rousseauistic opposition between the natural and the artificial. [5]   But
further quotation could only illustrate what is
already sufficiently evident.   Nowhere is Wordsworth praised for what he is, nowhere is he criticized
for what he is not, but everywhere he is described
in the general terms of contemporary admiration
and enthusiasm.

To Bagehot's treatment of other romantics little
objection can be made.   If he is guilty of any fault
it is that in two of the best of these essays, those on
Shelley and Hartley Coleridge, he makes the
slightest imaginable concession to contemporary
sentimentality.   Commenting on the tragedy of
Harriet Westbrook, he says of Shelley:

> This strange story is in various ways deeply illus-
> trative of his character.   It shows how the impulsive
> temperament, not definitely intending evil, is hurried
> forward, so to say, *over* actions and crimes which would
> seem to indicate deep depravity—which would do so
> in ordinary human nature, but which do not indicate
> in it anything like the same degree of guilt.   Driven by
> singular passion across a tainted region, it retains no
> taint; on a sudden it passes through evil, but preserves
> its purity.   So curious is this character, that a record
> of its actions may read like a libel on its life. [6]

Rousseau might have elaborated such a romantic paradox, but Dr. Johnson would have roared at it. In " Hartley Coleridge " eloquence must have its due. The world would be a wilderness, declares Bagehot, " if there were not some, to relieve the dull monotony of activity, who are children through life; who act on wayward impulse, and whose will has never come; who toil not and who spin not; who always have ' fair Eden's simpleness '; and of such was Hartley Coleridge."[6]   But I speak of venialities. Nearly all the rest is excellent. The " unsymmetrical genius " of Dickens, the intellectual melancholy of Clough, the sensitive nature of Thackeray, the " impulsive temperament " and abstract mind of Shelley are probed with the cold detachment of a surgeon and discussed with the verve of a *raconteur*. These studies seem the work of a contemporary, or a near contemporary, only in their freshness of impression and liveliness of manner. In depth of analysis and moderation of judgment they might pass as the distinguished product of fifty years later.

Bagehot brought to the study of literature almost every species of equipment but that of the literary historian. He had been educated for the Bar; he had acquired the specialized knowledge of an economist; he had gained practical experience as a banker, editor, and politician; and in the course of a studious life he had accumulated broad, heterogeneous information ranging all the way from biological science to Anglican theology. The result is that his essays seem to have an added dimension. The persons they describe appear not from the single aspect of their literary significance, but from the many aspects of their various interests and achievements. We hear of Jeffrey both as critic and as editor, of Crabb Robinson not only as a collector of literary lions, but as a successful member of the Bar. We become more definitely aware that there are sound politics in Shakespeare's plays and excellent political economy in Scott's novels. We are given the opinion of a politician upon the parliamentary career of Gibbon. In short, we feel that we are in the presence not of literary abstractions, but of total personalities. We see literature in its "connection with reality and affairs."[6]

At no time does Bagehot's peculiar training stand him in such good stead as when he delineates the past. Nor have his descriptions merely the charm of a close familiarity with many phases of life. Some historians have the faculty of making a past age vivid through the accumulation of encyclopædic detail. Bagehot had the faculty of talking about it like a contemporary. Intrinsically, his representations are not so circumstantial, and in some respects, not so vivid, as those of certain other first-class writers, yet his tone is more assured, more familiar. He creates the illusion of describing personal experience, and that illusion is worth a world of fact and rhetoric. What is the source of his peculiar power? He has himself observed that " the speciality of pursuits is attended with a timidity of mind."[6] Bagehot had the intellectual courage of a broad and versatile training. He writes with the ready confidence and easy adaptability of one who is accustomed to assume many points of view, to be at home in a great variety of surroundings, and to find beneath all the strange and multifarious phenomena of society that strange, familiar thing—human nature.

In his essays the literature, business, and politics of the eighteenth century seem the lively, intimate concerns of a few years back. The real founder of the Gibbon family, he relates,

> was the grandfather of the historian, who lived in the times of the " South Sea." He was a capital man of business according to the custom of that age—a dealer in many kinds of merchandise—like perhaps the " complete tradesman " of Defoe, who was to understand the price and quality of *all* articles made within the kingdom. The preference, however, of Edward Gibbon the grandfather was for the article " shares "; his genius, like that of Mr. Hudson, had a natural tendency towards a commerce in the metaphysical and the non-existent; and he was fortunate in the age on which his lot was thrown. It afforded many opportunities of gratifying that taste. Much has been written on panics and manias—much more than with the most outstretched intellect we are able to follow or conceive; but one thing is certain, that at particular times a great many stupid people have a great deal of stupid money.[7]

And so the narrative continues. A fireside conversation could not be more easy, nor the memories of youth more fresh and immediate.

In what might be called the familiar biographical essay Bagehot's equal is not easily found. In total output and sheer literary ability he cannot of course rank as an historian with Carlyle and Macaulay. The latter, in his essay on " History," set himself a very high ideal, which to an amazing degree he realized in his great history of England. He has described arts and manners, industry and commerce, " the crowds of the exchange and the coffee house," life in the cottage as well as in the palace.[8] With considerable completeness he has portrayed the great movements which lie behind superficial events. Where perhaps he has definitely fallen short is in the human insight in which he hoped to be pre-eminent. His characters are extremely colourful but rather empty; they tend to be either brilliant exteriors, or ponderous vivisections. He visits the crimes of his contemporaries upon the heads of their ancestors, and sees in all Tories, past and present, something inhuman and benighted. He deals with the private life of King James II as if he were impeaching that monarch in parliament, and even his most delicately sympathetic and intimate manner has something of the blare and clamour of the hustings. Where he chiefly excels, however, is in presenting the parade of history. I do not mean that he is simply another Froissart, that he describes mere ceremony and carnage. He delineates also the majesty of monarchial designs, the clash and excitement of public controversy, the pomp, rhetoric, and drama of parliament. He depicts, with unexampled vividness and to the unflagging military music of his prose, the whole sweep and march of public events together with their formal and secondary causes. But Bagehot takes us behind the scenes. He leads us from the throne room into the king's closet. In his easy, confidential way he introduces us to the great leaders who determine policy, and tells us their petty faults and their secret hopes. He focuses not on the outward drama and noise of events, but upon their inward and human signifi-cance. Beside the elaborate delineations of

Macaulay, his own brief sketches may seem to many readers rather slight, but they go deep, are bold and lifelike, and at the same time remarkably careful, both of the letter and the spirit of truth.

One of the most lively and sparkling of these brief works is that on Edward Gibbon. Unlike the great historian in his celebrated *Autobiography*, Bagehot has condescended to represent a human being. He has exhumed the man from his rhetoric and found below the ruins of the Roman Empire the comedy of a comfortable existence.[9] In " Lady Mary Wortley Montagu " he has with singular delicacy distilled a comedy equally brilliant, and a sketch only slightly less complete, from a long and gossipy correspondence. But perhaps the most remarkable members of Bagehot's gallery are his bores. Never were dull men made so entertaining. Never was stupidity so subtly and ingeniously explained. " Sir Robert Peel," " Sir George Cornewall Lewis," and the passages on Robert Harley, Earl of Oxford, in " Bolingbroke as a Statesman " are among the soundest and most entertaining pages in Bagehot.

A biographer should above all be truthful, and as a matter of fact Bagehot's salient quality as a thinker, and his greatest safeguard against the characteristic dangers of after-dinner writing, is undoubtedly what Arnold calls his " concern for the simple truth." That he should feel such concern is rather remarkable, for no man loved cleverness more, and it is possible to be almost infinitely clever, if only one is content to be wrong. But Bagehot was too much of a realist, hated moonshine too intensely, ever to be satisfied with sparkling in a

vacuum. He loved cleverness, but he was married
to truth. The consequence is, that one goes to
Bagehot not just to read Bagehot, but to read about
great authors, not to discover what ingenious and
beautiful notions can be spun around them, but
what sensible and just opinions can be developed
upon them. One may find stranger, more poetic
ideas in another critic, but what one seldom finds
in another critic are so many sound ideas so profoundly conceived and so brilliantly expressed. He
is a storehouse of sensible criticism, of the " simple
truth."

In his essay on Bishop Butler, Bagehot divides
philosophers into " gropers " and " seers."[10] The
former have no vision of the truth; they move
toward it, as it were with the aid of the tactual
sense alone. Such a philosopher was Aristotle, or
Butler. Seers are, like Plato, " picturesque "
thinkers:

> A thinker of . . . the picturesque order has a vision,
> a picture of the natural view of the subject. Those
> certainties and conclusions, those doubts and diffi-
> culties, which occur on the surface, strike him at once;
> he sees with his mind's eye some conspicuous instance
> in which all such certainties are realized, and by which
> all such doubts are suggested. Some great typical
> fact remains delineated before his mind, and is a
> perpetual answer to all hypotheses which strive to be
> over-subtle.[10]

Such was Bagehot's own mind. He had in extraordinary degree the power of seeing vividly the
general in the particular. No gift could be more
valuable to a thinker who must deal with the
infinite complexity of social and human phenomena.

Such an author must see clearly the one in the many, or he will fall into a thousand confusions.

Accordingly, Bagehot's works reveal everywhere the illuminating influence of type-idea. They abound in unforgettable delineations of national character, party character, type character of many kinds. One of the most striking features of the biographical studies is that he nearly always sees the individual through some aspect of the universal. Behind his picture of Milton stands the general type which is founded on "ascetic goodness," behind his picture of Butler that which is founded on "moral thoughtfulness." Mr. Caldwell is the typical Parliamentary leader, Lord Brougham the typical agitator, Pitt the typical administrative statesman. Shakespeare has an "experiencing," Macaulay an "inexperiencing," nature. Gladstone has an "oratorical temperament," and an "advocate's intellect." But most brilliant of all are his sketches of the typical Englishman, the typical Frenchman, the typical Whig, and the typical Tory:

> The essence of Toryism is enjoyment. . . . The way to keep up old customs is, to enjoy old customs; the way to be satisfied with the present state of things is, to enjoy that state of things. Over the "Cavalier" mind this world passes with a thrill of delight; there is an exultation in a daily event, zest in the "regular thing", joy at an old feast. Sir Walter Scott is an example of this. Every habit and practice of old Scotland was inseparably in his mind associated with genial enjoyment. To propose to touch one of her institutions, to abolish one of those practices, was to touch a personal pleasure—a point on which his mind reposed, a thing of memory and hope. So long as this

world is this world, will a buoyant life be the proper source of an animated Conservatism.[10]

But Bagehot's generalized portraits are not always so fortunate. He had what are perhaps some of the peculiar faults of the " picturesque " thinker. He craved the excitement of clarity and required the assurance of concreteness. I do not mean that he sacrificed truth, but he tended sometimes to simplify it, and also, as for example in certain of his writings on political economy, to slight those aspects of his subject requiring complex logic and elaborate abstract reasoning, in which concreteness is impossible and clarity difficult.[11] He was also inclined, as a " picturesque " thinker, to rest a little too securely in his vision, and since it is easier to take a clear view of few facts than of many, he sometimes snapped the picture too soon. Knowledge made him cautious and ignorance made him bold. He is sound and circumspect on politics and government, of which he knew much; and on literary theory of which he knew considerably less, he is bold and fallacious. In evolving his type-delineations he was occasionally rapid and hasty. Even the best of them are but the rapid conclusions of a man whom long observation of human nature has given a wise instinct, together with much vague data, for discovering truth. Many of them were doubtless struck off in the heat of the moment, and based upon single examples, or even fragments of examples. Consequently, it is not surprising that a few are superficial or specious. Arthur A. Baumann has pointed out that the type of the historian, as Bagehot presents it, is so far from sufficing for all members of the species that it does not even explain Macaulay himself, from whom it was deduced. Whereas the typical historian is maintained to be " a cold and insensible person," Macaulay was really " warm-tempered and warm-hearted; a good hater as well as a good lover; one of the most sympathetic and affectionate of men."[12] Despite a few glaring failures, however, Bagehot has on the whole succeeded admirably in being at once clear, brilliant, and truthful. Some of his types and generalizations have, I understand, been adopted by psychological science.[13] Indeed, with these brilliant creations Bagehot has himself erected a psychology and supplied us many new and vivid terms with which to think about human nature.

Some critics feel that Bagehot's truthfulness is impaired by defects of a totally different order. Mr. George Sampson speaks of " the hardness that somewhat mars his work—hardness, remember, not bluntness. His temper was of steel—keen, resilient, but undeniably hard. He seemed impatient of emotion and suspicious of any action born of its influence. He was in fact, an example of excessive rationalism."[14] Certainly there is in Bagehot's writings, not so much, I think, in his " temper," a quality which may be described as hardness. One feels nearly everywhere in the literary essays an enthusiasm for ideas and an indifference to persons, an eagerness to explore diseases and a carelessness of suffering, a readiness to criticize and an unwillingness to reverence or admire. This disposition appears most strikingly, I feel, in " Henry Crabb Robinson," in which one seems to obtain a disquieting glimpse into the clear, frigid depths of a critic's mind. Full justice, at least in the letter, is done the eminent diarist. His loyalty, his kindness, his generosity are all duly emphasized. His literary opinions are condemned, and his legal abilities are praised. His faults are indulgently explained. And yet, for all its tact and fairness, its humour and brilliance, the essay is in a sense slightly repellent. One feels somehow that Bagehot regrets not so much the loss of a lovable old friend as the extinction of a rare and amusing animal. He had treasured " Old Crabb " not for being kind, but for being grotesque. Perhaps he had always, in spite of his practical joke, unconsciously resented the diarist's interminable monologues. At any rate, the essay, though the memoir of a thirty years' friendship, is undeniably " hard." Mr. Sampson appears to think the essay on Clough, another old friend of Bagehot's, even harder, and perhaps he is right.

But after all, the object of criticism is presumably not to extend sympathy, but to discover truth, or at least to evolve just opinions. The question is, does Bagehot succeed in so doing? In my opinion he does to an exceptional degree. The portraits of Robinson and Clough are entirely in accord with the facts, and that of Robinson is surprisingly complete. No doubt a warmer artist might have found much more to express of what is good and lovable in Clough, and to omit this is certainly to neglect a part of the truth, yet it must be remembered that Bagehot wrote essays and not exhaustive monographs. Few could present more clearly the essence of Clough's mind and of his tragedy. Indeed, Bagehot's hardness does not materially restrict his

vision. Cool detachment is the natural adjunct
to clarity and justness of insight. A certain irrational cheerfulness is conducive to deep rationality.
Sad men must play with illusions. Serious men
cannot bear to be too serious. As a matter of fact,
Bagehot's critics are really objecting much less
to his matter than to his manner. It is regrettable
that he could not produce sympathetic, as well as
comic, portraits, but much more is it fortunate
that he could produce fair and accurate ones.
It would have been more graceful in him as a
man, perhaps, to describe Crabb Robinson with
gravity, but it would not have been more truthful
in him as a critic.

This limitation of manner springs from a want
rather of sympathy than of feeling. Feeling Bagehot
did not lack. On the contrary, he was a warm
friend, an affectionate son, and a passionate lover.
Indeed he was " impatient " not of emotion, but
of irrational emotion. Passion was strong in him,
but docile, tractable to the will and the conscience.
It fastened firmly to legitimate objects, and was not
inflamed by the forbidden and the mysterious.
Why? The answer must be found in the influences
of early training, in the tendencies of a moral
imagination and a disciplined mind. But at any
rate the result is clear. His strong, sufficient life
never knew the suffering and humiliation of serious
moral weakness, and what he had never vividly
felt himself, he was not inclined to pity in others.
He lacked somewhat the broad humanity which he
has himself attributed to King David.[15]

Perhaps his limitation of manner was also due to
a deficiency in the imagination and the faculty of

expression itself. His gift was critical and analytic, in no sense poetic or lyrical. His mind expressed thought so much more brilliantly than feeling that the one crowded the other out of his writings. Probably his warmest and most enthusiastic essay is that on Shakespeare, and it is probably also his worst. We can scarcely regret that he has not made a greater exhibition of his literary failings, nor deplore that, being a critic, he has displayed the virtues of a critical, and not of a poetic, temperament.

CHAPTER X

TECHNIQUE AND HUMOUR

BAGEHOT's general method of writing an essay, his " formula," owes much to contemporary practice, and particularly to that of Macaulay. The same hard, rational tone, the same long digressions, the same tendency to vary literature with politics and history, the same love of anecdote, of paradoxical statement, of striking theory, the same preference of persons to books are to be found in both authors. Indeed I might go farther and maintain that the essays of both fall into the same two general type-forms: the narrative and biographical, on the one hand, and the expository and critical on the other. " Lord Clive " might be compared with " Edward Gibbon," " Milton " with " Shakespeare—The Man." But the parallel is not exact and the notation of discrepancies would be too complicated a process to be worth attempting here. Differing greatly in that more fundamental part of method which depends on native qualities of mind, the two authors betray in their use of forms, devices, and conventions striking similarities, and these similarities indicate, as I shall attempt presently to prove, that the later has in considerable degree imitated the earlier.

Bagehot was interested, it will be remembered, in the criticism not so much of books as authors. In technique his character studies depend sur-prisingly little on the usual routine of enumerating

traits and illustrating them. His remarkable ability
to see particular character in terms of clear and
brilliant generalization permits him two avenues
of escape. Either he concentrates upon witty and
humorous narrative, and allows his character to
develop dramatically; or he elaborates a sparklingly
epigrammatic and paradoxical description of type
or principle, and cites his character as illustration.
These devices are of course not sharply segregated
in practice. In " Hartley Coleridge " and " Mr.
Clough's Poems " both are used side by side. In
" Edward Gibbon " and " Lady Mary Wortley
Montagu " the first, and in " John Milton,"
" Shakespeare—The Man," and " Charles Dickens " the second is markedly predominant.

In elucidating these two techniques I find myself
drawn inevitably to discuss " Edward Gibbon "
and " John Milton," of which I have perhaps
already said too much. In many respects " Edward
Gibbon " approaches the short story, or rather, the
brief tale. Each phase of Gibbon's life—his early
spiritual adventures, his military experience, his
love affair, his political career, his intellectual
development—is so described as to point to one
salient fact, that the great historian was an eminently
placid and comfortable man. Novelistic methods
are employed, but with restraint. The narrative
is only occasionally gathered up into scenes, and
these are seldom much elaborated, except with
quoted source material, which, in Gibbon's case,
is readily to be found in the *Autobiography*. Dialogue
is of course not attempted, but authentic remarks
and sayings, and even ordinary quotations from
authorities are frequently introduced in a highly

N

dramatic manner. Bagehot has occasion to observe that Lord North could hardly be angered: " ' No doubt,' he said, tapping his fat sides, ' I am that odious thing a minister; and I believe other people wish they were so too.' "[1] But Bagehot excels where most narrative artists are weak—in bare summary. Vivid and epigrammatic phrasing injects interest and humour into the most unlikely material. As a Member of Parliament Gibbon " quietly and gently supported the policy of his time."[1] After so wisely terminating his little affair with *Mademoiselle* Curchod, he was by his family " justly regarded as a most safe young man, singularly prone to large books, and a little too fond of French phrases and French ideas; and yet with a great feeling of common-sense, and a wise preference of permanent money to transitory sentiment."[1] Nearly all that Bagehot has to say about Gibbon might be deduced from " his wise preference of permanent money."

" John Milton " is perhaps the best example as well as the most complete embodiment of Bagehot's second method of character portrayal. He begins by maintaining that there are two kinds of goodness, sensuous and ascetic. Sensuous goodness depends upon a " sensibility to outward stimulus "—a characteristic from which, citing King David as an example, Bagehot elaborates a complete, highly integrated type. Ascetic goodness is founded upon the " protective instinct," upon a principle of " repulsion from the world," an " impulse . . . to start back from what may trouble us, to shun what may fascinate us, to avoid what may tempt us."[1] From this principle also Bagehot elaborates a type even more impressively complex in its details, and unified

in its central logic. Everything is now in readiness.
The contrasting moulds have been exhibited, and
King David has been fitted into the first. Accordingly Milton is introduced and triumphantly fitted
into the second. Nearly the entire remainder of
the essay contributes to prove that he is a striking
instance of ascetic goodness.

Witty and humorous in narrative, brilliant and
clear—if at times somewhat lengthy—in exposition,
Bagehot had, as a critic, little occasion to avail
himself of his descriptive powers. They appear to
have been considerable, and worthy of greater
cultivation. Touches like the following brief portrait of Crabb Robinson are extremely effective:
" His face was pleasing from its animation, its
kindness, and its shrewdness, but the nose was one
of the most slovenly which nature had ever turned
out, and the chin of excessive length, with por-
tentous power of extension."[1]   Bagehot was too
much interested in ideas to care much for exteriors,
and Crabb Robinson is the only one of his contemporaries whose outward appearance he has in
any sense attempted to describe.

Bagehot may be said to have three styles: one
literary, one philosophical, and one journalistic.
The first flourishes through the period ending in
1859, when he becomes editor of *The Economist*.
The last two develop in the period which follows.
The second and third differ from the first chiefly
in purpose and emphasis, and from each other only
in the degree of care with which they were written,
the one being rather studied, the other sometimes
ragged and slovenly. Bagehot's later writing is
almost unfailingly clear and vigorous, frequently

vivid and epigrammatic in phrase, and carefully, though not elaborately, rhetorical in structure. Yet in the main its virtues are utilitarian. The subtle refinements of art, the ornaments of the imagination are absent. What I have called his philosophical style is designed to convey truth to the learned and scientific; his journalistic, to impart fundamentals to the uninitiated. Sir Robert Giffin declares that in writing for *The Economist*, Bagehot

> had always some typical City man in his mind's eye— a man not skilled in literature or the turnings of phrases, with limited vocabulary and knowledge of theory, but keen as to fact and reading for the sake of information and guidance respecting what vitally concerned him. To please this ideal City man Bagehot would use harsh and crude or redundant expressions, sometimes ungrammatical, if tried by ordinary tests; anything to drive his meaning home.[2]

His literary style includes the virtues of the philosophical and journalistic, and much besides. It is equally clear, vigorous, and colloquial, but it is also infinitely broader in range, more varied in tone and structure, and richer in implication. It is highly flexible, and slips rapidly from witty, racy conversation to a nervous, intellectual eloquence. Occasionally it bursts out in flashes of genuine poetry, but attains its proper heights in paradox and epigram, in humour and satire. Its chief technical excellence is in vivid and striking phrase, yet it does not lack the firmness of strong rhetorical structure, and is sometimes rhetorical to a fault. Altogether Bagehot's prose reveals much natural talent and not a little deliberate art. Careful revision might have made it truly great.

His models of style were probably Hazlitt and Macaulay. Burke also he must have read with close attention, but then Burke, far more than Hazlitt, wrote in the grand style, and one suspects that Bagehot secretly felt the grand style, especially in prose, to be a breach of true English reserve. Writing so lofty, so poetic, so extravagantly passionate, could scarcely awaken emulation in a literary young business man. At any rate, little of his work suggests the great orator's influence— except perhaps here and there a touch in " The Letters on the Coup D'État," and especially one long passage on the Catholic Church, which has indeed something of the sustained power and eloquence, the compact and vigorous rhetoric of Burke.[3] But in the main Macaulay and Hazlitt were nearer to his taste. The one was a pattern of clear—perhaps too clear—exposition; the other an ideal of vivid and powerful writing. Both were masters of anecdote, rhetoric, brief narrative, of the essay form. What Bagehot could learn from other authors he probably found in these two.

When he becomes rhetorical, Bagehot approaches more closely the heavy obviousness of Macaulay than the subtle variety of Hazlitt. Macaulay's characteristic balance, antithesis, and series are frequently to be found in Bagehot. Indeed he is sometimes guilty, like his master, of developing these devices beyond the natural capabilities of the thought, summing up a discussion of hereditary moral weakness, for example, with the following sentence:

But, explicable or inexplicable—to be wondered at or not to be wondered at—the fact is clear; tendencies and temptations are transmitted even to the fourth generation both for good and for evil, both in those who serve God and in those who serve Him not.[3]

Again, after the manner of Macaulay's *History*, he suggests by a series of short, parallel clauses the rapid order of events in narrative: " The Napoleonic era has commenced; the term of the dictatorship is fixed and the consolidation of France is begun."[3] In passages of analysis Bagehot often, like his favourites, tends to an even more nervous and staccato rhythm. Hazlitt's portrait of Lord Jeffrey and Bagehot's of Francis Horner offer an interesting comparison:

> He is a master of the foils; he makes an exulting display of the dazzling fence of wit and argument. His strength consists in great range of knowledge, and equal familiarity with the principles and the details of a subject, and in a glancing brilliancy and rapidity of style.[4]
>
> .   .   .   .   .   .
>
> He never had the means of obliging any one. He was destitute of showy abilities: he had not the intense eloquence or overwhelming ardour which enthrall and captivate popular assemblies: his powers of administration were little tried, and may possibly be slightly questioned.[4]

I might trace to Hazlitt and Macaulay several other rhetorical devices employed by Bagehot, but such parallels are too difficult to establish, and speculation on them too tenuous, to be pursued very far. Let it suffice to say that in his considerable, though not obtrusive, use of rhetoric Bagehot appears to have learned much from his two more eminent predecessors.

Bagehot's style could scarcely be described as

" rich in imagery." To be sure, he has achieved
some very respectable poetic passages. Having told
how Cowper, while a literary young gentleman
living at the Temple, tries to commit suicide, he
exclaims:

> What a contrast is the " broad piece of scarlet
> binding " and the red circle, " showing plainly that I
> had been on the brink of eternity," to the daily life of
> the easy gentleman " who contributed some essays to
> the *St. James's Magazine*, and more than one to the
> *St. James's Chronicle*," living " soft years " on a smooth
> superficies of existence, away from the dark realities
> which are, as it were, the skeleton of our life,—which
> seem to haunt us like a death's head throughout the
> narrative that has been quoted![5]

In general Bagehot seldom attempts purely poetic
effects, and where he does, fails nearly as often as
he succeeds. The passage explaining the psychology
of nature worship in " The First Edinburgh
Reviewers " is nearly as bad as the opening of
" Hartley Coleridge " is good.[6] His best images
are apt and vivid rather than poetic. He is
most successful when he describes Lord Brougham
as " for many years rushing among the details of
an age," or when he likens the mind of Sir George
Lewis to " a registering machine with a patent
index." " The legitimate food of a self-relying
nature," he writes, " is early solitude."[7]

Some of his figures very closely resemble those of
Macaulay. He has the same taste for exaggerated
simile: " A French politician will no more cite as
authority the domestic policy of Colbert or Louvois
than we should think of going for ethics and
æsthetics to the bigamy of Lamech, or the musical

accomplishments of Tubal Cain."[8]   Or better,
and more poetical: Hartley Coleridge " could no
more have achieved football, or mastered cricket,
or kept in with the hounds, than he could have
followed Charles's Wain or played pitch and toss
with Jupiter's satellites."[8]   But there can be little
doubt that Bagehot found his best model for vivid
language in Hazlitt. One has only to compare such
passages of these two writers as I have already
quoted in Chapter Eight to perceive how carefully
and profitably the later must have studied the
earlier. And not only has he acquired much of
the vivid phrasing and epigrammatic force of his
model, but he has succeeded also in imparting to
his language that same occasional dash of racy
colloquialism.   In " Lord Brougham " he writes:

> There is a glare in some men's eyes which seems
> to say, " Beware, I am dangerous; *noli me tangere.*"
> Lord Brougham's face has this. A mischievous excita-
> bility is the most obvious expression of it. If he were
> a horse, nobody would buy him; with that eye, no
> one could answer for his temper.[8]

The chief difficulty with epigrams and paradoxes
is that if they please the reader very much, they
please the writer even more. Perhaps no modern
writer has produced so many epigrams as the
late Mr. Chesterton, but unfortunately Mr. Chesterton never sufficiently realized that epigram, repeated
once too often, becomes commonplace. Hazlitt,
Macaulay, and Bagehot were more moderate, but
when the mood was upon them, they frequently
pursued their idea till it staggered. Macaulay's
paradoxes are usually saved by vividness and
rhetoric, Hazlitt's by poetry and imagination, and

Bagehot's by the subtlety of the idea itself and the humour of the development. In expatiating on the political value of stupidity and the corresponding dangers of cleverness, Bagehot is long, but at least he is not in deadly earnest. He has the spice of humour and the elusiveness of irony.

His best sayings are, like Hazlitt's, to be found in his character sketches. Though immensely inferior in brilliance of statement, he has over Hazlitt the advantages of being much more just and much better humoured. He is never guilty, for example, of such bitter injustice as that in the following:

> Mr. Southey has not fortitude of mind, has not patience to think that evil is inseparable from the nature of things. His irritable sense rejects the alternative altogether, as a weak stomach rejects the food that is distasteful to it. He hopes against hope, he believes in all unbelief. He must either repose on actual or on imaginary good. He missed his way in *Utopia*, he has found it at Old Sarum—
> " His generous *ardour* no cold medium knows: "
> his eagerness admits of no doubt or delay. He is ever at extremes, and ever in the wrong![9]

In a sense Bagehot has written many more real epigrams than Hazlitt. He deals more in general statements, and these are usually humorous: " Decorum is the essence, pomposity the advantage, of tutors." And again, upon the same subject: " A schoolmaster should have an atmosphere of awe, and walk wonderingly, as if he was amazed at being himself."[10] Some of his remarks are extremely profound, the result of mature reflection on abundant knowledge and observation.

" Coleridge," he says, " is an example of mis-
formed mind in which not only may ' Faith ' not
produce ' works,' but in which it had a tendency
to prevent works. Strong convictions gave him a
kind of cramp in the will, and he could not act on
them."[10]   One feels that the following springs
directly from his personal experience: " There is
much quiet intellectual persecution among ' reasonable ' men; a cautious person hesitates before he
tells them anything new, for if he gets a name for
such things he will be called ' flighty,' and in times
of decision he will not be attended to."[10] Bagehot
has not the glitter of Hazlitt or Macaulay, but
what glitters in his writings is usually gold.

The chief excellences of Bagehot's style can be
summed up, in my opinion, under the head of
effective phrasing, and although this effectiveness
depends chiefly upon imagery and paradox, it
depends also upon a certain quietly apt, accurate,
and whimsically vivid use of words—the sort of
thing which in lesser degree Hazlitt achieves when
he speaks of Kemble playing Hamlet with a
" determined inveteracy of purpose."[11] Bagehot
goes far beyond his master in this lesser art, and it
is one of the most individual qualities of his style.
Indeed, his attitude toward language is excellent.
Hazlitt uses words much more powerfully, but
fiercely, recklessly. He seems always to be fighting something—if only a windmill. To Bagehot
words are a means of illumination. He uses them
with discretion and judgment, and sometimes he
turns them playfully, like a lantern, this way and
that, to get fantastic effects in the shadow or to
light up queer, dark little corners. In order not

to weary the reader I shall consider in this regard
only his use of adjectives. He speaks of Cowper as
being in his youth " a gentle and gradual, rather
than a forcible or rigorous learner," and again as
spending his days at the Temple in light study and
" tranquil negligence."¹² He refers to the English
schoolboy as " the small, apple-eating animal
whom we know."¹² One cannot but feel, he says,
a certain admiration for Lord Brougham. He has
" such an aggressive intelligence—so much *knocking*
mind."¹²

But although Bagehot's phrasing is nearly always
vivid, it is not always elegant and melodious.
Without a shudder he can write: " His range is
very varied; " and he is too fond of " ignoble "
words, especially such conversational connectives
as " anyhow " and " anyway."¹³ He will mar a
strong passage with a vague, cliché phrase. Explaining the value of the ceremonial and " theatrical "
elements in the English constitution, he writes:

> That which is mystic in its claims; that which is
> occult in its mode of action; that which is brilliant to the
> eye; that which is seen vividly for a moment, and then
> is seen no more; that which is hidden and unhidden;
> that which is specious, and yet interesting, palpable in
> its seeming, and yet professing to be more than palpable
> in its results; this, howsoever its form may change, or
> however we may define it or describe it, is the sort of
> thing—the only sort—which yet comes home to the
> mass of men.¹³

Such an expression as " the sort of thing " would
freeze the marrow of a really conscientious stylist,
yet Bagehot is content to introduce it at the most
important point in his discussion.

But perhaps his worst fault is that he fails in economy of phrase. In attempting to write one must learn first how to use words and then how to do without them. Bagehot never learned the second. I do not mean that he is thin or diffuse. Few writers are so compact in *thought*. One cannot read an essay of his without feeling that one has come in contact with a great many ideas, but one sometimes wishes that they were more briefly expressed. The truth is that he has enormous literary courage, and will write across a sheet of blank paper with as little trepidation as one would chat about the weather. His language has not only the tone, but something of the garrulity of conversation. He sometimes uses a cumbersome phrase where a single word would carry his meaning more vigorously. He has the talker's careless redundancy in transition: "Again, moreover, and in the course of time, the advance of ages and the progress of civilization appear to produce a new species of poetry."[13] Bagehot's gusto, and his low opinion of his readers' intelligence, also lead him to dwell unduly upon his ideas. It is true that he does not, like Hazlitt, whet them away to nothing in attempting to put an edge on them, but in his anxiety to be understood he is on occasion painfully obvious. He sometimes appears to be at low, when he is at high tension.

Perhaps one could not describe Bagehot's style better than to say it is worthy of so able a man. It is not one of the great Victorian styles, nor the style of a careful artist; but it is adequate; it is the faithful mirror of a brilliant mind. And indeed one feels in reading this author that one is in the presence of great powers of thought, rather than great powers of expression. I would not seem to undervalue, nor to imply that his writing is a mere patchwork from Hazlitt and Macaulay. It has not the poetic contentiousness of the one nor the exasperated vehemence of the other. It is much more reserved, more restrained. It implies a more reasoned judgment and a reflection more carefully matured. It is easier and more conversational, yet it is vigorous, spirited, and epigrammatic. Its peculiar excellences, including that effectiveness of phrase to which I have already called attention, depend upon qualities of humour which neither Hazlitt nor Macaulay possessed.

Of wit and humour Bagehot's command is so broad and inclusive that it is easier to begin by mentioning some of the varieties which he eschews rather than those in which he excels. His fun is never boisterous or farcical. It seldom reveals emotion or sympathy. It is seldom subjective and personal. He lacks the gift, so dear to Englishmen, of gracefully turning his humour against himself. He ironically pretends on occasion to be ignorant, naïve, stupid—he jests at his virtues, but never at his failings. Sometimes he laughs with the reader, sometimes he laughs at him, but he never laughs at Walter Bagehot. The omission is not, I think, necessarily significant, yet it may indicate a certain ὕβρις. That so clever a man could be so much amused by dull men, that a person who has clear, logical, satisfactory theories about everything should be so much delighted with those who never have a clear, logical, satisfactory notion about anything is undoubtedly suspicious. Perhaps it was with a glance of satisfaction at the clear efficiency within his own mind that Bagehot wrote, gaily and ironically, in 1852:

> By the sound work of old-fashioned generations— by the singular painstaking of the slumberers in church- yards—by dull care—by stupid industry, a certain social fabric somehow exists; people contrive to go out to their work, and to find work to employ them actually until the evening, body and soul are kept together, and this is what mankind have to show for their six thousand years of toil and trouble.[14]

But if in his humour he sometimes appears a little too assured, his fault is due not so much to com- placency as to a contempt for others, and even more perhaps, especially in his later years, to a native detachment of mind and a strong and settled reserve. He shrinks from obtruding his personality between the reader and the subject. " The Letters on the French Coup D'État " may seem to be an exception to this remark, but there he has a definite artistic reason for referring to himself. In pretend- ing to be a dull, ignorant fellow who takes only the most conventional view of a situation, he renders doubly shocking to his pious Unitarian readers the extremely paradoxical argument which he sets forth.

Of that kind of laughter which depends upon a deeply sympathetic and imaginative insight, which results from a perception of absurdities in oneself as well as in others, and which sees these absurdities against the background of the august mysteries of life and death—of this there is little in Bagehot. One rather striking example does indeed occur in " Hartley Coleridge ":

Hartley Coleridge was not like the Duke of Wellington.
Children are urged by the example of the great statesman and warrior just departed—not indeed to neglect
" their book " as he did—but to be industrious and
thrifty; to " always perform business," to " beware of
procrastination," to " NEVER fail to do their best ":
good ideas, as may be ascertained by referring to the
masterly dispatches on the Mahratta transactions. . . .
But

" What a wilderness were this sad world,
If man were always man and never child! "

And it were almost a worse wilderness if there were not
some, to relieve the dull monotony of activity, who
are children through life; who act on wayward impulse, and whose will has never come; who toil not
and who spin not; who always have " fair Eden's
simpleness ": and of such was Hartley Coleridge.
" Don't you remember," writes Gray to Horace
Walpole, "when Lord B. and Sir H. C. and Viscount D.,
who are now great statesmen, were little dirty boys
playing at cricket? For my part I do not feel one bit
older or wiser now than I did then." For as some
apply their minds to what is next them, and labour
ever, and attain to governing the Tower, and entering
the Trinity House,—to commanding armies, and
applauding pilots,—so there are also some who are
ever anxious to-day about what ought only to be considered to-morrow; who never get on; whom the earth
neglects, and whom tradesmen little esteem; who are
where they were; who cause grief, and are loved;
that are at once a by-word and a blessing; who do
not live in life, and it seems will not die in death:
and of such was Hartley Coleridge.[15]

Though marred by sentimentality, the passage is
in my opinion full of sincere feeling and poetic
imagination. It is pregnant with the suggestions
of the deeper meanings of existence. But in
general his laughter has no cosmic echoes. Its

implications are deep and penetrating, but seldom vast and tremendous. He laughs at men in their multifarious activities, not at man rearing his head among the stars.

But it is not so much in humour as in wit, in the cool, objective levity of the intellect, that Bagehot excels. Within this sphere he ranges all the way from the simplest plays upon words to delicious outbursts of keen and whimsical absurdity. His wit has two great merits: it almost never lacks point, and it is never ill-humoured. Even his puns, which are few, will bear a second thought. Gibbon's style, he says, is much too grand. " He *cannot* mention Asia *Minor*."[16]

Of Bagehot's epigrams, and of the difficulty of discussing them apart from his wit, I have already spoken. I have referred also to the sparkling comments which he scatters through his narratives. Many of these are delightfully whimsical and rather kindly, and might be thought not so much wit as a kind of lesser humour, or better yet, perhaps, a blend of the two. Theodora, Cowper's sweetheart, " never married. Love did not, however, kill her —at least, if it did, it was a long time at the task, as she survived these events more than sixty years." But then he adds, as though to remove any possible sting from his words: " She never, seemingly, forgot the past."[16] Some of his fun may seem to be mere gaity and to lack point. But let us take an example:

> History, it is said, is of no use; at least a great critic, who is understood to have in the press a very elaborate work in that kind, not long since seemed to allege that writings of this sort did not establish a theory of the universe, and were therefore of no avail. But whatever

may be the use of this sort of composition in itself and abstractedly, it is certainly of great use relatively and to literary men. Consider the position of a man of that species. He sits beside a library-fire, with nice white paper, a good pen, a capital style, every means of saying everything, but nothing to say; of course he is an able man; of course he has an active intellect, beside wonderful culture; but still one cannot always have original ideas. Every day cannot be an era; a train of new speculation very often will not be found; and how dull it is to make it your business to write, to stay by yourself in a room to write, and then to have nothing to say! It is dreary work mending seven pens, and waiting for a theory to " turn up." What a gain if something would happen! then one could describe it. Something has happened, and that something is history.[16]

I am very far from thinking that such wit lacks point. The passage implies a comment upon the whole psychology and motivation of authorship. And in general, though not inclined to find a deep significance in every one of his jokes, I feel that he very seldom fires into the air at random.

In his narratives Bagehot shows an extraordinary grasp of comic idea. In so far as biographical and critical essays can be comedies, " Lady Mary Wortley Montagu " and " Edward Gibbon " are such. Both contain a well-defined comic idea, treated with much skill, if intermittently and with slight detail. In the first essay, Lady Mary Pierrepont, a daring and restless woman of ideas, tempestuously woos and wins, with extravagant hopes of an ideal union, Mr. Wortley Montagu, whom after several years of conjugal life she discovers to be a very dull and timorous male. In the second essay, Gibbon, the comfortable man, is

o

represented in a series of highly unnatural postures and situations. He appears as the religious fanatic who peacefully subsides into scepticism, the lover who prefers a good income to a clever woman, the soldier who would rather dine than fight, the statesman who secretly fears he is the kind of man that a revolutionary mob would guillotine. In both of these narratives Bagehot evinces an extraordinary ability, without perversion of fact or serious omission, to keep his theme steadily and vividly before the mind of the reader. It is perhaps to be regretted that having written so many brief biographies, he never attempted a more extended one.

Chapter XI

AN OLD RELIGION IN A NEW WORLD

It is a commonplace to observe that the Victorian period is distinguished from all others by a tremendous expansion of material knowledge. The result was that men obtained an immensely wider control over the powers of nature, and therefore beyond all previous conception they multiplied physical comforts, devised mechanical contrivances, built factories, railroads, steamships, until, almost with surprise, they found themselves living in a new world. But having created it, what were they to think of it? The Victorian was *par excellence* a century of " problems," of which the chief—since all problems are said ultimately to be religious—was that of adapting an old religion to a new age. How could the possibility of unlimited wealth, luxury, and power be reconciled to Christian asceticism? How was the new illumination to be adjusted to nineteen hundred years of religious experience?

These were some of the difficulties that faced the shopkeepers of England, for nineteenth-century civilization was essentially middle class. Its history is the record of the triumph and bewilderment of that class. In a sense it represents the tragedy of Monsieur Jourdain.

When in 1832 they formally acquired the dominant power in the state, the middle class were for the most part Puritan, but theirs was a Puritanism much deteriorated.   It had been too long in the world, too long in contact with money and commerce.   Puritan piety had become mere respectability, Puritan valour mere efficiency.   They still had what Arnold called " a genius for conduct; " their concepts of duty were in many respects deep and sincere, but had unfortunately been extended, as sometimes happens in a zealous race, to include some of their vices.   One of the principal duties of a nineteenth-century Puritan, for example, was that of making money.   A great fortune was a glorious monument to the Lord.   By 1832 these glories abounded in rank profusion.   The countryside was covered with great brick factories and the sky was filled with chimneys and with smoke. Men rejoiced in their duty and beheld a vision of innumerable factories and smokestacks.   They conceived the digits of their bank balances multiplied into infinity.   What is perhaps even more remarkable, many of them did not forget heaven, nor even hell.   But most of these latter-day Puritans contemplated eternity in the spare moments of an engrossing business career.   God was becoming suspiciously like a golden image.   He moved only to nod approval to the clink of shining coins.   The more cynical members of the middle class gave themselves up to building gingerbread castles and truckling for titles and social prestige.   The more " serious " made money anxiously and piously. They accumulated wealth, and consoled themselves by not spending it.   The strictness of their manners and the sterness of their propriety reconciled them to the vanity of their lives.   Thus, measured by a severe standard, did the majority appear.   It must not be forgotten that the minority contained such men as Thomas Bagehot.

The increasing materialism of the age did not go unchallenged. Newman, Carlyle, Ruskin, and Arnold, themselves the sons of Philistines, denounced it with eloquence and power, and were actually read. It is characteristic of the English nation that these great moralists were widely celebrated and little heeded. They spread some bewilderment among thoughtful men, and that bewilderment was intensified by a set of problems which had forced themselves upon public attention.

There is of course much that is timeless about great minds and great ideas, but until the nineteenth century most ordinary men derived their theories of the visible world from Scripture. The Scriptural accounts, it is true, were not entirely consistent, but theologians were equal to the difficulty, and therefore, according to the general feeling, the material universe was, comparatively speaking, a cosy, cheerful, sinful little place, a sort of ante-room to the awful regions without, the spiritual universe of heaven and hell. All was clearly explained. The earth was about six thousand years old. It had been created, exactly in its present form, by the hand of God. He was occupied with His work for six days; and in that time He had created, with equal finality, the sun, the moon, the stars, all living things, and last of all, man, whom He fashioned in His own image and made the special object of His surveillance. Such a theory, though rather crude, was clear, simple, poetic, and moral. It served excellently to promote a spiritual attitude in ignorant and uncritical minds. But by the early decades of the nineteenth century upper middle class minds were somewhat less ignorant and uncritical. The results of the industrial revolution had given prestige to science and the scientific method. The romantic movement had caused men to look upon nature and the outward world not with fear and suspicion, but with interest and sympathy. Scientific theories were being propounded, scientific discoveries were being made, in every field of investigation. At the opening of the nineteenth century Treviranus in Germany and Lamarck in France set forth " the idea that from forms of life organically simple had arisen all higher organizations by gradual development."[1] It began to appear that the animal kingdom was not a settled hierarchy but an order vast and uncertain, subject to laws of endless change. In 1830 Sir Charles Lyell published his *Principles of Geology*, summing up recent geological study, and proving that the earth was of great age, that mountains, valleys, and the major features of topography, far from being eternal and immutable, were as shifting as the sea sands, building and unbuilding themselves incessantly according to natural laws. In 1859 Charles Darwin brought forth his *Origin of Species*. In that book he not only produced a great body of evidence to prove the fact of evolution, but offered in the natural selection theory what appeared to be the fundamental law of the animate world. The book was received first with ridicule, then with alarm, and finally with every variety of dismay and enthusiasm. The discoveries, so contrary to common religious belief, of Galileo, Copernicus, and Newton were brought before the

public mind more vividly than ever before. Most
orthodox thinkers held that Christianity depended
on revelation, and now revelation had in many
particulars been proved wrong. What was to be
done?

Kant had solved the difficulty—in so far as mere
logic could solve it—some sixty years before. He
maintained that there are two worlds, or aspects,
of experience. One is material and accessible only
to the senses and the ordinary reason. The other
is spiritual and known solely to the moral, or
" practical," reason. Each variety of reason is
supreme over its own sphere, and may not pronounce authoritatively upon that of the other. Of
the realm of spirit, a man can believe as his heart
dictates, without restricting his freedom, within
the realm of sense, to doubt or accept as reason
requires, for science can no more disprove the
existence of an unseen world of spiritual entities
than religion can lay down dogmas concerning
the world of sense.[2] Several English thinkers, like
James Martineau and his friends Hutton and
Bagehot, attempted a solution to the contemporary
religious problem with the aid of Kant's distinction.

Perhaps this distinction is somewhat facile.
Man conceives of other worlds in terms of the
images which he has formed of this, and though,
logically, he is perhaps free to believe in any kind
of heaven he chooses, he will probably be less
satisfied with one whose material aspects contradict
his knowledge of material phenomena.

But many Victorians were led not merely to
reform heaven, but to abolish it entirely. Indeed
imagination, even more than reason, induces belief.

The neat, bright walls of the old little world had fallen away, and men had found themselves in a great, mysterious universe, infinitely complex and splendid, dark even with the light of a billion suns, and extending endlessly into the abyss of time and space. The spectacle was fascinating, but there was scarcely room in men's minds for two such worlds. The spiritual receded to an infinite remoteness, and God diminished almost to the vanishing point. Indeed the trend of thought has ever since been toward materialism. The prophets of the new faith were triumphant. Had they not a formula? Newton had provided them with an explanation of the inanimate world, and now Darwin with an explanation of the animate. They had a key, and rejoiced to think of the universe as a keyhole. And who could say what the universe was, and what it might not become, when such an organism as man had arisen from such a thing as protoplasm? Had not England already been filled with factories and smoke stacks? The dignified march of progress had already become a rapid jog-trot. What might one not expect? Many looked forward with confidence to some " far-off divine event," a heaven or millennium to be achieved in time and space, and meanwhile, having relegated fundamental problems to the indefinite future, gloried in the mere activity of making money or accumulating fact.[3]

Others again, though fallen in spite of themselves into a sceptical attitude of mind, longed for the peace and security of faith. Such men as Arthur Hugh Clough and the youthful Matthew Arnold found themselves

" Wandering between two worlds, one dead,
The other powerless to be born."[4]

Some few, like Newman, mounted to a haven of
faith on a ladder of fine-woven logic. We may feel
that Newman was unmodern in his disparagement
of the intellect and narrow in his estrangement
from ordinary life, yet we must admire the beauty
and loftiness of his spiritual life: few modern
existences have shown so much sheer dignity. But
by far the majority of thinking Victorians slipped
into some form of compromise, and of such men
Tennyson, oscillating complacently between the
opposite poles of medieval spirituality and modern
materialism, is perhaps the most conspicuous
example. Certainly no age, with the possible
exception of the present, has shown so much mental
power and activity together with so little deep and
consistent sense of fundamental reality.

Bagehot's solution to the contemporary religious
problem is characteristically astute. It does not
involve compromise, but mediation. We should
strive, he says, " ' to make the best of both
worlds.' "[5] We must not presume to know too
much of the spiritual, nor allow ourselves to make
too much of the material. We must live humbly in
the one, moderately in the other, and broadly and
humanly in both, aspiring above all to develop a
healthy soul in a healthy body.[5]

Bagehot has one of those broad minds which
narrow people think inconsistent. I have referred
to him as a man of the world. He was also a
man resigned to the world. His attitude of mind
is in several respects typically religious, and like
all religious men he evinces a natural distrust of

ordinary life. " If there be," he declares, " any
truly painful fact about the world now tolerably
well established by ample experience and ample
records, it is that an intellectual and indolent happiness is wholly denied to the children of men." We
are bound to petty cares and petty toils. We are
" basely subjected to the yoke of coin." And in
deeper, more serious vein he speaks in the same
essay on " William Cowper," as perhaps I need
scarcely remind the reader, of the " dark realities
which are, as it were, the skeleton of our life."[5]

To a large degree the world is of course what
men make it, and one of the principal reasons why
Bagehot distrusted it so much was that he understood men so thoroughly. Few writers have
observed their fellows, good and bad, in so many
different walks of life, with so much clear, cold
detachment. He knew how weak is altruism, how
feeble is reason, how strong is passion, how powerful
is self-interest, how wayward impulse. He knew
how rare and difficult is progress, how short the
distance between savage and civilized man, how
long and tremendous the effort which was necessary
to cover that distance. He saw how little
material progress means moral progress:

> We live among the marvels of science, but we know
> how little they change us. The essentials of life are
> what they were. We go by the train, but we are not
> improved at our journey's end. We have railways,
> and canals, and manufactures—excellent things, no
> doubt, but they do not touch the soul. Somehow, they
> seem to make life more superficial. With a half-
> wayward dislike, some in the present generation have
> turned from physical science and material things.
> " We have tried these, and they fail," is the feeling.

" What is the heart of man the better for galvanic
engines and hydraulic presses?   Leave us to the old
poetry and the old philosophy; there is at least a life
, and a mind."⁶

Even amid the hilarious optimism which followed
the great books of Darwin, Bagehot remained
cautious and sober.

His psychology is traditionalistic, emphasizing,
as I have already observed, the fundamental dualism
of human nature.   Man is made up of a lower and
a higher self: the one essentially animal, and
dominated by the lusts and the desires; the other
essentially human or divine, and dominated by
the conscience or the moral will.   Most men's
lives represent a constant warfare between these
conflicting forces.   Of this ancient conception of
our nature, supported by so much experience
through so many ages, Bagehot has given several
interesting accounts, from which I quote one:

> Some men are born under the law; their whole life
> is a continued struggle between the lower principles
> of their nature and the higher.   These are what are
> called men of principle; each of their best actions is a
> distinct choice between conflicting motives.   One
> propensity would bear them here; another there; a
> third would hold them still: into the midst the living
> will goes forth in its power, and selects whichever it
> holds to be best.   The habitual supremacy of conscience
> in such men gives them an idea that they only exert
> their will when they do right; when they do wrong they
> seem to " let their nature go "; they say that " they
> are hurried away ": but, in fact, there is commonly an
> act of will in both cases;—only it is weaker when they
> act ill, because in passably good men, if the better
> principles are reasonably strong, they conquer; it is
> only when very faint that they are vanquished.   Yet

the case is evidently not always so; sometimes the wrong principle is of itself and of set purpose definitively chosen: the better one is consciously put down. The very existence of divided natures is a conflict. This is no new description of human nature. For eighteen hundred years Christendom has been amazed at the description in St. Paul of the law of his members warring against the law of his mind. Expressions most unlike in language, but not dissimilar in meaning, are to be found in some of the most familiar passages of Aristotle.[6]

This passage also clearly indicates a belief in the freedom of the will, and indeed Bagehot was far too practical a man to give credence to predestination or any variety of scientific determinism. To the doctrine that self-conquest, though difficult and seldom achieved in any high degree, yet lies largely within the power of every man, Bagehot adhered throughout his life, guarding himself repeatedly in *Physics and Politics* from the imputation that in accepting evolution he accepted a mechanistic interpretation of man's nature.

Many thinkers, if they may be so called, seem to regard the universe as an ingenious mechanism with an ingenious defect, a vast piece of machinery potentially perfect and efficient but for one tiny loose bolt. Naturally they know the bolt and are eager to give the necessary twist of the fingers. Needless to say, Bagehot was not such a thinker. From an author so little confident of human nature, so little impressed with the wonders of modern civilization, so distrustful, in short, of what might be called the world in its pride and presumption, one could hardly expect a novelty cure-all or a magic key. He seems to have felt that the really fundamental problems are those that remain with us from generation to generation, and that old-fashioned problems require an old-fashioned solution. The primary difficulty with mankind is man. Every means must be taken to strengthen his moral nature. He needs sound early habits, education, religion, the ethical inspiration of a high and serious literature. Bagehot's conservatism in politics proceeds also from his deep conviction of human frailty. Old customs and traditions are instruments of moral unity and bulwarks against appetite and desire. The constitution of a country is the visible expression of its inward ethical character and the fabric upon which its civilization chiefly depends. Reform should therefore be extremely cautious and gradual.

But if the world is so evil, should not the serious few retire from it and chasten themselves with meditation and self-abasement? So far Bagehot would not go. Never, even in the excesses of youthful romanticism, was he an admirer of cloistered holiness. Solitary contemplation is much easier and pleasanter than virtue practised among the difficulties and temptations of life. " That bodily penance is considered by most men easier than the everyday work of duty," he wrote his mother in 1845, " is quite evident from the history of all religions."[7]

Even more strongly than he objects to monastic, Bagehot objects to morbid, religion, and his ideas upon this subject can perhaps best be summed up as a criticism of Puritans and Puritanism. The " nightmare " which Calvinism conjures up may infuse a little healthy fear and reverence in crude and coarse minds, and a certain exaltation in harsh and insensitive ones, but in proportion as it is vividly realized it is morbid and dangerous: " A prolonged meditation on unseen realities is sufficiently difficult, and seems scarcely the occupation for which common human nature was intended."[8] The toughness of most minds is a natural protection against morbid doctrine. In fact, a low church divine like Dr. Arnold might do great good with his heavy and serious teaching:

> Dr. Arnold was almost indisputably an admirable master for a common English boy,—the small, apple-eating animal whom we know. He worked, he pounded, if the phrase may be used, into the boy a belief, or at any rate a floating, confused conception, that there are great subjects, that there are strange problems, that knowledge has an indefinite value, that life is a serious and solemn thing.[8]

But upon serious, imaginative students like Clough his teaching produced a disastrous effect. It led to morbid introspection, to a strained and exhausted attitude of mind, to " a fatigued way of looking at great subjects."[8] In the gentle, acquiescent mind of William Cowper teaching more harshly Calvinistic led to insanity itself. The Reverend John Newton represents nearly all that Bagehot considers most objectionable in Dissenters.

John Milton embodies all that he considers most admirable, but even in that great poet Bagehot finds, if not the morbidity, at least the harshness, the inhumanity, and the narrow asceticism commonly believed to be the typical vices of Puritan character. Perhaps no better illustration could be found of Bagehot's attitude toward a solitary and meditative religion than in the character study of Milton which

I have quoted in Chapter Ten.[9]   Though guarding himself from expecting too much of the world, Bagehot felt very deeply that to turn from it entirely was a grave mistake—not merely because such an act eliminates a major field of experience, but because it also greatly reduces the possibilities of experience in the remaining field.   We think of both worlds with the same mind and character, and as our life has been in the visible world of men —narrow and confined, or broad and human—so our thoughts and conceptions of the invisible world of the spirit are likely to be.   We should beware, therefore, of an unhealthy one-sidedness. We should also not commit the error of regarding our present life merely as a trial to be endured. Despite occasional hints to the contrary, which reflect a more strictly religious side of his character, Bagehot was in general thoroughly convinced that in this life virtue and intelligence can build a noble and lasting happiness.   It is true that he nowhere explicitly declares this opinion, but the whole trend of his thought implies it and renders it necessary. Certainly he would not so sternly criticize the ascetism of pious men, did he not think that a broad, human existence offered some real and substantial happiness.   But what is the nature of such happiness?

Obviously, it is something which results from " making the best of both worlds."   It is neither a purely religious peace and serenity nor a mere animal complacency.   It is the result neither of an entirely inward, nor an entirely outward working. Indeed, for mere aimless and superficial activity, which was the popular Victorian conception of a significant life, Bagehot had, Victorian business man though he was, the greatest contempt:

> What mankind really wish to economize is thought. Admirable speculators publish beautiful eulogiums on the employment of the faculties, and the universal creed is, that the exertion of the reason is the highest and truest of human enjoyments; yet if a steady observer really looks at actual life, he will see that men never think if they can help it—that they require to be goaded towards it—that they invent devices to avoid it—that, however greedy of enjoyment in other ways, they decline, if possible, to enjoy themselves in this.
>
> One of these devices is activity. People rush to and fro. They are never still. They go to eight committees in a day, taking care to be pretty late at each —they look at their watches the moment they get there —they spurt out rapid errors. If you suggest a little reflection before doing anything, they say, " Don't bother about that *now* "; and when all has gone wrong, they have the ready plea, " I was so occupied, I could not give *it* a thought." In their own circles, such men are always considered wonderful men of business. It is natural their wives and families should believe in them; for they spend so much toil and trouble, they make everybody so uncomfortable, in order to boil a pea, that those who know no better of course suppose that the pea is boiled.[10]

Even to a life of administrative routine, however useful it might be, Bagehot did not attach very high value. Contrasting the management of a joint stock bank with that of a private bank, he explains that the former is presided over by a manager, technically trained for his position and expected to devote his whole time to it:

> But a private bank of the type usual in London has no such officer. It is managed by the partners: now

these are generally rich men, are seldom able to grapple with great business of detail, and are not disposed to spend their whole lives and devote their entire minds to it if they were able. A person with the accumulated wealth, the education, and the social place of a great London banker would be a fool so to devote himself. He would sacrifice a suitable and a pleasant life for an unpleasant and an unsuitable life.[10]

But in seeking to render possible a fuller and nobler happiness, Bagehot would also curtail activity which might be thought a good deal more significant. According to Hutton:

Bagehot held with Sir George Lewis that men in modern days do a great deal too much; that half the public actions, and a great many of the private actions of men, had better never have been done; that modern statesmen and modern peoples are far too willing to burden themselves with responsibilities. He held, too, that men have not yet sufficiently verified the principles on which action ought to proceed, and that till they have done so, it would be better far to act less. . . . He would have been glad to find a fair excuse for giving up India, for throwing the Colonies on their own resources, and for persuading the English people to accept deliberately the place of a fourth or fifth-rate European power—which was not, in his estimation, a cynical or unpatriotic wish, but quite the reverse, for he thought that such a course would result in generally raising the calibre of the national mind, conscience, and taste.[11]

In short, there should be, in the life of a nation, an inward as well as an outward motion. The rough, utilitarian labours inevitable to a mundane existence should be balanced and elevated by an æsthetic, intellectual, and moral working which is vitally necessary to any permanent happiness. These

P

views amount really to nothing else than Aristotle's doctrine of σχολή, or leisure, which Bagehot conceives not, in the anæmic latter day manner, as a kind of æsthetical puttering, but as a way of life merging into the religious idea of a life of contemplation.

Bagehot's conception of happiness is, to be sure, not entirely spiritual. One would hardly expect a banker and economist utterly to condemn wealth, and indeed Bagehot considers it of great importance in making leisure possible and affording the means of rendering it elegant and artistic. Moreover, wealth, like position, which, as we have seen, he also considered very important, is an entry into the great world, and therefore a broadening and socializing influence.[12] Rightly used, it enriches leisure, and connects the delicate, intangible life of the mind with the hard, yet real and vital life of society.

To sum up, happiness depends on a proper balance between labour and leisure, between external and internal action; since the internal, to be broad and human, must be moral, obviously happiness must depend upon the pursuit of virtue and self perfection. Bagehot's idea of perfection, I need scarcely say, is of something large and harmonious. He conceives of virtue humanistically, as of a mean between extremes, an internal symmetry and comeliness, a fine poise and balance of soul. He objects to all excess, even an excess of goodness. " You can say nothing favourable of the first Christians," he says, " except that they *were* Christians. We find no ' form nor comeliness ' in them; no intellectual accomplishments, no caution in action, no discretion in understanding." In short, they were enthusiasts; the whole appeal of their faith was to " unheeding, all-venturing emotion."[13] The humanistic virtues are described and recommended in many ways and under many circumstances in Bagehot's writings. They are at the basis of his conception of English national character, and, as I have already in part observed, of his conception of the ideal writer:

> If any one were asked to describe what it is which distinguishes the writings of a man of genius who is also a great man of the world from all other writings, I think he would use these same words, " animated moderation." He would say that such writings are never slow, are never excessive, are never exaggerated; that they are always instinct with judgment, and yet that judgment is never a dull judgment; that they have as much spirit in them as would go to make a wild writer, and yet that every line of them is the product of a sane and sound writer. The best and almost perfect instance of this in English is Scott. Homer was perfect in it, as far as we can judge; Shakespeare is often perfect in it for long together, though then, from the defects of a bad education and a vicious age, all at once he loses himself in excesses. Still, Homer, and Shakespeare at his best, and Scott, though in other respects so unequal to them, have this remarkable quality in common—this union of life with measure, of spirit with reasonableness.[13]

Perhaps even better than he described these virtues, Bagehot illustrated them. Certainly it is not too much to say that he possessed the energy, the courage, the quickness of judgment, the versatility, the broad and practical view, the easy pliancy of a man who has played an important and varied role in the world of affairs, together with the detachment of mind, poise, moderation, and coherent personality of one who has calmly observed life and reflected upon it. In his *Pensées* Pascal writes:

> Je n'admire point l'excès d'une vertu, comme de la valeur, si je ne vois en même temps l'excès de la vertu opposée, comme en Épaminondas, qui avait l'extrême valeur et l'extrême benignité. Car, autrement, ce n'est pas monter, c'est tomber. On ne montre pas sa grandeur pour être à une extrémité, mais bien en touchant les deux à la fois, et remplissant tout l'entre-deux.[14]

Of Bagehot these words are peculiarly true, not merely with regard to a single virtue, but to his character as a whole. He was both a man of action and a philosopher, and he filled the space between.

If such, then, was the general nature of Bagehot's belief, by what process did he arrive at it? What is its logical basis? Though in some respects sympathetic to scepticism he was not really a sceptic— except as few of us are sceptics nowadays, in doubting that all new ideas are necessarily true, or that this gross, substantial world in which we breathe and walk is necessarily the only world.[15] But he was never a sceptic in the sense of attempting to undermine the reasonable certainties of life, nor did he, like Newman, minimize one kind of truth in order to exalt another. Indeed, Bagehot held that excessive doubt paralyses men. Writing " On the Emotion of Conviction," he declares:

> Intense convictions make a memory for themselves, and if they can be kept to the truths of which there is good evidence, they give a readiness of intellect, a confidence in action, a consistency in character, which are not to be had without them. For a time, indeed, they give these benefits when the propositions believed

are false, but then they spoil the mind for seeing the truth, and they are very dangerous, because the believer may discover his error, and a perplexity of intellect, a hesitation in action, and an inconsistency in character are the sure consequences of an entire collapse in pervading and passionate conviction.[16]

The plain implication of this essay is that men should feel passionately and vitally beliefs which they have formed with infinite coolness and caution.

Of abstract, metaphysical principles, especially when they were basic and sweeping, he disliked to speak, and therefore it is difficult to determine his ultimate logical position, but the key is probably to be found in Kant, of whom in his youth he was an earnest student.[17]   Bagehot seems to have held the view which I have already explained, that there are two distinct spheres of experience and, correspondingly, two methods of arriving at belief.   In the material sphere one arrives at belief from the evidence of the senses and the operation of reason; in the spiritual sphere, from the operation of reason and the intimations of the conscience.   Neither mode of thought can legitimately intrude upon the proper field of the other.   " Free, unprejudiced investigation of the facts and laws of the phenomenal world can never touch the foundations of faith. Natural science can lead to the knowledge only of the realm of the law of things.   It cannot give us the inner moral sense of those things."[18]   Likewise, theology cannot pronounce upon such matters as the origin of the world and the evolution of species. Indeed, without ever throwing theology or dogma overboard, Bagehot seems to have receded during the course of his career from a typical high Anglican position to one which involved denial of the literal truth of Scripture and assumption of a thoroughly modern attitude. He appears from an early time in his career as a writer to have been influenced both by German Biblical criticism and by the discoveries of modern science—particularly in the field of biological evolution. Writing in 1862 on " Clough's Poems," he observes that the human concept of God is evolutionary:

> The divinities of Olympus were in a very plain and intelligible sense part and parcel of this earth. . . . The God with whom the Patriarch wrestled . . . might have been wrestled with even if he was not; he was that sort of person. If we contrast with these the God of whom Christ speaks—the God who has not been seen at any time, whom no man hath seen or can see, who is infinite in nature, whose ways are past finding out—the transition is palpable.[19]

Certainly this passage does not suggest a literal belief in the Old Testament, and *Physics and Politics*, which applies evolutionary ideas to the study of society, is but a long, implicit denial of such a belief. Hutton writes of Bagehot:

> Certainly he became much more doubtful concerning the force of the historical evidence of Christianity than I ever was, and rejected, I think, entirely, though on what amount of personal study he had founded his opinion I do not know, the Apostolic origin of the fourth Gospel. Possibly his mind may have been latterly in suspense as to miracle altogether, though I am pretty sure that he had not come to a negative conclusion.[20]

Though more and more in his later days he tended to become the political and economic scientist, and was in general much impressed with the future of the scientific method; yet he never in any sense fell into unbelief or irreligion. Accepting the doctrine of evolution by natural selection, Bagehot never took a materialistic view of that doctrine. " Indeed, in conversation with me on this subject," relates Hutton, " he often said how much higher a conception of the creative mind, the new Darwinian ideas seemed to him to have introduced, as compared with those contained in what is called the argument from contrivance and design."[20]

And yet, despite his admiration for science, Bagehot seems, like Kant, to grant pre-eminence to the faculty of spiritual, rather than of physical, perception. But how, it may be asked, can such pre-eminence be conceded when the perceptions of that faculty have so little objective value? Is there not the greatest disagreement as to what constitutes spiritual truth? Do not many deny even such doctrines as the freedom of the will, the frailty of man, the fundamental dualism of his nature, and the necessity of self-discipline to the attainment of lasting happiness? Bagehot replies that although great differences certainly exist, there is among the wise and the best a significant uniformity:

> Persons who give credence to an intuitive conscience are so often taunted with the variations and mutability of human nature, that it is worth noticing how complete is the coincidence, in essential points of feeling, between minds so different as Butler, Kant, and Plato. We can scarcely imagine among thoughtful men a greater diversity of times and characters. The great Athenian in his flowing robes daily conversing in captious Athens —the quiet rector wandering in Durham coalfields—

the smoking professor in ungainly Königsberg, would, if the contrast were not too great for art, form a trio worthy of a picture. The whole series of truths and reasonings which we have called the supernatural religion, or that of conscience, is, however, as familiar to one as to the other, and is the most important, if not the most conspicuous, feature in the doctrinal teaching of all three.[21]

In a later writing, " The Ignorance of Man," he amplifies this view:

Beliefs altogether differ at the base of society, but they agree, or tend to agree, at its summit. As society goes on, the standard of beauty, and of morality, and of religion also, tends to become fixed. The creeds of the higher classes throughout the world, though far from identical in these respects, are not entirely unlike, approach to similarity, approach to it more and more as cultivation augments, goodness improves, and disturbing agencies fall aside.[21]

It is characteristic of one so detached as Bagehot that he was deeply influenced by men with whom he fundamentally disagreed. Certainly the two greatest influences upon his religious thought were Butler and Newman, yet against both he clearly felt a primary objection. They were too anxiously pious, too morbidly introspective. Their humanity was exalted, but not rich.

Perhaps of the two he was really more in sympathy with Butler, of whom in many respects he was the antithesis, for Butler was a shy, lonely, melancholy man, essentially a scholar, readier with his pen than his tongue, and caring little for the world or society. As a thinker he was confused and obscure —in Bagehot's vivid phrase, a " groper," feeling his way slowly and painfully to truth and fallacy.

On the other hand, he also resembled Bagehot in many ways. He was cautious, conservative, and practical. Though not a man of the world, he was as Bishop of Durham necessarily a man of affairs, and, like Bagehot, always wrote with a vivid sense of the everyday world outside his study window. He argued for the Christian mysteries on prudential grounds, shrewdly urging that it is safer to believe than to deny, and indeed his writings are a quaint and curious mixture of the prose of caution and the poetry of resignation.[22] Moreover, he tended to see virtue and truth in dull, prosaic people. He detested facile, abstract speculation, and preferred humble and reverent common sense to confident and presumptuous talent.[22] Altogether he was the kind of man Bagehot would consider " solid," and from whom he would be inclined to take suggestions. Of these suggestions, which are highly important to Bagehot's religious thought, I shall speak more fully later.

Newman's literary genius, his exalted life and character, his profound religion and dramatic conversion wrought a powerful fascination in the youthful Bagehot, who became a considerable admirer of the Church and even celebrated it in religious verse. In soberer years he took revenge with sharp criticism upon the great man by whom, in spite of himself, he had been influenced and moulded. Probably he never thought seriously of becoming a Catholic. He saw the enormous value of the Church as a repository of religious experience and an instrument of spiritual government, but he feared also, as Hutton puts it, " her tendency to use her power over the multitude for purposes of a

low ambition."[23] He seems also to have dreaded
her power over the cultivated and unusual mind.
She permits too little spiritual and intellectual
liberty.   Into the natural and symmetrical growth
of the free individual she interposes a violent and
constraining hand.   The typical Catholic, in
Bagehot's opinion, is too ready to believe at command, to force his own reasonings and intuitions
into conformity with the rigid law of the Church.
Newman scarcely attempts a searching and disinterested inquiry, and therefore, though amazingly
skilful in discovering the weaknesses of other men's
creeds, he does little to find and state a distinct basis
for his own.[24]

Yet Bagehot has also much in common with
Newman.   In fact he is himself in some measure
guilty of the very same faults.   I do not mean that
he opposes disinterested inquiry; but he does, like
Newman, distrust the intellect and magnify the
role of the imagination.   Man is not a reasoning
and sceptical, but a credulous and superstitious,
animal.   Regarding habit and imagination as
dominant factors in our nature, Bagehot also
resembles Newman in emphasizing the value of old
traditions and old institutions.

He was likewise imbued with the feeling—which
P. E. More finds so characteristic of Newman and
of " all deeply religious minds—that material
phenomena are unreal and that the only realities are
God and the soul."[25] To him, as to Newman, this
world of sight and sound, of creeping rivers and heavy
skies, of crowded streets and droning court rooms
seemed often highly incredible, a vast and intricate
veil concealing greater and more permanent

realities.[26]   This idea Bagehot expresses many times—and in Newman's own words. But that he had Newman's sense of the nearness of God, that he rested so tenaciously " in the thought of two and only two absolute and luminously self-evident beings, myself and my Creator," there is little reason to believe.[27] Seldom in his familiar letters and even more seldom in his formal writings has he expressed anything like strong personal feeling toward the Deity, or indeed like religious fervour. " I do not think that the religious affections were very strong in Bagehot's mind," writes Hutton, " but the primitive religious instincts certainly were."[28]   From any elaborate attempt such as Newman made to picture the invisible regions, to people them with spirits, to endow God with the qualities of personality, he seems to have shrunk with the instinctive fear of a practical man. As it appears in his published works, his religion has none of the splendour and brilliance of mysticism. It penetrates beyond external appearances, but chiefly to a moral reality. It is pre-eminently, and I think deeply, moral, a religion of action rather than of vision.

Newman's approach to the subject of religion is mainly psychological, and it was doubtless that element in his thought which attracted his young admirer. Bagehot frequently quotes him upon the subtleties of belief and, like him, as I have already hinted, makes conscience " the essential principle and sanction of religion in the mind."[29] In his essay on " Bishop Butler " Bagehot distinguishes two kinds of religion, natural and supernatural. The first arises from contemplating the beauties of external nature and is another curious instance of the seriousness with which he regarded the pantheism of Wordsworth. Of supernatural religion Bagehot writes in close parallel to Newman:

But . . . there is a religion of another sort, a religion the source of which is within the mind, as the other's was found to be in the world without; the religion to which we just now alluded as the religion (by an odd yet expressive way of speaking) of *superstition*. The source of this, as most persons are practically aware, is in the conscience. The moral principle (whatever may be said to the contrary by complacent thinkers) is really and to most men a principle of fear. The delights of a good conscience may be reserved for better things, but few men who know themselves will say that they have often felt them by vivid and actual experience. A sensation of shame, of reproach, of remorse, of sin . . . is what the moral principle really and practically thrusts on most men. Conscience is the condemnation of ourselves. We expect a penalty. . . . How to be free from this, is the question. How to get loose from this—how to be rid of the secret tie which binds the strong man and cramps his pride, and makes him angry at the beauty of the universe— which will not let him go forth like a great animal, like the king of the forest, in the glory of his might, but restrains him with an inner fear and a secret foreboding, that if he do but exalt himself he shall be abased; if he do but set forth his own dignity, he will offend ONE who will deprive him of it. This, as has often been pointed out, is the source of the bloody rites of heathendom.[30]

" Of course," continues Bagehot with a touch of his characteristic humour, " it is not this kind of fanaticism that we impute to a prelate of the English Church."[30] And yet, even in the elegant and refined religion of a rector of Stanhope and a

Bishop of Durham there remains, to be sure in a more exalted form, the same anxiety, the same consciousness of sin.

From these two kinds of religion, according to Bagehot, arise two divergent conceptions of the Deity: one, of a cheerful, comforting Being, whose smile, as it were, shines through all the forms of external nature; the other, of a watchful, jealous God, whose eye searches unceasingly the depths of the heart. The great problem of religious philosophy is how to reconcile these two conceptions. " How do we know that the Being who refreshes is the same as He who imposes the toil, that the God of anxiety is the same as the God of help? "[30] The solution to the difficulty lies in the assumption of an absolutely perfect Being. Upon this assumption Bagehot, like Butler, insists at considerable length.[31] He continues:

> It follows from the very idea and definition of an infinitely-perfect Being, that He is within us, as well as without us—ruling the clouds of the air, and the fishes of the sea, as well as the fears and thoughts of man—smiling through the smile of Nature, as well as warning with the pain of conscience.[32]

This statement is an interesting example of how far Bagehot could go in the direction of modern monism. But it should not be given an extreme interpretation, for with indiscriminate pantheism, or monism, he had fundamentally very little sympathy. The discussion as a whole is also noteworthy as a rather superficial treatment of what Bagehot, throughout his career, seems to have considered the central problem of religion: the reconciliation of the outward world with the inward, of superficial appearance with underlying reality. The most complete formulation of Bagehot's religious ideas appears in the essay on "The Ignorance of Man." The title is significantly the same as that of a sermon by Butler. Both writers see a necessity, and indeed a benefit, in our ignorance of the universe in which we live. Butler explains this ignorance as a valuable part of man's moral probation. It is nobler and more difficult to act virtuously with little, than with great knowledge. Knowing little of God's ultimate nature, we must have faith in Him. Knowing little of His justice, we must put trust in Him and do our duty. These bare ideas Bagehot develops into an elaborate, ingenious little system by which he explains the moral and religious significance of very nearly everything under the sun. The problems which he attempts to answer are those fundamental ones with which Butler also, in *The Analogy* and throughout his works, is continually occupied: the relation between morality and religion, between the visible and the invisible world.

Bagehot begins his essay on " The Ignorance of Man " by pointing out that between morality and religion there is an inconsistency; the one demands that we do good disinterestedly, the other offers us the reward of heaven and threatens the punishment of hell. The solutions commonly proposed are really no solutions at all. It is maintained that the desire for eternal life, by the very nature of the object, is raised above ordinary selfishness. Or it is said that the Gospel is merely common sense. " It aims to persuade sensible men of this world, on sufficient reasons of sound prudence, to sacrifice the present world in order to gain the invisible one."³² But how can a religion of self-sacrifice be reconciled with selfishness? Again it is urged, and with much more ingenuity, that men are " partly disinterested and partly not disinterested. They are desirous of doing good because it is good, and they are desirous also of having the reward of goodness hereafter."³² Yet man's nature is such that if you strengthen one of two co-operating motives, you weaken the other. If men saw heaven as clearly as St. Paul's, they would no more think of doing evil than of committing murder in the open street.

The reason why we conceive religion morally is that we ourselves are moral. " Our only ground for accepting an ethical and retributive religion is the inward consciousness that virtue being virtue must prosper, that vice being vice must fail." From these axioms we infer " a continuous eternity, in which what we expect will be seen."³² The natural theologian cannot improve upon this solution, for, arguing from evidences of design in visible creation, he can only show that God is clever, not ethical, nor immortal, nor capable of endowing His creatures with immortality. The believer in Revelation, also, is obliged to admit that the basis of his belief lies in his moral nature, for unless he is inwardly aware that God is veracious, he can place no credence in His word. The soundness and health of a man's religion depends on the soundness and health of his morality. " A superstitious mind permits a certain aspect of God's character, say its justice, to obtain an exclusive hold on it, to tyrannize over it."³³ Conscience is thus very nearly destroyed by the very idea which it originally suggested; true virtue becomes impossible. Or such a mind, depending upon Scriptures too exclusively, may forget their moral foundation, and so lose all sense of doing good disinterestedly. Its creed then becomes " an isolated terrific tenet," which may work all manner of hideous deformity.[33]

The whole structure of creation is so designed as to make men sound moralists. Why is the physical world so utterly irrelevant to the ethical, so full of unmeaning ingenuity and cleverness? It is a mere screen, a passing show to divert the eye. It is a-moral in order that it may distract our attention from heaven and hell, and lead us to act without anticipation of ultimate reward or punishment. Why is human life so pitifully short? If men lived forever the consequences of good and evil would become so clear as to make a free, disinterested attitude impossible. " The physical world now rewards what we may call the physical virtues, and punishes what we may call the physical vices."[33] On pain of ill health and legal punishment, it teaches moderation, prudence, courage, pertinacity, and civic restraint. It inculcates the preparatory virtues, and produces the sound-bodied, moderate, careful pagan out of which the good Christian must be developed. Why is the bulk of mankind apparently so completely bereft of any real significance? Why is it that they " lead a life in great part neither good nor evil, neither wicked nor excellent "? Why are they so torpid, so " decent in their morals, respectable in their manners, stupid in their conversation "?[33] To be sure, in order that the few may do good disinterestedly. If one half of society were extremely good and one half extremely bad, the happiness consequent to the one state and the misery consequent to the other would be so evident as to make conscience totally unnecessary. Our conceptions of duty must also be various and uncertain. Otherwise an " accumulated public opinion " would arise and destroy our virtue. And for the same reason the moral personality of God must, above all, be obscured from us.

But what of the religious or moral intuition upon which all this argument rests? Is it not often misleading, obscure, vague? It does indeed in primitive states of society give rise to a surprising variety of gods, superstitions, and rituals, but where men have attained to a high degree of culture, it forms the basis of a teaching which is surprisingly uniform the world over.

Whatever this essay may indicate—and with its latent obscurantism, its hard sanity, and its rather confident cleverness, it is with all its clarity extremely puzzling—certainly it reveals Bagehot as a distinctively ethical thinker. He would preserve the image of heaven only insofar as it does not interfere with man's harmonious development in this world. His true concern is with morality, and that morality, I need scarcely say, is humanistic.

The main emphasis throughout is upon the cultivation in man of a rounded and delicately proportioned character. We should build up the health of the body, as well as the health of the soul. We should avoid all excess, even—and here Bagehot's characteristic obscurantism becomes evident—an excess of knowing. We should guard

Q

against forming too clear an image of God's justice, or His wrath, or indeed any phase of His personality, for in so doing we are forced into a spiritual attitude which is strained and unnatural. And by no means should we, mere screen or veil though it is, neglect this world, for at the very least it affords an arena in which the whole of man's faculties may receive harmonious development. Finally the aristocratic tendencies of the humanist are conspicuous. The great majority of mankind are regarded as having very little moral significance, either for good or for bad. According to the plain implications of the argument, they merely form a background against which the extraordinary man may test and develop his virtue. For it is in him alone that virtue can enjoy that varied and harmonious development which Bagehot considers significant.

Several of the leading ideas in the essay are of course not very new or startling. Medieval theologians have sufficiently insisted that the world is a snare and a deception. They have told us that we must not presume to great knowledge. But the really striking feature of the essay is the great cleverness and ingenuity with which nearly everything is explained by a single principle: that ignorance makes man a sound moralist. The paradox becomes strangely convincing. Never was obscurantism so clear, nor metaphysics so solid and substantial. " The Ignorance of Man " reads like the account not so much of a religious creed or an abstract philosophy, as a scientific hypothesis, the kind of theory which a brilliant scientist might form and leave for the patient verification of after ages. In a hard, rationalistic moment one shrewdly suspects that Bagehot is right. Certainly, despite some weaknesses, his theory is peculiarly attractive to the reason. It is comforting for a clever man to feel the universe is so cleverly designed. But for the very reason that it is so hard, so rational, so ingenious, so pat, this philosophy does not satisfy the religious sense. Man does not want to believe that his best light is darkness, that he must not think too precisely of God for fear of becoming a bad moralist, that this universe which he sees all about him is but a wise hypocrisy and a beneficent deceit. Nor would the true mystic agree that the vivid expectation of a reward is inconsistent with a noble morality. A man may begin by doing good in the selfish hope of future payment and end by doing good for the love of God. Eventually he may look forward to heaven not with a narrow and personal emotion, but with a pure and selfless joy, anticipating the heavenly judgment not as a mere personal reward, but as the occasion and the means of a closer communion with God.

I certainly do not mean to imply that " The Ignorance of Man " is mere rationalism. It has none of the petty pride and presumption of rationalism:

> We must not be invited to approach the Holy of Holies without being made aware, painfully aware, what Holiness is. We must know our own unworthiness ere we are fit to approach or imagine an Infinite Perfection. The most nauseous of false religions is that which affects a fulsome fondness for a Being not to be thought of without awe, or spoken of without reluctance.[34]

Yet Bagehot's religion, though deep and genuine, could scarcely be called exalted and mystical. One has only to compare him with such men as Edmund Burke and John Henry Newman. There is no talk of angels in Bagehot. There is no vision out into the Empyrean, no speculation above the stars, no sovereign contempt of the world. Moreover, having no intense and absorbing image of God, no oppressive sense of His omnipotence, Bagehot has none of the mystic's harsh insistence on the naked and shivering weakness of man. Compared to Burke, he seems almost confident of human nature; he seems rather at home in the world; his religion seems almost comfortable and easy.

In general Bagehot's is a religion not so much of exalted meditation as of wise and moderate conduct. It is a religion of balance and sanity, rather than of poetry and intensity. Despite its freshness of statement and its novelty of idea, it is of course very old. Great conservatives of every age would feel at home with it and agree to its basic principles. Indeed, as Bagehot himself says of Bishop Butler:

> It is much in every generation to state the ancient truth in the manner which that generation requires; to state the old answer to the old difficulty; to transmit, if not discover; convince, if not invent; to translate into the language of the living, the truths first discovered by the dead.[34]

Chapter XII

THE POLITICS OF A NATURAL ARISTOCRAT

PERHAPS no writer has been more irreverent toward his spiritual fathers than Bagehot. Nearly everything he wrote on politics reveals the influence of Burke, yet nearly everything he wrote of Burke is sharp and critical. He exalted—and very rightly— the younger Pitt above the great Whig as a practical statesman, yet neglected to remark how much more than a practical statesman Burke was.[1] He cites the latter as an example of excessive party zeal:

> No one's reasons are more philosophical; yet no one who acted with a party went further in aid of it or was more violent in support of it. He forgot what could be said for the tenets of the enemy; his imagination made that enemy an abstract incarnation of his tenets.[1]

There is much keenness and much justice in this estimate. Certainly Burke was guilty of ludicrous exhibitions, of serious indiscretions, of grave mis-judgments—even of positive moral error. Frequently he behaved like a man possessed. He was carried away not merely by his passions, but by truth itself. Consequently, though he must on the evidence of his great published speeches always stand in the first rank as a philosopher, he deserves, as Bagehot saw, only a lesser place as a politician and a statesman. His total career presents a splendid tragic spectacle in which the sublimity of universal genius and the excess of heroic character are diminished by the comedy of the passionate and melodramatic Irishman.

Bagehot's hostility is of course characteristic. He could not hero-worship Burke because Burke was a hero. Indeed, what other man, existing in a prosaic age, plodding in the humdrum world of affairs, has ever been so truly a hero? Nearly all his failings resulted not from the cold meanness of vice, but from the noble excess of virtue. In all his words and all his actions there was the same unflagging depth and vehemence of feeling, the same massiveness of character, the same loftiness and purity of insight. He was a kind of tragic protagonist, strangely going on and on after the fifth act, playing his magnificent role endlessly in an unappreciative world. His great speeches remind us of the soliloquies of Hamlet and the outbursts of Othello. They were such as angels might listen to, though the House of Commons would not. His philosophy was a Ulysses's bow. No lesser mind could have bent it. Analysed narrowly and superficially to its logical consequences, it seems a mass of contradictions. Conceived as Burke conceived it, it seems the highest wisdom. Had Shakespeare been a political philosopher, he probably would have been such a political philosopher as Burke.

And had Burke flourished in 1850 Bagehot would never have voted for him. Bagehot had a firm conviction that affairs are dull, and best managed by dull men. He gave his approval to Sir George Cornewall Lewis, and sagely suspected the clever men. And yet his philosophy is so like Burke's that if the latter could be called the poetry, Bagehot might be called the prose, of conservatism.

Their approach to the study of politics is in many respects the same. Both insist upon constant observation of the facts, upon constant reference of idea to reality. Both are reluctant to enunciate a universal principle. Both abhor that abstract, *a priori* type of reasoning which deduces a whole theory from a few half truths, or produces an elaborate paper constitution from a logical vacuum. " I must see the men, I must see the things! " exclaims Burke. " I never govern myself, no rational man ever did govern himself by abstractions and universals . . . : he who does not take circumstances into consideration is not erroneous, but stark mad—*dat operam ut cum ratione insaniat*— he is metaphysically mad."[2]

Nothing [writes Bagehot] is such a bore as looking for your principles—nothing so pleasant as working them out. People who have thought, know that inquiry is suffering. A child stumbling timidly in the dark is not more different from the same child playing on a sunny lawn, than is the philosopher groping, hesitating, doubting and blundering about his primitive postulates, from the same philosopher proudly deducing and commenting on the certain consequences of his established convictions. On this account Mathematics have been called the paradise of the mind. . . . Read in Bacon, the beginner of intellectual philosophy in England, and every page of the *Advancement of Learning* is but a continued warning against the tendency of the human mind to start at once to the last generalities from a few and imperfectly observed particulars.[3]

Bagehot not only condemns sweeping generalization and facile deduction. He believes also in the words of Burke, that " nothing universal can be rationally affirmed on any moral or any political subject."

> Burke first taught the world at large . . . that politics are made in time and place—that institutions are shifting things, to be tried by and adjusted to the shifting conditions of a mutable world—that, in fact, politics are but a piece of business—to be determined in every case by the exact exigencies of that case; in plain English—by sense and circumstances.[3]

In short, both writers held with Aristotle that politics is not capable of scientific universality and exactitude. No universal laws, no algebraic formulæ, no science of politics is possible. *Physics and Politics* may seem to indicate that Bagehot came later to think the contrary. And indeed he did attempt to explain human society in terms of biological laws, but with important reservations. Society, he insists, is infinitely complex: "No nation admits of an abstract definition; all nations are beings of many qualities and many sides; no historical event exactly illustrates any one principle; every cause is intertwined and surrounded with a hundred others."[3] Natural selection can explain human phenomena only in a rather general and superficial manner. It can explain the mechanics of physical, but not of moral, causes, and moral causes create the physical. There is no law of the conservation of moral energy.[3]

In his extremely able book on *The Political Philosophy of Burke*, Professor MacCunn remarks of the great statesman:

> No one can go far into his pages without becoming aware that his thought is profoundly influenced by convictions which he takes for granted. Some of them are psychological, and some are metaphysical. That man is 'a religious animal'; that he is likewise a 'political animal'; that all ordinary men are creatures

in whom feeling, habit, even prejudice are apt to be stronger than reason; that they act on motives relative to their interests far more than on theories; that they are much quicker to feel grievances than to find remedies—these are amongst the principles of his psychology. He does not prove them. He does not feel himself called upon to prove them.[4]

But does he need to prove them? Such beliefs are to be sure incapable of scientific proof. They cannot be tried in the laboratory, nor verified with statistics. Yet mere assumptions they are not. They are substantiated by human experience, for they lie at the basis of man's soundest moral and religious traditions, whose fruits through many centuries have commonly been happiness and virtue, as those of specious philosophies have been misery and degradation.

Bagehot, like Burke, adheres to these psychological doctrines, as well as to certain other conceptions much more definitely metaphysical. Both believe in a perfect and omnipotent God and in His providence. Burke's ideas on this matter go farther and are a good deal more precise than Bagehot's. Politics, in a sense the most worldly of all subjects, he regarded from an unworldly point of view. This immediate earthly life in which he laboured so earnestly and struggled so passionately, he considered after all but a fleeting shadow across an immensely greater spiritual reality. His attitude was basically religious. At its centre was a brilliant moral imagination and a profound spirit of Christian humility. He believed all that is virtuous in our nature proceeds from God, and all that is weak, from our inherent frailty. We must be everlastingly grateful for the one, and strive everlastingly against the other. God has been good: " He who gave our nature to be perfected by our virtue," writes Burke, " willed also the necessary means of its perfection. He willed therefore the State—He willed its connection with the source and original archetype of all perfection."[5] Burke might be called a political mystic. Preferring peace to truth, he considers it dangerous to form a sharp, elaborate image of heaven, but he does establish a kind of secular heaven in the past. If God willed the state, then he willed all the moral effort which contributed to its formation—all the great and virtuous deeds, all the heroic and exemplary lives, all the wise laws, all the ethical and social habits so slowly and painfully learned. The march of divine providence is in one of its phases nothing else than the moral evolution of society. The implications of this doctrine are obvious. The slightest civic duty becomes a sacred obligation. Law becomes an object of deepest reverence, always to be implicitly obeyed, and to be changed—if any of human weakness seems to cling to it—only with the greatest caution and piety. In later life, so critical did Burke become of men's interior defects, so reverent of the outward forms of government, that he seemed unwilling to change anything whatever. A man should strive to lead a good life, and not trifle with what God has ordained. If abuses and injustices exist, they are a fit chastening for our sins. And yet it is one of Burke's greatest merits as a philosopher, despite the extreme caution of his old age, that he has managed in so many ways, and so vividly and effectually, to link spiritual truth with ordinary mundane life. Characteristically, he conceives church and state as but two aspects of a single society. This identity, he felt, should be embodied in a national church.

Bagehot is much more worldly minded. He is strongly against any close union of church and state, and though much that he says clearly implies belief in the divine nature of society and the sacred character of civic duty, yet he is reticent upon these points, and his usual tone in political discussion is decidedly secular. The reasons are various. He was not extremely eloquent, and he probably felt that he could sway practical men more effectively by solid prose than hollow poetry. It was also one of his principles, as we have seen, that man should not pry too curiously into the ways of God. Finally, his faith, though deep and abiding, was not so intense and compelling as Burke's. He was not troubled by a vision of Paradise.

It is impossible to write of Burke without paradox, for even in his fundamental concepts of government there appears what might be called a wise inconsistency. He speaks of the state as an organism, and as a society of independent individuals held together by " artificial " contract. He speaks of the British Constitution as a mere human contrivance and as a kind of divine revelation. He regards politics as a mere business and as a sacred philosophy. These contradictions can of course be resolved. It may be said that men contrive wisely because they receive divine revelations. Burke himself has on several occasions carefully pointed out that the state is neither an organism nor a mere aggregation of individuals. Human society can be reduced to the laws neither of biology nor of formal logic. Yet, though apparently recognizing the limitations in his theory, Burke has not attempted to rectify them. He has not attempted any clear, logical synthesis. Rather, like a practical statesman, he has preferred to avoid the intricacies of abstract theory and to seize the convenient principle ready at hand, to oppose half truth to half truth. When folly and error have leaned to one extreme, he has leaned to the other. He has been superficially inconsistent but, by and large, remained true to justice and moderation. He has maintained opposite truths, and he has maintained them validly, because he has been large enough to fill all the space that lies between them. Indeed —though this point should not be forced—there may be said to lie at the basis of Burke's philosophy not so much a series of principles as a series of fulcrums. There is not so much a harmony of logic as a harmony and balance of soul.

Burke's reluctance to theorize springs from a variety of causes. As a practical man of action he was impatient of mere ideas. He detested the empty, abstract theorizing of the French revolutionaries. He was something of a mystic and disliked to imprison the living truth within the iron box of formula. He felt that irreverent inquiry destroyed much valuable belief. Above all, he had an Englishman's prejudice against ultimate principles and elaborate systems. In his " Reflections on the Revolution in France " he contrasts the few English revolutionary theorists, like Price and Priestley, with the great body

of conservative English subjects in the following
manner:

> Because half a dozen grasshoppers under a fern
> make the field ring with their importunate chink, whilst
> thousands of great cattle, reposed beneath the shadow
> of the British oak, chew the cud and are silent, pray do
> not imagine that those who make the noise are the
> only inhabitants of the field; that, of course, they are
> many in number; or that, after all, they are other than
> the little shrivelled, meagre, hopping, though loud
> and troublesome, insects of the hour. [5]

Bagehot also has worshipped the British cow,
sometimes solemnly and sometimes mischievously.
And yet, like Burke, he has been preserved from
the effects of his idolatry by the fineness of his
spiritual balance.   I have already tried to explain
that in his literary theory he is at times extremely
inconsistent—and perhaps more reprehensibly than
Burke—without injury to his fundamental soundness.   In his politics he is much less open to
criticism.   It is true that " The Letters on the
Coup D'État " and certain passages in *Physics
and Politics* imply a secular view of the state,
while other passages in *Physics and Politics* seem
to imply a religious view. [6]   At times he encour-
ages a searching, rationalistic attitude in politics,
and again he opposes it.   But in general he is
too cautious to be inconsistent.   He soberly analyses the fact before him, and seldom uses it as
a springboard to project himself into the dizzy
regions of ultimate principle, where inconsistency
is so easy and so glaring.   Few nineteenth-century
political philosophers were content with so little
abstract " system."   One has only to compare

The English Constitution with Mill's *Representative Government.* The first is the flesh and bone of factual analysis. The other seems in contrast but a skeleton of theory. Bagehot analyses the representative government immediately before him. Mill arrives at the ultimate conditions necessary for all good representative governments. Undoubtedly, for much the same reasons as Burke, Bagehot tends to be an obscurantist.

" The Letters on the Coup D'État " are the first of Bagehot's longer and better known political works. They represent an application of the ideas of Burke to a political situation in the nineteenth century. For a man of twenty-five they are an extraordinary production. It is not remarkable that so young a man should write brilliantly, or that he should deal cleverly with ideas, but it is very remarkable that he should see deeply into all the complexity and passion and prejudice of a real situation unfolding itself immediately before him. I have already spoken of that situation: The French republic was dying of fear. Everybody expected a revolution. Trade was at a standstill. The stock market had collapsed. People did nothing but talk in the streets and tremble. Suddenly Louis Napoleon, president of the republic, seized the government and put down the extremists. In his first letter Bagehot maintained that the president was justified, especially if he merely intended to retain control until the will of the people could be ascertained. But then the president brought out a constitution which gave him practically absolute power. The people seemed to approve. In his subsequent letters Bagehot contended for the new arrangement, basing his argument upon two great general principles: that self-preservation is the first law of societies, and that the government of a country should be adapted to its national character.

The first of these, with Burke as well as Bagehot, was an axiom which hardly needed explanation.[7] Civilization cannot exist without a social fabric, and that fabric is the result of infinite effort through many generations. The Prince-President was justified in not permitting momentary passion and violence to destroy what only time could build up again.

In his next letter Bagehot contradicted himself rather unnecessarily. The revolution of 1789, he declared, was an immense benefit to the French nation, precisely because it destroyed the whole social structure of the past and cleared the field for the inventive genius of Napoleon I. Having sacrificed logic to no particular advantage, he then affirmed on the authority of Burke that " politics are made up of time and place " and that " institutions are shifting things, to be tried by and adjusted to the shifting conditions of a mutable world."[7] The events of 1848 had taught people that by far the most important of these conditions is national character. An elaborate paper constitution is but so much paper, if its laws are not vitally adapted to the ἦθος, the social habits and moral capacities, of the nation for which it is intended.

A clever people like the French are, according to Bagehot, quite incapable of self-government. Men who are continually having new ideas unfortunately want to carry them into effect. They see that old laws are imperfect and they wish to abolish them.

They want new governors every week, and a new constitution every month. And yet they agree in nothing except in their hatred of what is old and established. Everybody has his own panacea. Clever people are incapable of corporate discipline. Moreover, the French are extremely impressionable, volatile, excitable, and in the heat of passion they carry every idea to an insanely logical extreme. Obviously, such people must be protected from themselves by a strong executive power. Only gradually, as they grow in calm and stupidity, can they hope for greater freedom and political responsibility.

Stupidity, then, is essential to self-government:

> What we opprobriously call stupidity, though not an enlivening quality in common society, is Nature's favourite resource for preserving steadiness of conduct and consistency of opinion. It enforces concentration; people who learn slowly, learn only what they must. The best security for people's doing their duty is, that they should not know anything else to do; the best security for fixedness of opinion is, that people should be incapable of comprehending what is to be said on the other side.[8]

> . . . . . .

> What I call a proper stupidity . . . chains the gifted possessor mainly to his old ideas; it takes him seven weeks to comprehend an atom of a new one; it keeps him from being led away by new theories—for there is nothing which bores him so much; it restrains him within his old pursuits, his well-known habits, his tried expedients, his verified conclusions, his traditional beliefs.[8]

An important aspect of Bagehot's attitude toward thought is summed up in his concept of stupidity, and therefore I should like to inquire a little into the meaning which he gives the term. " It is no doubt whimsical," observes Woodrow Wilson, " to call ' large roundabout common sense,' good judgment, and rational forbearance ' stupidity '."[9] President Wilson's remark well explains much of the positive significance of stupidity. On several occasions Bagehot does indeed use the word almost interchangeably with " common sense," as for example when he begins an encomium on Sir Robert Peel by exclaiming, " Was there ever such a dull man? " and ends with " Who is like him for sound sense? "[10] The moral connotation of stupidity is perhaps rather inadequately summed up by " rational forbearance." Bagehot, like Burke, tended to draw an opposition between intellect and moral intuition. Mere intellect analyses tradition into absurdity, and conscience into prejudice. Both writers felt also that rational inquiry destroys the moral grandeur of old institutions. In *The English Constitution* Bagehot emphasizes that the crown would lose much of its ancient prestige and ethical power in the nation if its constitutional weakness were generally understood.

The concept of stupidity is identified not merely with common sense and morality. It represents also an objection against certain kinds of thought. The first of these is of course facile abstract logical deduction, which Bagehot detests as heartily as Burke. In " The Letters on the Coup D'État " metaphysical deduction is several times connected with French cleverness, and scientific induction with English stupidity. Sir Leslie Stephen's interpretation is therefore partly correct: " ' Stupidity ' is invaluable just so far as it involves a tacit demand that theories should be checked by plain practical application."[11] But Bagehot does not confine his objection to error and sophistry. As I have already intimated, he shares the British reluctance to pry into first principles. Mr. Robert Lowe, he believed, was not entirely suited to be Chancellor of the Exchequer; he was not, like Mr. Caldwell, " an eminent master " in the art of being dull:

> [Mr. Lowe] cannot help being brilliant. The quality of his mind is to put everything in the most lively, most exciting, and most startling form. He cannot talk that monotonous humdrum which men scarcely listen to, which lulls them to sleep, but which . . . they suppose is " all right." . . . Mr. Lowe always ascends to the widest generalities; the *axiomata media*, as logicians have called them—the middle principles, in which most minds feel most reality and on which they find it most easy to rest—have no charms for him.[12]

Plainly, Bagehot dislikes general principles not merely because they are remote from the facts, but because they are exciting. Indeed, he seems to think nothing so dangerous for a popular government as the habit of uniting thought with excitement. No one who has read at all in the history of revolutionary movements can easily disagree with him. When the multitude grows enthusiastic about ideas and sets itself up as a judge over them, it may learn to prize clarity, brilliance, or cleverness, but seldom truth. For truth is not always adjustable to popular understandings and popular prejudices. It is often resistant to the touch of rhetoric and cannot always be rendered neat and clear, or glamorous and alluring. But error is infinitely pliant. It is better, therefore, that a nation should sleepily respect a dull and prosaic common

sense than that it should intoxicate itself with a
facile and specious cleverness. It is better that
true leaders should pretend to be dull than that
eloquent demagogues should seem to be wise.

Bagehot's antipathy to certain kinds of thought
led him to a noticeable prejudice against all
thought. His suspicion of pre-eminent ability
appears plainly in his under-estimation of Burke
and his over-estimation of Sir George Cornewall
Lewis. It is manifest in his abundant praise of
English stupidity, in his theory that truth is prosaic
and statistical, and in his reiterated contention that
dull government is safe government.[12] In his later
years this tenacious obscuranticism seems more and
more to have conflicted with his growing enthusiasm
for the scientific method, and with the spirit of
free inquiry which that enthusiasm engendered.
Yet in his late essay on " Mr. Lowe as Chancellor
of the Exchequer " he is unable to take a definite
and consistent stand. He asserts that Lowe is too
brilliant to be successful and yet concludes:

> But there is a profound truth in the saying that
> " men of pre-eminent ability are always safe "; not
> of course that so wide a phrase is to be taken exactly
> to the letter, but that there is a " reserve fund " in
> the highest ability which will enable it to pull through
> scrapes, to remedy errors, to surmount disasters, which
> would ruin and bury common men.[13]

In the essay on " Intellectual Conservatism,"
written only five years after " The Letters on the
Coup D'État," he pleads for " a statesmanlike
consideration of problems—a wise and patent weigh-
ing of facts," " a real mastery of the reasons, a real
familiarity with the moral grounds—to say nothing

of the political consequences—of the existing state of things."[13]　Moreover, the longer works of his later years, treatises like *Physics and Politics*, and *The English Constitution*, are in themselves, as Stephen observes, a eulogy and a recommendation of scientific thought.

A word or two more of " The Letters on the Coup D'État " will suffice.　Their manner is cynical and drastic, but their substance cautious and conservative in the extreme.　Bagehot was very far indeed from condemning the French to everlasting despotism.　He merely felt that at the time they were unprepared for complete self-government. The constitution of Louis Napoleon, if faithfully carried out, would afford them a modified freedom which might, with favourable results, be gradually increased.　Perhaps Bagehot's greatest error was in placing any confidence in a mere political adventurer.　It was difficult, however, for a conservative critic to do anything else.　The Prince-President was the one strong man in a distracted nation.

During the fifteen years which elapsed between " The Letters on the Coup D'État " and *The English Constitution*, Bagehot wrote for the journals a great number of shorter political essays. Many of these have permanent value.　Naturally, most of them are first hand studies of the current political situation.　A few are historical.　Bagehot's attitude toward history is that more of the statesman than of the scholar.　He is thorough, accurate, unprejudiced, but he is interested in the past primarily as a means of explaining and illuminating the present.

Perhaps the longest and most significant of the

studies thus undertaken is " The History of the Unreformed Parliament, and its Lessons," an essay of about fifty pages, which appeared in 1860, when electoral reform was beginning once more seriously to be considered. The work is in itself a penetrating analysis of certain principal aspects of the eighteenth-century constitution, and an interesting preliminary to the more elaborate analysis which was to follow seven years later. Bagehot shows no aristocratic prejudice in favour of the eighteenth century. He felt that the older government, despite the many brilliant leaders that graced it, was definitely inferior to its later development. Widespread corruption rendered it weak at precisely the times it should have been strong, for a purchased majority knows no loyalty to opinion: when the minister was victorious, it was steady and powerful; when the minister seemed about to be beaten, it made haste to support the opponent who was most likely to obtain control of the treasury. All Members of Parliament were not corrupt in those days, however, and Bagehot maintains that the unreformed constitution did at least adequately perform one important function of representative government: it represented the intelligent opinion of the country. Had it not done so, had those been permitted to vote who had no enlightened conviction—such was the feeling of the common people that they would probably have chosen the Stuarts and absolutism rather than the Guelphs and liberty. Indeed the clear moral of the " History " is that electoral reform should be exceedingly cautious, that there is no infallibility in numbers, that a great share of power must always be left in the hands of the " wealthier and more instructed classes " who mould the most enlightened public opinion.[13]

The " History" is also a vivid illustration of the manner in which Bagehot perceives behind the maze of political forms the real seat and nature of power. It is this ability, developed early and exerted long, which makes *The English Constitution* so great a book.

Even more keenly perhaps than he read the past, Bagehot read the living scene before him. He studied governments all over the world. Naturally he was interested in the rise of Prussian bureaucracy and in the vicissitudes of French experiment, but to America he turned with peculiar interest, for the United States represented that type of equalitarian democracy toward which England herself was tending. " Lancashire," writes Bagehot, " is sometimes called ' America-and-water ': we suspect it is America and very little water."[14] No doubt he suspected also that Lancashire was becoming an ever more considerable ingredient in the English mixture. In England the franchise had been extended, and class distinctions were fading. In America there was already universal manhood suffrage, and even fewer social distinctions than at the present time. Bagehot observed the results of equalitarianism with close attention. It is true that he never visited America. Perhaps Lancashire was sufficient. But he must have met many Americans in England. He kept up with current American developments, and read extensively in Hamilton, Morris, Madison, and other American political writers. He gives abundant evidence of having studied De Tocqueville's typically French analysis of American democracy. The judgment at which he arrived is not altogether flattering. He greatly admired Washington and respected the aristocratic tradition in American history; he pays high tribute to American political character; but for Jeffersonian democracy he has no enthusiasm. In his opinion, to make the common man supreme in the state is to reduce the whole of political life to his level. It is to make commonplace, vulgarity, ignorance, passion supreme. It is to drive able men out of public life, to expose policy and polity to the momentary whims, the passionate contentiousness, and the unreasoning vanities of the multitude. The wise framers of the American Constitution were well aware of these truths, but being forced to compromise with the extremists, they tried to avoid the dangers of popular government, not by giving dominant power to the educated and propertied classes, but by various ingenious and complicated devices, such as that of the indirect election of the president. " Their ingenuities have produced painful evils, and aggravated great dangers; but they have failed of their intended purpose—they have neither refined the polity, nor restrained the people."[15]

Indeed Bagehot was not a great admirer of the American Constitution. It is absurd to suppose, he declares in " The American Constitution at the Present Crisis," " that the limited clauses of an old state paper can . . . forever regulate the future."[15] American history, and especially the great crisis of the Civil War, reveals that the American Constitution has one great defect: instead of uniting the

executive and the legislature, as in English government, it erects between them a strong and unnecessary barrier. Many unfortunate consequences
result. When the British prime minister cannot
command a majority in the House of Commons, he
either gives way to a minister who can, or he
appeals to the voters in a general election. When
the president of the United States is confronted
by an adverse majority in Congress, he may half-
heartedly carry out measures of which he does not
approve or he may bring government to a standstill. At some of the most important moments of
American history (as when the House impeached
President Johnson at the conclusion of the Civil
War) deadlocks have occurred. Again, American
government is not dramatic; it does not adequately
perform its teaching function; and consequently,
the public are not deeply interested in it. When
the prime minister of England introduces a vital
measure, the opposition bends every effort to
defeat him. There is a great discussion, and great
public excitement. If defeated, the minister resigns.
In America the fate of government almost never
depends on discussion. No matter what they do
or say, American presidents and American con-
gressmen remain in office until the end of their
terms, and therefore, except in extraordinary
instances, the public pays little attention to its
representatives until election time. The habit of
indifference, varied with intervals of intense excitement, grows upon the nation, and is, in Bagehot's
opinion, one of the most serious evils in American
political life.

A third great defect of American government

results from the way in which political parties select candidates for the presidency.   In Bagehot's day, the candidate was chosen by " a very complicated apparatus of preliminary meetings, called caucuses," of which the modern convention is a modification.[15] This method of nomination is, according to Bagehot, " singularly disastrous ":

> Every statesman who has been long tried in public life must have had to alienate many friends, to irritate many applicants by necessary refusals, to say many things which are rankling in many bosoms.   Every great man creates his own opposition; and no great man, therefore, will ever be President of the United States, except in the rarest and most exceptional cases. The object of " President makers " is to find a candidate who will conciliate the greatest number, not the person for whom there is most to be said, but the person against whom there is least to be said.[15]

Many a " dark horse " has won in the presidential race; many an " arch mediocrity " has sat in the presidential chair.   At the outbreak of the Civil War, perhaps the most tragic hour in American history, an unknown was chief executive of the nation.   We have not the Constitution to thank that Abraham Lincoln proved to be a great man. Nor are Americans deprived of the services of distinguished statesmen only through their mode of nominating candidates for the presidency.   In Bagehot's opinion it is not worth a great man's while to be a cabinet officer.   According to the unfortunate theory of the separation of powers, such an official cannot be a member of the legislature.   He is deprived of a parliamentary career. Usually, therefore, he is called to his post without previous political experience and has no political future. Very few cabinet officials have ever become president of the United States. In short, the American Constitution provides no adequate apparatus for the training, testing, and proper selection of great national administrative statesmen.

Undoubtedly, Bagehot's criticism of America is unduly stringent. Not only was the raw, rough, equalitarian young democracy a denial of some of his fundamental ideas, but it was unlovely æsthetically in his eyes. Certainly he overstates the evils which have resulted from defects in the Constitution. We continue to have able presidents. We continue to have able cabinet officers. Rather ironically, in seeing the future of Britain in America, he was even more right than perhaps he imagined, for English democracy has grown like the American not only socially, but politically as well. The English Constitution, the basic principles of which Bagehot seemed to feel were so secure, has come since its golden period more and more to resemble the American.

It is one of the unfortunate characteristics of modern patriotism that nations, as nations, are seldom humble. They feel it a patriotic duty to heed nothing but praise, and fiercely to resent adverse criticism. In America this pious resentment has happily become less fierce. We should not altogether reject Bagehot's judgment of us because it is severe. It is certainly not an entirely false judgment, for its error lies not so much in discovering fictitious faults as in exaggerating real ones. It is the kind of criticism to which Americans should listen.

CHAPTER XIII

THE LONGER WORKS

IN studying the American Constitution, Bagehot
seems to have learned much about the English.
Probably the disadvantages of the separation of
powers in the one brought home to him with
peculiar force the existence, and the value, of the
unification of powers in the other. His essay on
" The American Crisis " contains an illuminating
comparison of the two governments, and in *The
English Constitution* this comparison is elaborated
at length. No doubt he had intended for many
years to write upon the constitution of his country,
for his book shows every mark of careful preparation. Indeed, the whole of his earlier life and
reading was a preparation. One has only to
glance over the titles of his essays to perceive how
wide must have been his reading in the history,
the literature, the biography, the private letters
and the public documents of those centuries in
which the peculiarly modern development of the
constitution took place. Undoubtedly he derived
many suggestions from earlier political theorists.
In De Lolme's *Constitution of England* he found in
embryo his own idea of dividing the constitution
into its effective and dignified parts.[1] In John
Stuart Mill's *Representative Government* he found,
stated as general principles, ideas which proved
peculiarly applicable to the English system—in
particular the ideas that government must perform

a teaching function and that indirect election is excellent " when the electors are not chosen solely as electors, but have other important functions to discharge, which precludes their being selected solely as delegates to give a particular vote."² From the speeches of Edmund Burke he imbibed those fundamental ideas upon government which contributed so much to make his book not merely a photograph of a passing stage of constitutional history, but a philosophical work of permanent significance. The greatest part of his materials were derived of course from personal observation and study of the immediate fact before him—that great spectacle of political and official life which was the momentary embodiment of English government.

Before the publication of Bagehot's book, the orthodox theory was that the British Constitution was made up of a beneficent mixture of monarchy, aristocracy, and democracy, in which each part checked the excesses and the defects of the others. Bagehot was the first authoritatively to deny and refute this view. In order clearly to understand the English Constitution, he maintained, one must recognize that

> it contains a simple efficient part which, on occasion, and when wanted, *can* work more simply and easily, and better, than any instrument of government that has yet been tried; and it contains likewise historical, complex, august, theatrical parts, which it has inherited from a long past—which *take* the multitude—which guide by an insensible but an omnipotent influence the associations of its subjects,

—and particularly of its humbler and more ignorant

subjects.[3] The theatrical parts are of course the
monarchy and the House of Lords. Monarchial
government, as such, is strong government for
two reasons. In the first place, it is intelligible
government, for however complex in administra-
tion and ceremonial, it is essentially simple. " The
action of a single will, the fiat of a single mind, are
easy ideas," but " the nature of a constitution, the
action of an assembly, the play of parties " are
complex and difficult facts.[3] Democracy might
have been comprehensible to the Athenian citizens,
who were really an aristocratic few, but it could
scarcely have been so to their slaves, who constituted
the bulk of the population. A great modern
nation must provide adequate and understandable
government for both classes, and therefore a
constitution like the English, which superimposes
the clarity and poetry of monarchy upon the more
opaque benefits of democracy, presents an ideal
combination. Again, monarchy acquires a peculiar
sanctity in the eyes of men. No one regards the
House of Commons or the prime minister as sacred,
but the king, who owes his position not to human
choice but to ancient right, seems hedged with a
strange divinity. And oddly enough, the king of
England, as he has lost real power, has gained
enormously in his influence over the imaginations
of men, both ignorant and educated, and the
holiness which attaches to his person has come to
inhere also in the laws and institutions of his
government. The English monarch is valuable in
other ways. He is the head of English society. He
symbolizes morality. He is a disguise or screen,
behind which the real rulers of the nation can

change without alarming excitable people. He had certain effective functions: on the advice of his minister he dissolves parliament and creates peers; he names the incoming prime minister, and at least in Bagehot's day, could exercise some real choice when no party had a clear majority in the House; he had considerable influence over foreign policy and possessed, in all the business of government, " the right to be consulted, the right to encourage, the right to warn."[3]

The House of Lords, in its dignified capacity, was also very important. " Nobility is the symbol of mind." It awakens even in the coarsest men " the sensation of obedience. . . . It prevents the rule of wealth—the religion of gold."[4] And even if the respect for rank, like that for gold, is but an idolatry, at least " in the competition of idolatries the true worship gets a chance." But " in reverencing wealth we reverence not a man, but an appendix to a man; in reverencing inherited nobility, we reverence the probable possession of a great faculty—the faculty of bringing out what is in one."[4] As an efficient body the House of Lords could only revise and suspend the legislation of the Commons. If it dared to defy a strongly decided public opinion, the prime minister might advise the king to create a sufficient number of peers to reverse the vote. The advantages of the House of Lords were several. Being wealthy, it was free from the sinister influences sometimes exerted upon the Commons; enjoying its power independently of popular favour, it was independent of the caprices and sudden fluctuations of popular feeling; having ample leisure, it escaped the distracting routine which prevented the Commons from giving proper consideration to important problems. The defects of the House were perhaps even greater. Being made up almost entirely of great landowners, who acquired their position by birthright rather than by competition, and who were trained in habits of idleness rather than of industry, it tended to be partisan, mediocre, and sleepy. Bagehot suggested that these weaknesses might in some measure be remedied by introducing into the House of Lords a considerable number of " life peers," or distinguished men to hold seats during life.

The House of Commons had five principal functions: electoral, expressive, teaching, informative, and legislative. All of these it performed, on the whole, tolerably well. Its great excellence was of course the union of the executive and the legislature. The House itself chose the prime minister. Indeed, because of party alignments, it was continually in an attitude of potential choice. A premier supported by a considerable party majority was reasonably assured of some continuance in office, yet he might not go too far. He might not insist too much on the extreme ideas of his party, or the great number of moderate men, who were in a majority in every English parliament, would vote him down. But parliament itself might not grow too capricious and unruly, or the prime minister could threaten dissolution, and force every member to seek re-election at the polls. Under the British system the crisis came, not as in the American, at regular election intervals, but following an adverse vote upon some crucial public question. There was a great debate, upon which the fate of the ministry, often of the parliament, depended. Therefore the public attended to the debate, and therefore parliament accomplished its teaching function. In Bagehot's day the Commons had not, like the American electoral college, become the mere pledged mouthpieces of the nation. They were too important. They responsibly decided on all vital matters of legislation, and therefore they responsibly decided on who should be chief executive. The premier was actually chosen by the chosen of the nation. Its expressive function the House performed very well, except that it gave no representation to the working classes, which, Bagehot felt, ought to control one or two of the large constituencies. Had they done so, the House would have better fulfilled its informative function. It would have better expressed particular grievances and aired particular complaints. The House passed good laws, though badly formulated; in short, it legislated well, and because it was well led and well chosen. England was a " deferential " country.[4] The many had a traditional respect for the few, not because they had any appreciation of education and ability, but because the authority of education and ability had stood the test of time, gained the prestige of long survival, and was surrounded by theatrical appendages which inspired respect. The people of England therefore preferred to be ruled by men of education and wealth rather than by members of their own class.

The English Constitution is perhaps the best example of Bagehot's mature work. It has not the verve and spirit, the youthful sparkle and brilliance of " The Letters on the Coup D'État," but in closeness of logic, in fullness of analysis, in firmness of organization, in thoroughness of treatment, it is far superior to the " Letters," and indeed unique among Bagehot's writings. It reveals in supreme degree his extraordinary ability to penetrate behind outward forms and appearances to the vital essences of sovereignty and power. It reveals his statesman's gift of political imagination, his ability to predict and visualize the working of proposed new laws and forms. What this gift means to a political writer one can understand by comparing Bagehot's treatment of electoral reforms with that of Mill, or more specifically, Bagehot's rejection of Thomas Hare's electoral plan with Mill's advocacy of it. However much he may admit that men have behaved like sheep in the past, Mill always hopes they will behave like philosophers in the future.[5] Bagehot steadfastly sees men as they are. Altogether, his book presents an amazingly real and vivid picture of the government of a great country. Yet it is the picture of a government which no longer exists. Under its theatrical mask of petrified forms the English Constitution has still continued slowly and subtly to shift and change. Since 1881, party lines have been greatly strengthened. The wide extension of the suffrage has rendered it increasingly difficult for independent candidates to contest elections at their own expense; and as candidates have grown docile, parties have grown more autocratic. Having once learned, under the tutelage of Joseph Chamberlain, the advantages of rigid discipline, they have

s

demanded that their representatives pledge themselves to elaborate programmes and absolute
obedience to certain colourful, much advertised
party leaders. The result is that the House of
Commons has come somewhat to resemble the
American electoral college. Its members have
become mere voting machines, mere delegates
elected to choose and blindly to support a minister.
Cabinet dictatorship has grown with the decline
of the House, and bureaucracy has grown with
the growth of cabinet dictatorship, for government
has extended its sphere too widely, become too
complex and technical, adequately to be controlled and supervised by a handful of party
politicians. The permanent bureaucracy has absorbed so much power that it now threatens to
overshadow British democracy itself.

These tendencies Bagehot foresaw only in part.
Superficially, his book is the classical account of
the Constitution in its golden period—as it once
was; as it may, with the inevitable modifications of
new conditions, again be; but as it is no longer.
Yet essentially, *The English Constitution* is something more than this. It is a true "classic,"
and for several reasons. In the first place, though
it gives no adequate account, it does imply a
penetrating criticism, of the twentieth-century
English Constitution—a criticism which modern
authorities, admirably as they have written on their
subject, might well consider more carefully. Again,
as I have already indicated, Bagehot's book describes
the functions which all representative governments
should perform.[6] Finally, it contains a philosophy
of politics.

This philosophy is of course that, largely inspired by Burke, which I have already described. Certain aspects, however, come out in *The English Constitution* with peculiar prominence, and are worthy of some elaboration at this time. I have already spoken in the chapter on religion of Bagehot's tendency to discount the importance of the lower classes. His political views are not different, and closely parallel those of Burke, whose distrust of the political capacities of the common people is famous: " No legislator, at any period of the world, has willingly placed the seat of active power in the hands of the multitude: because there it admits of no control, no regulation, no steady direction whatsoever."[7] And again: " Indeed, arbitrary power is so much to the depraved taste of the vulgar . . . that almost all the dissensions which lacerate the commonwealth, are not concerning the manner in which it is to be exercised, but concerning the hands in which it is to be placed."[7] Bagehot's view is as realistic, and his language often nearly as violent. He feared nothing more than the extension of the franchise. In " The History of the Unreformed Parliament " he writes:

> The lesson of the whole history indubitably is, that it is in vain to lower the level of political representation beneath the level of political capacity; that below that level you may easily give nominal power, but cannot possibly give real power; that at best you give a vague voice to an unreasoning instinct, that in general you only give the corruptible an opportunity to become corrupt.[8]

Again, writing several years after the Reform Act

of 1867 an introduction to *The English Constitution*, he acknowledges a fear that the two great political parties may bid against each other for the support of the working man. Statesmen, he warns, have now a grave responsibility. They must appeal to the best, not to the worst, instincts of the ignorant masses. To be feared above all is a political combination of the lower classes for their own objects. Such a combination would inevitably mean " the supremacy of ignorance over instruction and of numbers over knowledge."[8] Indeed every type of extreme democracy evokes from Bagehot the strongest language of opprobrium. For what he calls " constituency government "—the twentieth-century system by which the Member of Parliament is chained to an elaborate programme and rendered the mere automatic mouthpiece of the voters—he has the greatest contempt: " Constituency government is the precise opposite of parliamentary government. It is the government of immoderate persons far from the scene of action, instead of the government of moderate persons close to the scene of action."[8] In other words, though it may seem a paradox, true " parliamentary," or representative, government is at its best always an aristocracy. It is government by the chosen few, and those few are the more excellent according as the great mass of the people possess that quality of " deference " to the higher powers which Bagehot prizes so highly in the English.

That England was faced in the Victorian era by an unprecedented social problem, that the industrial revolution had inflicted on the poor an almost inconceivable misery and degradation—one would never suspect from reading Bagehot. Some of his writings seem to indicate a belief that all curable evils were rectified by the middle of the century. The time to be an agitator, he declares in *The English Constitution*, was in 1820. By 1870 there could be no worse trade. " A man can hardly get an audience if he wishes to complain of anything."[8] Charles Dickens's later novels largely undid the good accomplished by his earlier. In the earlier he aroused the people against real abuses; in the later he continued dangerously and unnecessarily to excite the public mind after the abuses had all been removed.[9] Again, Bagehot concedes that, subjected to the temptations of the great towns, and to the monotony of modern industrial life, the common people are under a tremendous pressure, and stand in danger of losing " all deep moral feelings." His remedy is characteristically conservative. He proposes no alleviation of conditions or material betterment of the people, but " an effectual culture of their conscience," upon the means of accomplishing which he is rather vague.[9]

But though not particularly sympathetic toward the lower classes, Bagehot was, especially after the growing influence of democracy became more clearly evident, at least ready to do them justice. For hasty and sentimental philanthropy, and for any attempt to establish a " poor man's paradise " he felt always the greatest disgust, but after the Reform Act of 1867, he decided that statesmen could avoid class war only by making every possible concession to the common people:

They must avoid, not only every evil, but every

appearance of evil; while they have still the power they must remove, not only every actual grievance, but, where it is possible, every seeming grievance too; they must willingly concede every claim which they can safely concede, in order that they may not have to concede unwillingly some claim which would impair the safety of the country. [9]

To be sure, this is not open-hearted justice, but at least it is justice.

Both Burke and Bagehot, I need scarcely say, believe that society is by nature, not equalitarian, but aristocratic. Inevitably there appears an " upper ten thousand," the people of wealth and power, of culture and refinement, which form a class from whom the leaders of the nation, in arts and sciences as well as in politics, are chiefly drawn. Sometimes, presumably, the constitution of this class becomes impaired, or its political powers are greatly curtailed, but the state is usually best governed by its representatives, and no amount of ingenious political machinery, or efficient bureaucracy of ordinary men, can supply the want of really great leaders. For Burke, the " natural aristocracy " of England was largely represented by the hereditary nobles and gentlemen, among whom, however, those who rose by merit might, though with difficulty, take their place. As the owners of land, the possessors of special privilege by law, the members of this class are the interested protectors of all privilege and law, the natural guardians of the Constitution. Receiving in youth every benefit of education and training, growing up in an atmosphere of responsibility and public business, raised—at least in theory—above the ordinary

infirmities of their nature by the pride of rank and
family reputation, they are at once the proper
guides and governors of the state, and " a graceful
ornament to the civil order," " the Corinthian
capital of a polished society."[10] To Bagehot the
nobility are decidedly less glamorous, though he
approved of them as having given, in a blundering
sort of way, predominance to the select few. He
was much impressed with their " theatrical " value,
and preferred them to the new plutocracy as
symbolizing mind rather than mere wealth or
power, as representing a more human excellence,
" the probable possession of a great faculty—the
faculty of bringing out what is in one."[11] But for
him the real aristocracy was one in which intelligence and ability are at least prominent qualities;
it was that society of all the talents which inevitably
forms in a nation, and particularly in a great
capital, and for which the aristocracy of title and
wealth acts as a framework and a cementing
element. Bagehot's conception is plainly much less
formal than Burke's, much more inclusive and
modern. He regards aristocracy much less as a
kind of hallowed circle, and much more as a free
society of individuals who have won, or precariously
inherited, a high place in the competition of life.

It is only natural that, laying upon the aristocrat
large and grave responsibilities, Bagehot should
form a high ideal of his character and way of life.
This ideal, which is of course humanistic, I have
already described at length in the chapter on
religion.

In his essay on " Darwinism in the Theory of
Social Evolution " Giddings says:

It was not until the publication of *The Descent of Man* in 1871, when controversy over *The Origin of Species* had raged through twelve years of intellectual tempest, that the full significance of natural selection for the doctrine of human progress was apprehended by the scientific world. Mr. Spencer saw it when the *Origin of Species* appeared. Mr. Darwin himself had perceived that he must offer a credible explanation of the paradox that a ruthless struggle for existence yields the peaceable fruits of righteousness. But it was neither Mr. Spencer, nor Mr. Darwin who first recognized the specific phase of the life struggle in which the clue to the mystery might be sought. The gifted thinker who made that discovery was Walter Bagehot, editor of the *London Economist*, whose little book on *Physics and Politics*, or *Thoughts on the Application of the Principles of Natural Selection and Inheritance to Political Society*, was published first as a series of articles in *The Fortnightly Review*, beginning in November, 1867.[12]

In some respects *Physics and Politics* is less impressive than *The English Constitution*. The logic is not so concentrated, the analysis not so elaborate and conclusive, nor the organization so firm and consequent. Yet the book is certainly one of Bagehot's most interesting productions, and a striking instance of his breadth and adaptability. Indeed its subject is immensely, almost hopelessly, extended, and must have required a preparation of intensive reading in unfamiliar fields. To trace in any detail the many items of that reading, and the many suggestions which were doubtless obtained from it, would be an extremely difficult task, which I shall scarcely attempt. For his leading idea of. natural selection Bagehot is of course indebted to Darwin. He also quotes at considerable length Thomas Huxley, Herbert Spencer, and other

scientific philosophers of lesser note.[13] His knowledge of primitive society was largely derived from
the works of the eminent anthropologists Sir John
Lubbock and Sir Edward Burnett Tylor, and from
those of Sir Henry Maine, the great authority on
ancient legal history. Indeed, Sir Henry Maine
has contributed largely to a number of his primary
conceptions, including that of the religious sanction
of early law.[14] In formulating his principles of
order and progress in the evolution of communities,
Bagehot probably obtained suggestions from the
similar discussions in Coleridge's *Church and State*
and Mill's *Representative Government*.[15] Mill's little
book he seems to have read to great advantage—
particularly the remarks on arrested civilizations,
the early advantages of slavery, and the relationship between government and social development.[15]

Bagehot's purpose is, as I have said, to explain
the evolution of societies. He postulates first an
" age of isolation," a period of confusion and disorder, in which a polity began to grow up—what
kind scarcely mattered—because polity was the
one thing necessary.[16] A feeling of community
developed among members of the same family,
then among people of the same blood. " Strong
and eager individuals got hold of small knots of
men, and made for them a fashion which they were
attached to and kept."[16] A sort of " chance
predominance " created a model of behaviour which
all members of the group were led irresistibly to
imitate, and thus a national character came into
existence.[16] Gradually, what Bagehot calls a
" *cake* of custom " was formed.[17] An elaborate
framework of tradition, custom, and taboo arose,

which imposed, by the force of religious sanction and the penalty of supernatural punishment, a rigid control on the fierce waywardness of savage nature. Disciplined communities overcame the undisciplined, and imposed their manners upon them, for the vanquished tend naturally to imitate the victors. " Civilization begins, because the beginning of civilization is a military advantage."[17] Civilization continues because, except in certain minor respects, the greater the civilization, the greater the military advantage. There is a selection by conflict. Law, morality, religion, the arts and sciences tend to develop because they make for a better war machine. To the preliminary age of isolation succeeds an age of " nation-making," in which the process of cohesion in societies is apparently intensified and operates on a larger scale. " Bagehot wisely discriminates," writes Professor Bristol, " between the process of race making (confined mostly to prehistoric times), and that of nation making, a modern phenomenon."[18] Of the first process he cautiously says little. He maintains that the second results from the action of two forces—those of imitation and persecution. Even in civilized man, the inclination to mimicry is strong. Almost in spite of ourselves we tend to imitate prominent men, to copy the new fashions and mannerisms, to believe what other people believe. In the savage this sense, like those of sight and hearing, is many times fresher and keener. Moreover, all primitive peoples fiercely persecute nonconformity, because they feel a strong group liability. They believe that any offence against the sacred ways of the tribe brings guilt not only upon the offender, but upon the whole community. The efficacy of these forces was further augmented by certain varieties of social selection.

In early states of civilization there is a great mortality of infant life, and this is a kind of selection in itself— the child most fit to be a good Spartan is most likely to survive a Spartan childhood. . . . I suppose, too, that there is a kind of parental selection operating in the same way and probably tending to keep alive the same individuals. Those children which gratified their fathers and mothers most would be most tenderly treated by them, and have the best chance to live, and as a rough rule their favourites would be the children of most " promise," that is to say, those who seemed most likely to be a credit to the tribe according to the leading tribal manners and the existing tribal tastes.[19]

But once the cake of custom has been formed, the difficulty is to break it again. Continual progress presupposes continual possibilities of change. If the cake of custom is never broken, and the tyranny of the old established ways becomes so great that new variations are suppressed as soon as they appear, further advancement is impossible. Certain civilizations, like the Chinese and the Indian, have attained to a comparatively high level before being, as it were, petrified by custom. Indeed progress in its more advanced stages is the exception, and possible only for a society capable of some change and innovation, in short, for a " free state," which " means a state . . . in which the sovereign power is divided between many persons, and in which there is a discussion even among those persons."[19] Councils and assemblies are not uncommon among primitive peoples, but are usually concerned only with practical undertakings. If discussion is to affect a state fundamentally, it must be fundamental, a discussion of primary issues and basic principles; and such discussion inflames the passions, blinds the reason, and incites to violence. A nation continually torn by civil war can scarcely advance. A progressive nation is necessarily one which can discuss exciting subjects without too much excitement. In Athens and Rome, the aristocratic and popular parties conducted a long constitutional debate which led to much innovation and development. This process was furthered by the broadening influences of trade and colonization.

" Civilized ages inherit the human nature which was victorious in barbarous ages, and that nature is, in many respects, not at all suited to civilized circumstances."[19] In primitive life problems are plain and simple, and best dispatched by vigorous and incessant action. For this reason " an inability to stay quiet, an irritable desire to act directly, is one of the most conspicuous failings of mankind."[19] We love action so much that we never have time to plan. Even philosophers are so eager to think that they never have time to judge, and often expand into a tremendous system what were better left as a little suggestion. If many business men could be persuaded to trade cautiously four hours a day, they would grow rich, but they trade hastily for eight, and are ruined. The habit of discussion prevents hasty action. It ensures elaborate consideration, makes men sober and thoughtful, renders them tolerant, and frees them from the barbarous prejudice of early custom. Above all, it develops that quality of " animated moderation " which Bagehot finds so admirable in the Englishman.[20]

At the conclusion of the book, the author asks whether there has been any real progress. He recognizes that upon this question, particularly in its artistic, moral, and religious aspects, the greatest divergence of opinion exists. Even the meaning of the term itself is hotly disputed. Nevertheless, there has been, he feels, some definitely verifiable advancement which nearly everyone would admit. Men have improved their methods of warfare, multiplied their means of happiness, and increased their command over the powers of nature. These advantages are not merely external; they depend also on a certain type of character. They are perhaps best summed up, in Spencer's phrase, as an increased adaptation to environment.[21]

Pointing out that progress has been the exception rather than the rule, Bagehot asks what has caused progress. In the first place, nature offers a reward to ability wherever it occurs, and particularly to high and instructed ability. But favourable social conditions can greatly increase such rewards. Indeed mankind can advance only in groups, the members of which must be sufficiently similar to co-operate easily together. Within competing groups social selection preserves the best institutions, the best types of character, and the best religions—those which " fortify " and give a " confidence in the universe."[22]

Among modern authorities on sociology there is a considerable range of opinion as to the value of *Physics and Politics*. Mr. F. N. House declares that Bagehot has shown himself merely a brilliant phrase maker and that nearly all the ideas of his book were already " implicit in the writings

of predecessors, particularly Sir Henry Maine."[23]
But most authors agree with F. H. Giddings that
he " arrived at conclusions which to-day we recognize as belonging to the theoretical core of scientific
sociology."[24]   Certainly the social significance of
imitation, persecution, discussion, and natural selection between competing social groups was never
before so clearly realized nor so brilliantly described
as in *Physics and Politics*.   And certainly also
the book has had a strong influence on those who
have since expressed these concepts, including,
oddly enough, the later Darwin himself.   Professor
Lichtenberger sees clearly the effect of Bagehot's
ideas on *The Descent of Man*.[25]   But *Physics and
Politics* is not merely a landmark.   It is also a
classic, having two very distinct elements of
permanence.   It deals not with mere abstract
theory, but with solid human nature.   Insofar as I
am qualified to judge, Harry E. Barnes is right in
saying: " Bagehot's ' Physics and Politics ' remains
as valuable as ever, for he dealt with those fundamental psychological foundations of group action
which time is not likely to change in any material
manner."[26]   Moreover, the work has literary value.
Other books may present the same ideas in a more
modern, but scarcely in a more vivid, form.   It is
not only informative, but pleasantly informative.

It should also be observed that in this work
Bagehot makes a final comment on his theory of
valuable stupidity.   In early and unstable societies
ideas are dangerous because they introduce varia-
tion and excitement at a time when men need
discipline and restraint.   But in proportion as men
grow moderate and wise, ideas become valuable,

and all steady progress in a nation depends upon developing the ability calmly to discuss and evaluate them. The doctrine of discussion is the proper answer to the doctrine of stupidity. Even more, perhaps, it is the completion of that doctrine, for Bagehot still condemns the excited and extravagant discussion of false ideas. He now recognizes, in addition, how invaluable is the calm discussion of sound ideas. In this work he also pays a generous tribute to science as a force in human advancement.

Sir Robert Giffin has already written so well—and I am so little competent to write—upon Bagehot's economic works, that I shall say relatively little of them, and indeed I am more interested in the human, than in the technical, aspects of his thought.[27] In a sense the economic writings are very human. " Why was Bagehot a success in so many fields? " asks Mr. J. M. Keynes. " The answer leaps to the question. Bagehot was a psychologist—a psychological analyser."[28] He was not so much a theoretical economist as a psychologist of finance. In abstract theory he was somewhat deficient. His forte consisted in analysing, predicting, and describing the practical and personal aspects of business and public affairs. He wrote of economics like a statesman, almost like a novelist, and just as a novelist has a sure tact and imagination for conceiving the thoughts and actions of his characters in the most dramatic circumstances, so Bagehot had a sure tact and imagination for predicting the thoughts and actions of the politician and the business man in the most complicated political and commercial situations.

Lombard Street (1873), his first great economic

work, is a typical product of this visualizing and prophetic faculty. It is not merely an analysis of the London money market, but a forecast of its tendencies, a criticism of its weaknesses, and a recommendation for their cure. It was designed not only to give information, but to sway public opinion, and to produce action. It points out that the whole structure of English, and at that time, of continental, credit was ultimately dependent on the gold reserve of the Bank of England. Consequently there was tremendous pressure on the Bank, and if the reserve were ever allowed to go down to the " apprehension minimum," there was grave danger of a widespread panic. *Lombard Street* explains for the first time, though as Mr. Keynes protests, with some theoretical superficiality, the nature of panics and business cycles, and suggests a procedure by which the Bank should cope with them. It lays down a policy for the Bank and recommends reforms, extremely wise and conservative, for its government, and for the whole British credit system. It predicts the decline of private banks and the increase of joint stock banks. *Lombard Street* was, as Mr. Keynes puts it, " levelled at the magnates of the City and designed to knock into their heads, for the guidance of future policy, two or three fundamental truths."[28] Its language is appropriate to its purpose. It is filled with City phrases and expressions, and is in style not only simple and clear, but plain and utilitarian. There is much repetition and little complication. A layman can follow the argument with ease. To a surprising degree *Lombard Street* has accomplished its object. Much of what Bagehot advocates has been carried into effect, as much he predicts has come true. But the very change in conditions which it brought about has rendered the book somewhat obsolete. It is still read, however, and rather widely used as a textbook in colleges and universities. Essentially, *Lombard Street* is the vivid and interesting record of a great reform, effected by a statesman who never sat for a constituency.

In one other respect Bagehot has done important work in *Lombard Street*. I quote Sir Robert Giffin:

In describing . . . the working of economic phenomena in the mass in business societies constituted like that of England at the present time, he has really been doing preparatory work for the solution of problems which can only be solved statistically. All that relates to the Bank reserve, to the increase of bank-note circulation at certain seasons or in certain years, to the succession of good and bad years in business, to the tendency of money to be dearer at one season than at another and in one year than in another, to the special danger of panics at certain times, involve statistical considerations; and without being strictly a statistician, still by his quantitative sense Bagehot has given an idea of how the statistics would tell, and has prepared the way for the more exact study. [29]

The *Economic Studies* are perhaps the best known of Bagehot's writings on political economy. They were intended to form a work of three volumes, but at the time of Bagehot's death in 1877, less than two hundred pages had been written. As Sir Robert Giffen observes, these studies were no doubt an outgrowth of the inquiry begun in *Physics and Politics*.[29] In the first page of that book we read:

A new world of inventions—of railways and of tele-

T

graphs—has grown up around us which we cannot help
seeing; a new world of ideas is in the air and affects us,
though we do not see it. A full estimate of these
effects would require a great book, and I am sure I
could not write it; but I think I may usefully, in a few
papers, show how, upon one or two great points, the
new ideas are modifying two old sciences—politics
and political economy.[30]

But a serious illness led Bagehot to alter his intention
of executing this plan within the limits of a single
book. *Physics and Politics* shows the effect of the
" new ideas " only on politics. The *Economic
Studies*, written several years later, reveals the
effect on political economy. It is an amusing
feature of this book, as of *Physics and Politics*,
that an author so superbly civilized should find so
much instruction in savage life. Essentially, *Economic Studies* constitutes an inquiry, first into
the logical foundations and the history of economic
thought, and second into the stages of actual
economic development in the world itself. The
earlier theorists seem to assume that economics is
applicable, literally and concretely, to all men in
all ages. Bagehot points out that it is in the first
place, like any science or any theory, by nature
abstract. It isolates a particular set of causes and
traces out their effects on human society. It
regards man not in the totality of his nature, but
as an economic animal. Its laws are absolutely
true only in the ideal world where economic causes
alone exist; of the real world they are true but
relatively and in part. Moreover, they apply
almost exclusively to great modern economic
societies like the English, where contract is free,
and labour and capital are easily transferable.

Nowadays men and money move, with but very little impediment, to the points where wages and profits are highest. But in primitive societies there is very little capital, and even when it exists it is never loaned. Every man practises every craft. There is no transference, because there is no division, of labour; and when a division of labour grows up, it is a rigid and petrified structure by which the worker is chained to his native place and his original trade by every variety of legal and customary bond. Early societies must be stable, and therefore polity prohibits movement. In the light of this investigation Bagehot considers in order some of the founders of political economy, describes them as men and thinkers, points out some of their fundamental errors, and makes suggestions toward a more satisfactory theory. He concludes with an elaborate analysis into the cost of production, in the course of which he attacks the views of his contemporaries, Mill and Cairnes.

It was apparently impossible for Bagehot to keep living personalities out of any book—even out of a book on " the dismal science." The *Economic Studies* contains clever and amusing sketches of Adam Smith, Malthus, and Ricardo, and was eventually to contain several other portraits of a more elaborate nature. It is also, as Bagehot himself observes of *The Wealth of Nations*, filled with " just maxims fresh from the life."[30] Indeed, never was abstruse theory so concretely, so vividly conceived and presented. Throughout this work Bagehot has endeavoured to put the abstract problems of his science clearly before his imagination, and to check and correct accepted views by his own keen psychological insight and broad knowledge of commercial realities. The result is a book as fresh and influential as it is vital and interesting.

Bagehot's longer works show him to be eminently capable both of sustained logic and of complex and elaborate analysis. They do not, however, reveal him to be particularly at home with abstractions. Even Sir Robert Giffen admits that Bagehot's work on the more abstract phases of economics is of secondary excellence. I am inclined to think he was not so much incapable, as impatient, of such thought, for as I have already explained, Bagehot was a " thinker of the picturesque order." He craved the excitement of a clear vision, and retreated from those aspects of a subject in which such vision was impossible. In any event, it is remarkable that an author writing long books on difficult subjects should remain deeply attracted to the human and dramatic aspects of truth. One is inclined to speculate how such a man came to write so much on the abstruse subjects of government and finance, but whatever the reason, we should be grateful for being taught so clearly to see that this mechanized world is after all still very human at the core, and that the greatness of a nation may depend on the quality of its national character even more than on the quantity of its coal and iron deposits.

Chapter XIV

CONCLUSION

THE imagination rules mankind, said Pascal, and experience confirms what he said.[1] The imagination is a mysterious, terrible power, lying partly within, and partly without, our control. It is the avenue through which outward things reach into our minds and mould our thoughts. It stores up sense impressions, and subtly combines and re-creates them into a new world—often a pathetic dream—inside the brain. It is the storehouse of the past and the factory of the future. It presents, sometimes according to our will and sometimes against it, pictures of the present, past, and future, of the possible and impossible, of the desirable and the undesirable. It is the medium by which we conceive, realistically or phantastically, of the world and life about us, and according to its inward images we think and act. Usually, what sets us dreaming affects us most, and eventually sets us acting. A man has a vision of himself, or of success, or of wealth, which he attempts to realize. Or again some great fact, or phantasy, may burn itself in upon his imagination, and dominate his life. The writings of famous reformers suggest that on the whole they have been less influenced by their often elaborately logical programmes of action than by some radiant vision of what they expected the world ultimately to become. The records of history and literature indicate that few soldiers ever had any rational understanding of why they fought, but that numberless soldiers have fought and died for their vision of some great hero, like Napoleon, or for the visions and pictures clustering around their ideas of patriotism and country.

Every man's life is finally a problem of the imagination. After all each man must live alone with his dream of a world and, if he would be happy, he must make that " dream " as true and valid as he can. Obviously his success will depend not merely on the images which he forms of the visible and the palpable world, but on the conceptions with which he grasps at ultimate moral and religious realities, and since these realities are remote from sense phenomena, he can hope to visualize them only through a veil of illusion. The nature of his illusion and the quality of his imagination must therefore be the supreme index of an author's real power and thought.

It must be confessed that Bagehot himself does not fully appreciate how much the problem of life is a problem of the imagination. He does not grant to that faculty its full role. He assigns it a major part in the attainment of scientific knowledge.[2] He rather vaguely concedes its importance to poetry.[2] He considers it immensely valuable as a medium by which certain political ideas may be impressed on the masses.[2] But that it has any function beyond these, that it might give new vitality to truth already known, or interpret and vivify, as in religion, truth not easily comprehensible to the human mind, he does not definitely admit. In the sphere of practical action he would confine its effect pretty largely to the masses. The poor and ignorant, he seems to believe, are inevitably subject to the vagaries and superstitions which the fancy engenders, but the intelligent and educated should see things as they are and act according to reason. In short, Bagehot appears to be rather more keenly aware of the dangers, than the advantages of the imagination. " It is often said," he remarks, " that men are ruled by their imaginations; but it would be truer to say they are governed by the weakness of their imaginations."[2]

In one or two instances alone does he take a profounder view. In *The English Constitution* he points out that the English monarch is a religious symbol, and he seems to imply that in terms of that symbol all Britons attain to a deeper and more moving conception of the state and of civic duty. But his language is vague, and one is inclined to place greater emphasis on a passage concerning Disraeli, which I quote a second time only because it is so significant:

Had Mr. Disraeli been a man of deeper and more original imagination than he is, he could not have surrendered as he has done, at every crisis of his career, to the ascendant influence of the hour. He has never had a political faith,—he probably does not know what it means. No man has invented so many political theories. No living politician's fancy has been half so prolific of suggestions for new bases of political creed. . . . Those who knew his early fictions and *Coningsby* well, recognized last session, in India Bill No. 2, unmistakable traces of the same mind. The same unsound imagination which filled Mr. Disraeli's novels with the most flimsy and eccentric theories of history, society, and political organization,—which invented the " Venetian-Doge " theory of the English Constitution,—the doctrine of the absolute ascendancy of the " Caucasian " race,—the gospel of " Young England," . . . and a thousand others,—has been equally visible whenever Mr. Disraeli has attempted to win the admiration of the House of Commons by any proposition of a directly constructive nature. No politician has ever shown, in the bad sense of the word, so *romantic* a political imagination,—in other words, a fancy so little imbued with the laws of real life, so ready to revolt against those laws, and put feeble idealities in their place.[3]

But though of key importance, this passage is unfortunately a little ambiguous. Does Bagehot mean that a profounder imagination than Disraeli's would conceive theories of greater literal truth, or theories which are at the same time true and compelling, which at once satisfy the sense of reality and take the imagination? The context seems to indicate the second meaning, of which Bagehot's discipleship of such men as Burke and Newman might seem a confirmation. The whole tendency of his thought, however, is contrary.

What Bagehot aspired to do in his own thinking was of course to see things, with scientific detachment, exactly as they are; and doubtless in considerable degree he succeeded. As a matter of fact his ideas have a colour, a vitality, a motive force entirely their own, and looking back over those ideas we must conclude that they proceeded from an imagination that was profoundly realistic, deeply penetrated with a sense of the comic and the humorous, and in a peculiar manner critical and ingenious. Bagehot saw life not sentimentally, nor idyllically, nor phantastically, but with a deep insight into its true character and a delightful perception of its absurdities and contradictions.

He was also capable of conceiving great truth, human, moral, and spiritual, but with a quality of imagination which, despite its excellence, has somewhat limited his scope. " The Ignorance of Man " is a wise and brilliant essay, yet it is little read. It has produced no disciples. Why? Because men are not moved by a religious vision so little solemn and awful. They are not content with an ingenious heaven, nor can they worship a clever and dexterous God. They do not like to think of the visible universe as a subtle hypocrisy, however beneficial to the soul. Bagehot is in some respects a sounder, and certainly a more modern, thinker than Newman, yet his religious works, I need scarcely say, will be much less remembered. People feel that a lofty subject should be treated with lofty imagination.

His discussions of politics and government reveal a similar limitation, though in this case many may consider it a fortunate one. Both Burke and Bagehot realized that in the lowest and most obvious sense the English Constitution was but a body of useful political habits, and they knew very accurately what those habits were. Yet both felt also that the Constitution was something more. To Burke it was a structure ancient and mighty, the work of English heroes and of the English race, a kind of vast, invisible cathedral of moral accomplishment, through whose Gothic windows, in holy and gorgeous light, shone the Eternal Wisdom. In a higher sense it was in itself a divine meaning echoing through the centuries in the souls of men, a second covenant or revelation, conferring mighty benefits and laying awful obligations. To Bagehot also the Constitution was ultimately something sacred perhaps; but immediately it was something useful and ingenious. It was another sage and politic deception; an "organized hypocrisy;" on the surface an impressive array of outmoded antiquities, below, a gleamingly efficient modern machine. It captured the imagination of the ignorant and satisfied the reason of the educated. It was the subtlest and most perfect of all governments, slowly worked out by a stupid and blundering race. Plainly Bagehot's picture, despite the paradoxes, humorous or serious, is more literally realistic than Burke's, for the British Constitution was in the nineteenth century, and is to-day, in considerable degree veritably a sage and politic deception. Bagehot lost some of the spiritual significance of English constitutional history, perhaps, but the bare, present fact he saw sharply and clearly. And therefore he will probably be read by sober men in a prosaic age, but could never, like Burke, have inspired a great conservative movement in a revolutionary age.

But why should these two great political philosophers conceive almost the same truth in terms so widely different? I have already attempted to answer this question in the chapter on religion.[4] Burke saw so keenly and vividly the misery and wickedness of the world that he required a consolatory vision into the glories of heaven. Bagehot never saw, perhaps, quite into the depths nor up to the pinnacles, and therefore he could observe the great middle regions more plainly and justly. Burke's merit is largeness and nobility of insight, Bagehot's, clarity and ingenuity of insight.

What Bagehot really enjoyed, and what he usually produced, was a clever and epigrammatic truth. Never ceasing to protest that real verity is dull and tedious, he always made it vivid and exciting. He loved to call sterling virtues by cynical names, to find sage council in muddling stupidity, to clothe sound, inescapable common sense in phantastic and exotic dress. The substance of his thought is sanity itself, its idiom is cleverness, wit, humour, irony. Indeed he was, in his earlier years, as alarming to safe men as congenial to their real tastes. In his later years, however, he strove to convince them as well as agree with them. He curbed his love of ingenuity and moderated his language. The result was that the other pre-eminent quality in his imagination, what might be called its marvellous transparency, its remarkable power of picturing with a minimum of illusion the bare essence of things, became more definitely paramount. In *The English Constitution*, for example, he vividly describes the royal family in all its valuable glamour and prestige, yet keeps clearly in mind throughout that after all it consists but of " a retired widow and an unemployed youth."⁵ He loved to see things as they might look to an inhabitant of Mars. President Wilson speaks of his " scientific imagination."⁶ The phrase is excellent.

Burke elevates and inspires. Bagehot amuses, exhilarates, enlightens. He is for those who can bear to see the veils torn away and look upon things as they are, who love cleverness with substance and truth with excitement. At times there is true poetry in his sanity, and nearly always there is sanity, which is ever valuable and rare in the criticism of an age which has produced so much impressive and poetic nonsense.

Among nineteenth-century thinkers Bagehot was perhaps not one of the greatest, yet he was certainly one of the most universal. As a writer and thinker he did not enjoy the luxury of pre-eminent genius, but he possessed a breadth and balance which such genius frequently lacks. He included within himself much of the past and therefore much of the future. In an age of various and widespread confusion he applied with cool common sense and keen penetration an ancient and profound philosophy to an immense variety of problems, both old and new.

BIBLIOGRAPHY

Bibliography of the Works cited in this Book.

Archer, Richard Lawrence: *Secondary Education in the Nineteenth Century.* Cambridge: University Press, 1921.

Arnold, Matthew: *The Works of Matthew Arnold.* De Luxe ed. London: Macmillan and Co., 1903. 15 vols.

Athenæum, Rules and Regulations, 1874. London, 1874.

Bagehot, Walter: *The Love Letters of Walter Bagehot and Eliza Wilson. Written from November* 10, 1857, *to April* 23, 1858. London: Faber and Faber, 1933.

Bagehot, Walter: One hundred and seventy-seven unpublished letters, 1832–1853.

Bagehot, Walter: *The Works and Life of Walter Bagehot.* Ed. and biographer Mrs. Russell Barrington. London: Longmans, Green and Co., 1915. The works in 9 vols., the life in 1 vol. (Vol. I contains two memoirs by R. H. Hutton.)

Barnes, Harry E.: " Some Typical Contributions of English Sociologists to Political Theory," *The American Journal of Sociology,* xxvii (March 1922), 573–81.

Barrington, Mrs. Russell: *The Servant of All; Pages from the Family, Social, and Political Life of My Father James Wilson.* London: Longmans, Green and Co., 1927. 2 vols.

Barrington, Mrs. Russell: See *The Works and Life of Walter Bagehot.*

Baumann, Arthur A.: " Walter Bagehot," *The Fortnightly Review,* n.s. xcviii (September 1915), 568–74.

Belliot, H. Hale: *University College, London.* London: University of London Press, 1929.

Birrell, Augustine: " Walter Bagehot," *The Collected Essays and Addresses of the Rt. Hon. Augustine Birrell.* London: J. M. Dent and Sons, 1922. 3 vols. ii. 213–35.

Birrell, Augustine: *William Hazlitt.* English Men of Letters Series. London: Macmillan and Co., 1902.

Bristol, Lucius Moody: *Social Adaptation, A Study in the Development of the Doctrine of Adaptation as a Theory of Social Progress.* Harvard Economic Studies, Vol. xiv. Cambridge: Harvard University Press, 1915.

Brownell, W. C.: *The Genius of Style.* New York: Charles Scribner's Sons, 1924.

Buffon, George L. L.: *Discours Sur Le Style.* Paris: Société D'Édition, 1926.

Burke, Edmund: *The Works of Edmund Burke.* Boston: Charles C. Little and James Brown, 1839. 9 vols.

Butcher, S. H.: *Aristotle's Theory of Poetry and Fine Art.* 4th ed. London: Macmillan and Co., 1927.

Butler, Joseph: *The Works of Joseph Butler, D.C.L. Sometime Bishop of Durham.* Ed. W. E. Gladstone. Oxford: The Clarendon Press, 1896. 2 vols.

Chilcott, J.: *Chilcott's Descriptive History of Bristol, Ancient and Modern. . . .* 4th ed. Bristol: J. Chilcott, 1840.

Coleridge, Samuel Taylor: *Biographia Literaria.* Ed. J. Shawcross, Oxford: The Clarendon Press, 1907. 2 vols.

Coleridge, Samuel Taylor: *The Complete Works of Samuel Taylor Coleridge.* Ed. W. R. R. Shedd. New York: Harpers and Brothers, 1884.

De Lolme, John Louis: *The Constitution of England; or An Account of the English Government, and Other Monarchies in Europe.* Ed. W. H. Hughes. London: J. Hatchard and Son, 1834.

Drummond, James: *The Life and Letters of James Martineau·* New York: Dodd, Mead and Co., 1902. 2 vols.

Encyclopaedia Britannica. 14th ed. " Langport."

Giffen, Sir Robert: " Bagehot as an Economist," *The Fortnightly Review*, n. s. xxvii (April 1880), 549–67.

Grant-Duff, Sir Mountstuart Elphinstone: *Out of the Past.* London: J. Murray, 1903. 2 vols.

Green, L. H.: " The Works of Walter Bagehot by Mrs· Barrington," *The Economic Review*, xxiv (October 1914), 463–6.

Hazlitt, William: *The Collected Works of William Hazlitt.*

Ed. A. R. Waller and Arnold Glover. London: J. M. Dent and Co., 1902. 12 vols.

House, Floyd Nelson: *The Development of Sociology*. 1st ed. New York: McGraw-Hill Book Co., 1936.

Hutton, Richard Holt: " The Metaphysical Society," *The Nineteenth Century*, xviii (August 1885), 177–96.

Hutton, Richard Holt: See *The Works and Life of Walter Bagehot*.

Keynes, John Maynard: " The Works of Walter Bagehot," *The Economic Journal*, xxv (September 1915), 369–75.

Lichtenberger, James Pendleton: *Development of Social Theory*. New York: Century Co., 1923.

Longinus: *On the Sublime*. Ed. W. Rhys Roberts. 2nd ed. Cambridge: University Press, 1907.

MacCunn, John: *The Political Philosophy of Burke*. New York: Longmans, Green and Co., 1913.

Macaulay, Thomas Babington: *Criticial, Historical, and Miscellaneous Essays*. Boston: Houghton, Mifflin and Co., 1886. 6 vols.

Martin, A. Patchett: *The Life and Letters of the Right Honourable Robert Lowe, Viscount Sherbrooke*. London: Longmans, Green and Co., 1893. 2 vols.

Mill, John Stuart: *Utilitarianism, Liberty, and Representative Government*. Everyman's Library. London: J. M. Dent and Sons, 1910.

Moore, Edward Caldwell: *An Outline of the History of Christian Thought Since Kant*. New York: Charles Scribner's Sons, 1918.

More, Paul Elmer: *Shelburne Essays*. Second Series. New York: G. P. Putnam's Sons, 1906. Eighth Series, Boston: Houghton Mifflin Co., 1913.

Morley, John: *Recollections*. 3rd ed. London: Macmillan, 1918. 2 vols.

Murray, Robert Henry: " Bagehot's Seminal Mind," *Studies in the Political and Social Thinkers of the Nineteenth Century*. Cambridge: Heffer and Sons, 1929. 2 vols.

Newman, John Henry: *Apologia Pro Vita Sua, Being A History of His Religious Opinions*. London: Longmans, Green and Co., 1891.

Newman, John Henry: *Fifteen Sermons Preached Before the University of Oxford Between A.D. 1826 and 1843.* London: Longmans, Green and Co., 1909.

Pascal, Blaise: *Pensées et Opuscules.* Ed. Léon Brunschvigg. 17th ed. Paris: Librairie Hachette.

Plenge, Johann, ed. and trans.: *Walter Bagehot's Das Herz der Wirtschaft: Die Lombarden-Strasse.* Essen, 1920.

Political Economy Club ...: *Minutes of Proceedings* 1899–1920; *Roll of Members and Questions Discussed* 1821–1920. Vol. vi. London: The Macmillan Co., 1921.

Saintsbury, George: *A History of Criticism and Literary Taste in Europe.* Edinburgh: William Blackwood and Sons, 1904. 3 vols.

Sampson, George, ed.: Introduction to Walter Bagehot's *Literary Studies.* London: Latchworth, 1912.

Spingarn, Joel Elias: *The New Criticism.* New York: Columbia University Press, 1911.

Stephen, Leslie: " Walter Bagehot," *Studies of a Biographer.* New York: G. P. Putnam's Sons, 1907. 4 vols. iii. 144–74.

Tennyson, Hallam: *Alfred Lord Tennyson, a Memoir by his Son.* London: Macmillan and Co., 1897. 2 vols.

Walter Bagehot, In Memoriam. Privately printed, 1878.

White, Andrew Dickson: *A History of the Warfare of Science With Theology in Christendom.* New York: D. Appleton and Co., 1896. 2 vols.

Wilson, Woodrow: " A Wit and A Seer," *The Atlantic Monthly,* lxxxii (October 1898), 527–40.

Wilson, Woodrow: " A Literary Politician," *The Atlantic Monthly,* lxxvi (November 1895), 668–80.

Zeitlin, Jacob: *Hazlitt on English Literature.* New York: Oxford University Press, American Branch, 1913.

NOTES

Consecutive references to the same author are grouped in threes and designated, both in the text and in the notes, by the same index number. A separate note and number is assigned to each different author, except where the ideas of two or more authors are being compared in the same passage of the text.

CHAPTER I

[1] Quoted by Mrs. Russell Barrington, *The Works and Life of Walter Bagehot*, x. 458. Volume X of this edition contains a life by Mrs. Barrington, Volume I, two memoirs by R. H. Hutton. The *Life* will be referred to in these notes as " Mrs. Barrington," the first and longer of the memoirs, which, only, I shall quote, as " Hutton."

[2] "Langport," *Encyclopaedia Britannica*, 14th edition.

[3] Hutton, p. 3.

[4] Mrs. Barrington, p. 60.

[5] Mrs. Barrington, p. 61.

[6] Quoted by Mrs. Barrington, pp. 86, 84.

[7] Hutton, p. 33.

[8] Quoted by Mrs. Barrington, pp. 64–5.

[9] Mrs. Barrington, p. 28.

[10] Bagehot, " Hartley Coleridge," i. 189. A simple Roman numeral following a Bagehot title will indicate a volume number of Mrs. Barrington's edition.

[11] Quoted by Mrs. Barrington, pp. 64, 77.

[12] Mrs. Barrington, p. 81.

[13] J. Chilcott, *Descriptive History of Bristol*, pp. 207–9.

[14] R. L. Archer, *Secondary Education in the Nineteenth Century*, pp. 56, 60–1.

[15] Unpublished letters: October 1840; March 2, 1841; November 7, 1841.

[16] Unpublished letters: April 11, 1840; May 16, 1841; May 1, 1840.

[17] P. 84.

[18] Quoted by Mrs. Barrington, p. 65.

[19] Unpublished letter, May 26, 1842.

[20] Mrs. Barrington, p. 84.

[21] P. 3.

[22] Unpublished letters: March 7, 1840; May 15, 1842.

[23] Quoted by Mrs. Barrington, p. 89.

[24] Unpublished letters: May 21, 1838; February 26, 1840; October 4, 1839.

[25] *The Love Letters of Walter Bagehot and Eliza Wilson*, p. 184.

CHAPTER II

[1] Bagehot, " Shakespeare—The Man," i. 219.

[2] P. 3.

[3] *University College, London*, pp. 1, 6, 78.

[4] Unpublished letters: October 15, 1842; September 2, 1846; September 9, 1846.

[5] Belliot, *University College*, pp. 82–3.

[6] Quoted by Mrs. Barrington, p. 115.

[7] Unpublished letter: about November 1846.

[8] Quoted by Mrs. Barrington, p. 102.

[9] " Oxford," i. 170.

[10] P. 4.

[11] " William Pitt," iv. 5–6.

[12] Pp. 7, 8.

[13] Quoted by Mrs. Barrington, p. 146.

[14] "Shakespeare," i. 252; " Henry Crabb Robinson," v. 52, 53.

[15] P. 9.

[16] Mrs. Barrington, p. 106.

[17] P. 3.

[18] Quoted by Mrs. Barrington, p. 63.

[19] Mrs. Barrington, pp. 65, 66.

[20] Quoted by Mrs. Barrington, pp. 73–4.

[21] Unpublished letter: October 8, 1839.

[22] Quoted by Mrs. Barrington, p. 411.

[23] i. 196, 199.

[24] Quoted by Mrs. Barrington, p. 171.

[25] Hutton, p. 15.

[26] Quoted by Hutton, pp. 19–20.

[27] " Letters on the French Coup D'État," i. 109, 110.

[28] Pp. 20, 22.

[29] Unpublished letter, March 1, 1849.

[30] Hutton, p. 25.

[31] Bagehot, " Coup D'État," i. 106, 86–111.

CHAPTER III

[1] Mrs. Barrington, p. 205.

[2] Quoted by Mrs. Barrington, pp. 225, 29, 81.

[3] Quoted by Mrs. Barrington, p. 457. L. H. Green, " The Works of Walter Bagehot by Mrs. Barrington," *The Economic Review*, xxiv (October, 1914), 464.

[4] Quoted by Mrs. Barrington, p. 213, 211.

[5] Hutton, p. 29.

[6] P. 218.

[7] P. 31.

[8] *Love Letters*, p. 88.

[9] Quoted by Mrs. Barrington, p. 247.

[10] A group of obituary notices appears in a small paper-covered volume called *Walter Bagehot, In Memoriam*, privately printed in 1878. The references given are in most cases incomplete, and I have supplemented them as far as I could. They appear in the order which they have in the booklet. As the date is in every case that of Bagehot's death, 1877, it is omitted, and should be understood as the volume reference where

only a page reference is given. R. H. Hutton, " Walter Bagehot," *The Fortnightly Review*, n. s. xxviii. 453–84; R. H. Hutton, " Mr. Walter Bagehot," *The Economist* (March 31), 349–51; R. H. Hutton, *The Spectator*, 1. (March 31), 394–95, 401–3; E. D. J. Wilson, *The Examiner* (March 31); R. H. Inglis Palgrave, " Walter Bagehot, The English Economist," *The Bankers' Magazine*, xxxi (May), 841–43; " Intellectual Detachment," *The Contemporary Review*, xxix (May), 1151–2; Percy Greg, *The Standard* (March 27); J. G. and E. J. B., *The Inquirer* (April 7); D. A. Aird, *The Civil Service Review* (March 31); *The Echo* (March 25); *The Dundee Advertiser* (March 27); *The York Herald* (March 28); *The Pall Mall Gazette* (March); *The London Daily News* (March); *The London Daily Telegraph* (March); *The Scotsman* (March 26); *The London Times* (March 27), 9; *The Langport Herald* (March 31); George Walker, " Walter Bagehot and the Economist," *The New York Nation*, xxiv (April 5), 204–5; J. W. C., *The New York Inquirer* (April 12); *The New York Public*, xi. 243; A. P. M., " The Late Walter Bagehot," *The Melbourne Review*, ii. 216–17; C. V., " Walter Bagehot," *La Revue Politique et Littéraire*, xix. 953; Max Wirth, *Die Neue Freie Presse* (April 6).

¹¹ " The Works of Walter Bagehot," *The Economic Journal*, xxv (September 1915), 370.

¹² The account of Bagehot's courtship, as well as the fragmentary quotations which appear from p. 52 to the end of the chapter, is derived from the *Love Letters*.

¹³ P. 45.

¹⁴ See pp. 146–55.

¹⁵ *Love Letters*, pp. 49, 56–7, 67.

¹⁶ *Love Letters*, pp. 99, 59, 61–2.

¹⁷ *Love Letters*, p. 86.

CHAPTER IV

¹ *Essays and Addresses*, p. 133.

² " Memoir of the Right Honourable James Wilson," iii. 302–35.

³ " Walter Bagehot," *Studies of a Biographer*, iii. 158.

⁴ Bagehot, " Sir George Cornewall Lewis," iv. 189.

⁵ Quoted by Mrs. Russell Barrington in *The Servant of All; Pages from the Family, Social, and Political Life of My Father*, ii. 137.

⁶ Quoted by Bagehot in " James Wilson," iii. 342.

⁷ Quoted by Mrs. Barrington, p. 17; Mrs. Barrington, p. 300.

⁸ Quoted by Mrs. Barrington, pp. 385, 457–8.

⁹ Bagehot, " Pitt," iv. 35, 36.

¹⁰ Mrs. Barrington, p. 386.

¹¹ P. 42.

¹² A somewhat puzzling comment on Bagehot as a politician occurs in *The Life and Letters of the Right Honourable Robert Lowe, Viscount Sherbrooke*, ii. 352, by A. Patchett Martin, who writes:

" He [Bagehot] appears, however, to have had one grave defect, inherent in the literary character, of allowing his pen to run away with him. At all events, in an electioneering manifesto addressed to Mr. Hutton, he used a phrase which the Conservatives construed into a charge of personal corruption against Disraeli, whereupon, on the principle of choosing the lesser of two evils, they expressed their determination of supporting

Mr. Lowe. Mr. Bagehot wrote: ' Mr. Disraeli, indeed, believes that by influence and corruption the mass of the voters may be made to aid him. But I do not believe that a Government based on influence and corruption is possible in England.' "

It is surprising that so cautious and cool a person as Bagehot should make so bold a statement, but the suspicion of any immorality always aroused peculiar indignation in him, and he seems also, especially in his later years, to have been bitter against Disraeli.

[12] Pp. 41–2.

[14] ix. 131.

[15] *Political Economy Club; Minutes of Proceedings* 1899–1920; *Roll of Members and Questions Discussed* 1821–1920, pp. viii, ii, xvii, 351.

[16] *Alfred Lord Tennyson, A Memoir by his Son*, ii. 167.

[17] ii. 370–1.

[18] " The Metaphysical Society," *Nineteenth Century*, xviii (August 1885), 177–96.

[19] Quoted by Mrs. Barrington, pp. 69-70, 378.

[20] " Some Typical Contributions of English Sociologists to Political Theory," *American Journal of Sociology*, xxvii (March 1922), 579.

[21] Mrs. Barrington, p. 404.

[22] Quoted by Mrs. Barrington, pp. 416, 418.

[23] *Das Herz der Wirtschaft*, p. vii.

" Bagehot as an Economist," *Fortnightly Review*, n. s. xxvii, April (1880), 558.

[25] P. 451.

[26] *Athenæum, Rules and Regulations* (1874), p. 9.

[27] Lord Morley, *Recollections*, i. 87.

[28] Quoted by Mrs. Barrington, p. 35.

[29] i. 193; " Pitt," iv. 7.

[30] Quoted by Hutton, pp. 44–5, 43.

[31] Bagehot, " Pitt," iv. 7.

[32] Quoted by Mrs. Barrington, pp. 359, 367.

[33] Pp. 377, 442–3.

[34] Mrs. Barrington, pp. 453–4.

[35] Giffen, " Bagehot as an Economist," *Fortnightly Review*, n. s. xxvii (April 1880), 567.

CHAPTER V

[1] " Béranger," iii. 11–13; " Charles Dickens," iii. 97; " Wordsworth, Tennyson, and Browning or Pure, Ornate, and Grotesque Art in English Poetry," iv. 304.

[2] "William Cowper," ii. 2–3; "Wordsworth, Tennyson, and Browning," iv. 268, 308.

[3] " The Preface to the First Edition of the Poems, 1853," *Works*, xi. 275; " Joubert," ix. 290–1. A Roman numeral following an Arnold title will refer to a volume of the De Luxe edition of his works.

[4] See p. 169.

[5] *Poetics*, ix. 3–4.

[6] S. H. Butcher, *Aristotle's Theory of Poetry and Fine Art*, pp. 137–8, 150.

[7] " Wordsworth, Tennyson, and Browning," iv. 272–3, 287; " Mr. Clough's Poems," iv. 130.

[8] " Henry Crabb Robinson," v. 61.
[9] Quoted by Mrs. Barrington, p. 248.
[10] " Wordsworth, Tennyson, and Browning," iv. 277; " The First Edinburgh Reviewers," ii. 52–3; " Wordsworth, Tennyson, and Browning," iv. 314.
[11] *A History of Criticism and Literary Taste in Europe*, iii. 543.
[12] " Sterne and Thackeray," iv. 244–5; " The Waverley Novels," iii. 50–2.
[13] Samuel Taylor Coleridge, *Biographia Literaria*, i. 202.
[14] " Percy Bysshe Shelley," ii. 255–60. The same idea is hinted at in " John Milton," iii. 205–6.
[15] Arnold, " Preface to the Poems, 1853," xi. 277–9; Hazlitt, " Schlegel on the Drama," *Contributions to the Edinburgh Review*, x. 81. A Roman numeral following a Hazlitt title will refer to a volume of the Waller and Glover edition of his works.
[16] " Wordsworth, Tennyson, and Browning," iv. 280. Arnold speaks (" Preface to the Poems, 1853," xi. 279) of classic art as that in which there is " not a word wasted, not a sentiment capriciously thrown in." All quotations from Bagehot which appear from pp. 97–103 of this book are to be found in " Wordsworth, Tennyson, and Browning," iv. 267–315.

CHAPTER VI

[1] *Biographia Literaria*, ii. 8–11.
[2] " Wordsworth, Tennyson, and Browning," iv. 279–80; " Hartley Coleridge," i. 205–7 (Aristotle, *Poetics*, xxiii–xxiv); " Wordsworth, Tennyson, and Browning," iv. 293.
[3] " Thomas Babington Macaulay," ii. 117; " Milton," iii. 190–1.
[4] i. 205–6.
[5] Bagehot, " Wordsworth, Tennyson, and Browning," iv. 280–1, 289–92.
[6] Arnold, " Preface to the Second Edition of the Poems, 1854," xi. 294.
[7] iv. 275; " Hartley Coleridge," i. 206; " Sterne and Thackeray," iv. 247.
[8] ii. 252–3; " Béranger," iii. 2–3; " Edinburgh Reviewers," ii. 75–7.
[9] " Béranger," iii. 5–7; iii. 38–9; " Edward Gibbon," ii. 163–4.
[10] " Milton," iii. 177–8; " Dickens," iii. 91–2 (Butcher, *Aristotle's Theory*, p. 340); iv. 299–300.
[11] iii. 95.
[12] *Aristotle's Theory*, pp. 334, 336.
[13] " Sterne and Thackeray," iv. 241; " The Adventures of Philip on his Way through the World," ix. 283–4; " Dickens," iii. 94–5.
[14] " Sterne and Thackeray," iv. 241; " Edinburgh Reviewers," ii. 82, 83; " Hartley Coleridge," i. 209.
[15] iv. 131.
[16] G. L. L. Buffon, *Discours Sur le Style*, p. 11.
[17] " Gibbon," ii. 161; " Sterne and Thackeray," iv. 241; " Macaulay," ii. 119–20.
[18] *The Genius of Style*, pp. 38, 51.
[19] " Gibbon," ii. 161; " Hartley Coleridge," i. 203; " Macaulay," ii. 122.

²⁰ Brownell, *Genius of Style*, pp. 66–9; Bagehot, " Milton," iii. 188.
²¹ " Adam Smith as a Person," vii. 25; " Béranger," iii. 13; " Physics and Politics," viii. 21. Although " Physics and Politics," " The English Constitution," " Lombard Street," and " Economic Studies " are of book length, and should therefore be italicised—as in the text—here I have put them in quotation marks to indicate they are single books within *The Works and Life of Walter Bagehot*.
²² " William Cowper," ii. 48.

CHAPTER VII

¹ " Edinburgh Reviewers," ii. 51; " Sterne and Thackeray," iv. 230; " Wordsworth, Tennyson, and Browning," iv. 280.
² " Gibbon," ii. 157; " Shakespeare," i. 228; " Edinburgh Reviewers," ii. 74.
³ " Crabb Robinson," v. 58; " Macaulay," ii. 89; " Physics and Politics," viii. 142–3.
⁴ " Milton," iii. 208.
⁵ *The New Criticism*, p. 3.
⁶ ii. 64.
⁷ " Wordsworth, Tennyson, and Browning," iv. 308, 307, 314; " Shakespeare," i. 218.
⁸ Bagehot, " Clough," iv. 117–18; " Macaulay," ii. 122; " Shelley," ii. 218–20; " Sterne and Thackeray," iv. 257–8; " Macaulay," ii. 112–13; " Milton," iii. 200; " Gibbon," ii. 155–6.
⁹ " Macaulay," ii. 96–8.
¹⁰ *On the Sublime*, xiv.
¹¹ Bagehot, " Wordsworth, Tennyson, and Browning," iv. 292, 267.

CHAPTER VIII

¹ Birrell, *William Hazlitt*, p. 123; Jacob Zeitlin, *Hazlitt in English Literature*, pp. xxxiii, lxxii; Bagehot, v. 61.
² Mrs. Barrington, p. 382.
³ Bagehot, " Shakespeare," i. 228, 239.
⁴ See pp. 170–1.
⁵ Birrell, *Hazlitt*, p. 123; Hazlitt, " Mr. Southey," *The Spirit of the Age*, iv. 269–70; Bagehot, " Shakespeare," i. 228–9. Compare also Hazlitt, " On the Knowledge of Character," *Table Talk*, vi. 308, with Bagehot, " English Constitution," v. 162–3.
⁶ Hazlitt, " Sir Walter Scott, Racine, and Shakespear," *The Plain Speaker*, vii. 345; Bagehot, " Waverley Novels," iii. 70–1.
⁷ Hazlitt, " On Shakespeare and Milton," *Lectures on the English Poets*, v. 47; Bagehot, " Shakespeare," i. 233–5.
⁸ Hazlitt, " Mr. Brougham—Sir F. Burdett," *The Spirit of the Age*, iv. 318; Bagehot, " Lord Brougham," ii. 299–307.
⁹ Hazlitt, " Mr. Jeffrey," *The Spirit of the Age*, iv. 315; Bagehot, " Edinburgh Reviewers," ii. 62.
¹⁰ Saintsbury, *History of Criticism*, iii. 257; More, " The First Complete Edition of William Hazlitt," *Shelburne Essays*, ii. 74.

¹¹ " On Gusto," *The Round Table,* i. 79–80.
¹² " Sir Walter Scott," iv. 248–52; " Sir Walter Scott, Racine, and Shakespear," *The Plain Speaker,* vii. 341.
¹³ " Edinburgh Reviewers," ii. 75, 76; " Hartley Coleridge," i. 190.
¹⁴ Mrs. Barrington, *The Servant of All,* i. 142.

CHAPTER IX

¹ " Shelley," ii. 215.
² " Bagehot," *Studies of a Biographer,* iii. 154.
³ " Wordsworth, Tennyson, and Browning," iv. 268; " Béranger," iii. 12; " Wordsworth, Tennyson, and Browning," iv. 280.
⁴ " Waverley Novels," iii. 57, 58, 59; " Mr. Disraeli," ix. 3–4; " Cowper," ii. 38–9.
⁵ " Hartley Coleridge," i. 213, 215; " Edinburgh Reviewers," ii. 74–7; " Béranger," iii. 10–11.
⁶ " Shelley," ii. 247; i. 187; " Brougham," ii. 305.
⁷ " Gibbon," ii. 127–8. See also " Lady Mary Wortley Montagu," iv. 69–70.
⁸ Thomas Babington Macaulay, " History," *Critical, Historical, and Miscellaneous Essays,* i. 426.
⁹ See pp. 177–8, 193–4.
¹⁰ i. 281–2, 307; " Macaulay," ii. 100. See also ii. 100–5.
¹¹ See p. 276.
¹² Arthur A. Baumann, " Walter Bagehot," *The Fortnightly Review,* n. s. xcviii (September 1915), 572; Bagehot, " Macaulay," ii. 89–92.
¹³ R. H. Murray, *Studies in English Social and Political Thinkers of the Nineteenth Century,* p. 221.
¹⁴ George Sampson, ed., *Walter Bagehot's Literary Essays,* pp. xii–xiii.
¹⁵ " Milton," iii. 183.

CHAPTER X

¹ ii. 155–6, 148; iii. 182, 183; " Crabb Robinson," v. 53–4.
² " Bagehot as an Economist," *Fortnightly Review,* n.s. xxvii (April 1880), 556.
³ i. 107–10; " Hartley Coleridge," i. 200; " Coup D'État," i. 93.
⁴ Hazlitt, " Jeffrey," *The Spirit of the Age,* iv. 315; Bagehot, " Edinburgh Reviewers," ii. 68.
⁵ " Cowper," ii. 18.
⁶ See pp. 152, 191.
⁷ " Brougham," ii. 285; " Lewis," iv. 189; " Pitt," iv. 6.
⁸ " Coup D'État," i. 97; " Hartley Coleridge," i. 188–9; ii. 307.
⁹ " Mr. Southey," *The Spirit of the Age,* iv. 263.
¹⁰ " Hartley Coleridge," i. 197; " On the Emotion of Conviction," v. 103; " Physics and Politics," viii. 62.
¹¹ " Hamlet," *Characters of Shakespear's Plays,* i. 237.
¹² " Cowper," ii. 8, 9; " Clough," iv. 120; " Brougham," ii. 318.
¹³ " Dickens," iii. 80; " English Constitution," v. 164; " Hartley Coleridge," i. 206.

[14] " Coup D'État," i. 84.

[15] i. 187–8. The verse quoted is from Hartley Coleridge's " Sonnet to Childhood."

[16] " Gibbon," ii. 161; " Cowper," ii. 13; " Gibbon," ii. 157.

CHAPTER XI

[1] Andrew Dickson White, *History of the Warfare Between Science and Theology*, i. 62–3.

[2] Edward Caldwell Moore, *An Outline of the History of Christian Thought Since Kant*, pp. 40–3.

[3] Alfred Lord Tennyson, " In Memoriam."

[4] Arnold, " Stanzas from the Grande Chartreuse."

[5] " Clough," iv. 116; " The Ignorance of Man," iv. 105; ii. 13, 18.

[6] " Brougham," ii. 323; " Shelley," ii. 216–17.

[7] Quoted by Mrs. Barrington, p. 147.

[8] " Cowper," ii. 26; " Clough," iv. 120, 121.

[9] See pp. 178–9.

[10] " Thinking Government," ix. 249; " Lombard Street," vi. 170.

[11] P. 38.

[12] See pp. 44–5.

[13] " Gibbon," ii. 170; " Physics and Politics," "viii. 130.

[14] Blaise Pascal, *Pensées et Opuscules*, pp. 490–1.

[15] Hutton, pp. 19–20.

[16] v. 110.

[17] Hutton, p. 19.

[18] Moore, *Christian Thought Since Kant*, p. 41.

[19] iv. 115.

[20] P. 18.

[21] " Butler," i. 290; iv. 111.

[22] Joseph Butler, *The Analogy*, i. 365; " Sermon XIII: Upon the Love of God," *Fifteen Sermons*, ii. 240–1; " Sermon XV: Upon the Ignorance of Man," *Fifteen Sermons*, ii. 268–9. All citations of Butler will be from the W. E. Gladstone edition of his works. A simple Roman numeral following a Butler title will indicate a volume number of that edition.

[23] P. 15.

[24] Bagehot, " Clough," iv. 122–3.

[25] " Cardinal Newman," *Shelburne Essays*, viii. 45.

[26] Bagehot, " Hartley Coleridge," i. 189–92.

[27] John Henry Newman, *Apologia Pro Vita Sua*, p. 4.

[28] P. 15.

[29] Newman, *Oxford University Sermons*, p. 18.

[30] " Butler," i. 273–4, 277.

[31] Butler, *Analogy*, i. 362.

[32] " Butler," i. 278; iv. 91–3.

[33] iv. 100, 104, 105.

[34] iv. 107; " Butler," i. 284.

CHAPTER XII

[1] " Pitt," iv. 3; " Milton," iii. 200.

[2] Quoted by John MacCunn, *The Political Philosophy of Burke*, pp. 6–7.

[3] " Coup D'État," i. 107–8, 98; " Physics and Politics," viii. 6–7, 40,.

[4] MacCunn, p. 13.

[5] " Reflections on the Revolution in France, and on the Proceedings of certain Societies in London relative to that Event," *The Works of Edmund Burke*, iii. 121, 108. A simple roman numeral following a Burke title will indicate a volume number in the Little and Brown edition of his works.

[6] viii. 77.

[7] See p. 190; see pp. 231–2.

[8] " Coup D'État," i. 102, 106.

[9] " A Wit and a Seer," *The Atlantic Monthly*, lxxxii (October 1898), 532.

[10] " Coup D'État," i. 101.

[11] " Walter Bagehot," *Studies of a Biographer*, iii. 171.

[12] " Mr. Lowe as Chancellor of the Exchequer," v. 113; " Dull Government," ix. 239–43; " Average Government," ix. 244–9.

[13] " Mr. Lowe as Chancellor of the Exchequer," v. 115; ix. 257; iii. 271.

[14] " Mr. Gladstone," iii. 276.

[15] " The American Constitution at the Present Crisis," iii. 384, 350, 376–7.

CHAPTER XIII

[1] J. L. De Lolme, *The Constitution of England, or an Account of the English Government*, pp. 178, 180, 195.

[2] Pp. 347, 295.

[3] " English Constitution," v. 166, 182–3, 212.

[4] " English Constitution," v. 222, 223, 119–20, 272.

[5] *Representative Government*, pp. 298–312; " English Constitution," v. 264–71.

[6] See pp. 255–6.

[7] " An Appeal from the New to the Old Whigs, in Consequence of Some Late Discussions in Parliament, Relative to the Reflections on the French Revolution," iii. 416, 415.

[8] iii. 250; v. 127, 262, 274.

[9] " Dickens," iii. 101; " Principles of Political Economy," viii. 231; " English Constitution," v. 127.

[10] Burke, " French Revolution," iii. 165.

[11] " English Constitution," v. 223.

[12] F. H. Giddings, quoted by J. P. Lichtenberger, *Development of Social Theory*, pp. 277–8.

[13] viii. 4, 5, 135.

[14] F. N. House, *The Development of Sociology*, p. 161.

[15] " On the Constitution of Church and State according to the Idea of Each," *The Complete Works of Samuel Taylor Coleridge*, vi. 38–40; Mill, *Representative Government*, pp. 197–200.

[16] viii. 27, 33, 25, 24.

[17] viii. 18, 34.

[18] L. M. Bristol, *Social Adaptation*, p. 178.

[19] " Physics and Politics," viii. 68–9, 102, 120.

[20] viii. 130.

[21] Paraphrased by Bagehot, " Physics and Politics," viii. 135.

[22] viii. 141, 140.

[23] *Development of Sociology*, pp. 160–1.

[24] Quoted by J. P. Lichtenberger, *Development of Social Theory*, p. 283.

[25] *Development of Social Theory*, p. 283.

[26] " Some Typical Contributions of English Sociologists to Political Theory," *American Journal of Sociology*, xxvii (March 1922), 579.

[27] " Bagehot as an Economist," *Fortnightly Review*, n.s. xxvii (April 1880), 549–67.

[28] " The Works of Walter Bagehot," *Economic Journal*, xxv (September 1915), 369, 371.

[29] " Bagehot as an Economist," *Fortnightly Review*, n. s. xxvii (April 1880), 566, 558.

[30] viii. 1; " Economic Studies," vii. 211.

CHAPTER XIV

[1] *Pensées*, pp. 362–3.

[2] " Economic Studies," vii. 101–2; " Shelley," ii. 255–6; " English; Constitution," v. 185–6, 182.

[3] " Disraeli," ix. 3–4.

[4] See p. 228.

[5] v. 182.

[6] Woodrow Wilson, " A Literary Politician," *Atlantic Monthly*, lxxv. (November 1895), 677.

INDEX